Looking Out/Looking In

Looking Out/Looking In

INTERPERSONAL COMMUNICATION

Second Edition

Ron Adler
Santa Barbara City College

Neil Towne
Grossmont College

Holt, Rinehart and Winston
New York   Chicago   San Francisco   Atlanta   Dallas
Montreal   Toronto   London   Sydney

To Sherri and Bobbi

Credits appear following the table of contents

Library of Congress Cataloging in Publication Data

Adler, Ron
Looking out/looking in : interpersonal communication.

Includes bibliographies and index.
1. Interpersonal communication. I. Towne, Neil, joint author. II. Title
BF637.C45A34 1978 301.14 77-13597

ISBN 0-03-018221-2

Printed in the United States of America

8 9 0 1 2 3 4 5 039 8 9 7 6 5 4 3 2 1

We have been gratified by the reception the first edition of *Looking Out/Looking In* has received. It has been used in more than 300 colleges and universities, as well as in other places, such as medical schools, and it has been sold in commercial bookstores. *Looking* has been used not only as a text for interpersonal communication courses, but also in psychology of adjustment classes, counseling groups, and professional, business, and industrial training programs.

We like to think that one reason for the success of the book has been its ability to speak to students. Too often texts seem to be written primarily for the authors' colleagues, without enough attention given to the needs or interests of the real consumers. In our case, we've often been told that *Looking* is a book that students keep long after the class is over, rereading it themselves and sharing it with family and friends. This is the best compliment we can receive, for it tells us that our readers think the material here has value for them beyond the walls of the classroom and the immediate payoff of a grade.

Our goal in this second edition has been to keep the basic elements which have made *Looking* a success: the assumption that awareness of one's present ways of communicating and exposure to alternatives can lead to change; a strong emphasis on experiential learning through exercises and other activities; demonstration of many ideas through a wide range of readings; attractive format; and a style of writing that is, we hope, simple without being simplistic.

At the same time we have tried to make our revision more useful by making several changes from the first edition. Most notably, we've entirely rewritten Chapters 1 and 2. In response to many suggestions, Chapter 1 contains much expanded material on communication models; the need for improving communication skills; and advice on how and when to engage in self-disclosure, risk taking, and the expression of thoughts and feelings. Chapter 2 is now totally devoted to a discussion of the self-concept and its critical role in influencing communication. In addition to these major changes, we have added many new readings and rewritten many parts of the text in Chapters 3 through 8. Along with updating the end-of-chapter suggestions for further readings and adding many film references to these sections, we have included a new feature, "Roads Not Taken," at the end of each chapter. In each of these sections we have suggested additional ways of exploring the topics covered in the text, so that students may have guidelines for pursuing a topic further, whether for a class project or simply out of curiosity.

As this edition goes to press, we want to look ahead by making a request of you. If you can think of any ways in which we can make *Looking Out/Looking In* suit your needs better, please let us know. We're optimistically anticipating doing a radically revised third edition of the book in a few years, and the best way to ensure its relevance is to learn what our users want. What subjects have we ignored, and what topics would you like to see handled differently? Do you have any favorite activities or reading selections you would like to see

Preface

included? If so, drop us a line in care of the publisher, and we'll be in touch with you. As we said in the preface to the first edition, this book is for you.

• • •

Many instructors around the country have told us that they are enthusiastic about using *Looking Out/Looking In*, but have had a difficult time designing suitable methods for evaluating how well their students have understood the material. Recognizing that grading is an important part of most educational systems, we have offered several detailed evaluation methods in the *Instructor's Manual* that is available for this book. After several years of experience with the contents of *Looking*, we and our colleagues have found each of these evaluation methods to be highly workable. The *Instructor's Manual*, which was prepared by Patricia Palleschi of Loyola Marymount University in consultation with us, also offers some general suggestions on using the book and, for each chapter, specific suggestions on the class activities and sample test questions; in addition, there are a suggested syllabus and an annotated bibliography. We wish to express our gratitude to Pat Palleschi for undertaking this task. The *Manual* may be obtained through a local Holt representative or by writing to Communication Editor, College Department, Holt, Rinehart and Winston, 383 Madison Avenue, New York, N.Y. 10017.

We are grateful to the following users of the first edition for their constructive suggestions: Paul Aschenbrenner, Hartnell College; Robert C. Bohan, St. Petersburg Junior College; Perry Carmichael, Mesa College; Marilyn Carter, El Centro Community College; Steve Collins, Modesto Junior College; Catherine R. Cowell, Angelo State University; Tracey L. Dunn, Lewis and Clark Community College; Edward K. Everroad, Scottsdale Community College; Robert H. Fogg, Millersville State College; Larry Galloway, Green River Community College; Joyce Gammon, Ventura College; Jeffrey C. Hahner, Pace University; Helen Hildebrandt, Oregon College of Education; Connie J. Jenson, Golden West College; Bob Jones, St. Petersburg Junior College; William E. King, St. Petersburg Junior College; Gary G. Konow, Aquinas College; H. Peter Kuiper, Fresno City College; Bonnie Lind, Iowa Western Community College; Jim Ludlow, Modesto Junior College; Janet Larsen McHughes, Southern Illinois University; Gordon Owen, New Mexico State University; Margaret C. Park, St. Louis Community College; Robert P. Pellack, Bergen Community College; Duane Petterson, University of Montana; Roberta K. Ray, Montana College of Mineral Science and Technology; Deborah Stelzleni, Lewis and Clark Community College; Harold Wennstrom, El Camino College.

We wish to express our appreciation also to Roth Wilkofsky and Pamela Forcey, our editors at Holt, for their assistance during all stages of the book. Finally, we are again glad to acknowledge the contributions of Janet Bollow, designer of both the first edition and this edition. Most of the credit for the attractive appearance of both editions goes to her.

Ron Adler
Neil Towne

Contents

Credits

N.B.

Categories such as chapters are somewhat arbitrary. Many of the ideas in this book would have fit in several places besides where you will find them. To remind you of this, *Looking Out/Looking In* is cross-indexed, using the symbol you see here. Each time a topic arises that also applies to another chapter, the index finger will point you to where else it belongs.

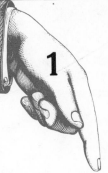

1

A First Look

You cannot teach a man anything.
You can only help him discover it
within himself.

Galileo

Introducing Ourselves

We want to begin by introducing ourselves. The word *we* you'll be reading throughout this book refers to us, Ron Adler and Neil Towne. We live in Southern California, where we make our living teaching interpersonal communication at the college level. We like our work: it helps us grow, helps our students get along better, and is fun. In fact we often think that we get as many rewards from our students as they do from us. Although we do share many things in common, we want to tell you that there are differences, too.

As we write this Ron, the younger by fifteen years, lives near the ocean with his wife Sherri and two daughters, Robin and Rebecca, ages four and one. Ron enjoys being a dad and husband most of the time, although he often longs for more quiet moments than he can find.

Ron likes trees, old houses, views, mail-order catalogs, and food, which he is able to enjoy without adding too many pounds. Daily jogging along the ocean and improving his skills at carpentry help him to relax and balance his life. In addition to coauthoring this book Ron has written two others by himself and is at present working on a third. He enjoys having written books, but will admit that he has a hard time writing them. Ron always seems to be too busy but realizes that this is the life-style he's chosen for himself for the time being, and wouldn't choose to have it any other way. When all is said and done, Ron feels lucky to have a fine, caring family, his share of close friends, and work he enjoys.

Neil finds it hard to believe that he has been teaching for more than twenty years. Although his hair is turning gray, his enthusiasm for life is evident in both his teaching and his play. Neil has a love affair going with his family. Bobbi, his wife, accounts for many of the positive things in his life and manages the home front, which is currently populated by six youngsters ranging from eleven to twenty-one years old. Neil and Bobbi belong to three P.T.A.s and are boosters of the local community college and U.S. Navy, with which the oldest son now travels.

Life for the Townes is not dull. If it isn't Little League, it's making out college applications, piano lessons, a new diet, wanting to see the latest movie, silk-screening Christmas cards, getting angry with each other, pro-

A First Look

ducing a puppet play of the Nativity, a picnic at the beach with friends, studying, feeding friends, dividing up home chores, watching a sunrise from the jogging course, leaving Dad alone while he works on the book, loving one another, and occasional summit meetings when the pace threatens to destroy what's left of their domestic tranquillity. Neil, it seems, is constantly presented the opportunity to work at interpersonal communication both at home and in the classroom!

Introducing This Book

We'll be sharing more about ourselves throughout the book. For now we hope this introduction has given you a brief idea about who we are. Our attempt to establish a personal style of writing is deliberate. We would like to think of our relationship with you as a conversation, a face-to-face meeting of real individuals, and not a treatise by faceless authors addressed to nameless students. We assume that you are in many ways like the people we get to know in our classes—so as you read on, realize that we are thinking of you.

Our goal in putting this book together was to provide a useful tool for helping you to improve your interpersonal communication skills. In other words our emphasis is practical rather than theoretical. Since this communication course may be the only one you ever take, we believe strongly that it needs to do more than "talk about" the subject: we hope it will actually help you find more satisfying ways to behave. If at the end of the course you have learned only to list the rules for good listening, identify defensive behaviors, or recite definitions of communication, we'll have failed to meet our goal. The kinds of results we are hoping for include relationships that run more smoothly, friendships that are becoming more meaningful, or a newfound ability to speak up when you want to.

Changes like these don't just happen magically. They come through new awareness, discovery, and learning on your part. To promote these goals we have filled *Looking Out/Looking In* with exercises and other activities, which you'll find printed in colored type. These activities fall into two categories. Some are designed to help you recognize more clearly your present styles of communicating, so that you can explore just how well they work for you. A second type of activity is aimed at showing you alternatives to those already existing styles. These are alternatives that research and experience suggest work well for most people, and we believe they will work for you if you are willing to learn them well.

One word about these new alternatives for communicating: To master them will require a fair amount of practice on your part. It just isn't realistic to expect that even the best ideas will work immediately for you. Rather, they'll take some practice, some false starts, and a certain amount of patience to master.

Gilly Caskey Lee
Hello Jay Mac Bobbi
Jane Eleanor Hello Ed
Jack Lois Neil Joe
Sherri Hello Jenny
Rich Sarah Karen Di
Hello Millie James
Don John Rebecca Hello Candy Al Wayne Frank Giles Ole Hello
Jeannie Sheila Robin Dave Mark Hello Wanda Gordon Audrey
Sean Gene Hello Joan Linda Dani Janet Patty Etta Steven
Hello Emmett Rabbit
Bill Greg Mimi Bob
Luke Hello Laura
Roth Matthew Lee
Marc Shayne Hello
Chevvie Vala Reda

MY
NAME
IS
ZEKE

Becoming Acquainted with Your Group

Having introduced ourselves as authors and told you something about the book, it's time for you to meet the other people who make up your group. You'll soon find that they will be important to you.

Name Calling

1 Assemble your group, including instructor, so that everyone can see each other easily; a circle works well.

2 The first person (ask for a volunteer) begins by giving his or her* name to the whole group, speaking loudly enough to be heard clearly by everyone. ("My name is Sheila.") The instructor may want to repeat what he's heard to check whether the speaker has been heard correctly. If you're not sure of a name, ask to have it repeated.

3 The group member seated on the first speaker's left will then give his own name followed by the first speaker's. ("My name is Gordon, and this is Sheila.")

4 Now the person to the left of the second speaker gives his name, followed by the second and first speakers' names. ("My name is Wayne, this is Gordon, and that's Sheila.") This procedure is followed around the whole group so that the last person names everyone in the class. This sounds like it'll be impossible for the last few people, but when you try it, you'll be surprised at how many names you'll remember.

5 Things to watch for:

a. If you forget a name, don't worry: that person will help you after you've had a little time to think.

b. If you don't catch the speaker's name, ask to have it repeated.

c. You may want the person who begins the activity to end it also. After that, anyone who wants to should try to "name 'em all."

d. Above all, keep the atmosphere informal. As you know, personal comments and humor have a way of lessening pressure.

*It's difficult to find a way of handling pronouns that don't discriminate against one sex or the other. For the rest of the book we'll shift back and forth between *he* and *she* as a way of both preventing bias and maintaining word economy. (See Chapter 7 for more thoughts on sexism in language.)

Now that you have started to become acquainted with the others in your class, let's look at some of the benefits of working in such a group. First, the sharing of thoughts and experiences that you'll find here can show you that you're not the only person who wants to communicate better. It's probable that many of the people you encounter every day are trying to appear more confident and skillful than they feel. They most likely put on this show of "having it all together" in the belief that others will like them better if they appear nearly perfect. If you're fooled by such acts, you probably think that you are the only one who finds it difficult to express yourself comfortably and well. In reality this most certainly isn't true, and in this group you'll find that most members share the same goals as you and have the same difficulty reaching them. This isn't because the people here are less well adjusted than those you'll find elsewhere, but simply because there will be more honesty here.

A second advantage of belonging to your group is the amount you will be able to learn from other members. Many will have found ways of overcoming difficulties you now have, and hearing their experiences can often give you new ideas about how to handle issues in your life. Some members might also serve as especially good models of desirable ways of communicating, so that you can learn a great deal simply by watching the way they behave.

A third benefit of exploring interpersonal communication in a group will become clear when you begin practicing the new skills presented throughout this book. Then you'll see that your classroom can become a kind of safe laboratory in which to try out new ways of behaving. This advantage of working with others is valuable because it helps you avoid the risk and anxiety that would come if you had to try out these new styles in the "outside world," where people might not look at your first and possibly fumbling attempts with much understanding. Since most of the techniques that follow will be new to the group, you'll all be able to try out new behaviors, make mistakes, and adapt accordingly with members of the group who understand what's going on.

To continue the process of getting to know one another, here's an exercise that will add some new information to go with the names you've already learned.

Introductions

1 Form dyads (groups of twos). If possible, pair up with someone you've *not* known previously. The instructor or facilitator should use himself to even out the dyads if necessary. In any event, someone should introduce the instructor.

2 Each member of a dyad will interview the other. Try to allow about twenty minutes for this.

a. You should find *three* unique things to tell the group about the person you're introducing. These may be actions, characteristics, or experiences that set your partner apart from other people. (For example, the fact that he graduated from Lincoln High School probably isn't so important as the fact that he's thinking about getting married, quitting school, et cetera.) Remember that most people feel uncomfortable talking about themselves, so you'll have to probe to get those *unique* aspects from your partner.

b. Use the *name* of the person you're introducing instead of the pronoun *he* or *she*. This will help everyone learn names.

3 After you've interviewed each other, get the group back together and proceed around the room introducing your partners until everyone has been introduced.

4 Unpacking: Discussing the Activity.

a. This experience was different from the usual way you get to know someone. What parts of it did you like? Were there parts that you didn't like? Why?

b. Now that you know more about each other, have your feelings changed about any of the individuals? How? Have your feelings changed in regard to the group? How?

A First Look

The Shields

Among the People, every person possessed a Shield of one kind or another. One of the most important things to understand about these Shields is that they were never intended to give physical protection in battle. They were not made to turn away arrows or bullets, or for people to hide behind. Usually they were much too thin and fragile for this. Sometimes they were made from the tough hides of bears or buffalo bulls, but more often they were covered only with the soft skins of deer, antelope, coyote, otter, weasel, or even mice. They were then hung with eagle plumes, cedar pouches, tassels of animal fur, and many other things. They were also painted with various symbolic figures.

In the case of the Personal Shields, all of these different things represented the individual Med-

icines and Clan Signs of the men who carried them. These Signs told who the man was, what he sought to be, and what his loves, fears and dreams were. Almost everything about him was written there, reflected in the Mirror of his Shield. . . .

These Shields were carried by the men among the People in order that anyone they met might know them. Even when they rested in their lodges, their Shields were always kept outside where all could see them. They might be hung up by the lodge door, or up by the smoke hole, or on a tripod near the lodge, according to each person's own Medicine Way. But they were always kept outside, where the People might see and learn from them.

Hyemeyohsts Storm, *Seven Arrows*

Your Personal Shield

1 Perhaps a good way to begin this activity is to read the short selection taken from Hyemeyohsts Storm's *Seven Arrows* that you'll find on page 9.

2 Now your task is to construct your own shield. You can consider your efforts satisfactory if when you finish you feel good with what you have produced.

3 Perhaps some of the following might be appropriate to present on your shield:

    a. people important to you
    b. things you like to be associated with
    c. places you like or would like to be
    d. personal traits that you're happy about
    e. ways you'd like others to see you
    f. talents and skills you have
    g. anything else you feel is an important part of you

4 On the next page is the outline of a shield. We suggest that you work with at least an 8½-by-11-inch sheet of paper. Sometimes it is decided that the whole group should work with a uniform size. *It is not necessary that you be an artist!* In completing this activity some of our students have made use of the following:

    a. drawings, designs, photos, words and/or pictures clipped from magazines, newspapers, etc.
    b. paint, felt-tipped pens, crayons, rub-on letters, etc.
    c. imagination—remember the idea is to let "you" show

The Need for Better Communication

Sometimes we are only vaguely aware of those things that are the closest to us. Just as we usually take the air around us for granted because it's always there and not visible, we often ignore the process by which we express ourselves and understand others. But just as the atmosphere can slowly become polluted without our noticing it and thus affect our physical health, the manner in which we communicate can break down and in so doing lead to many problems. In the next few pages we want to show you the critical role communication plays in meeting everyday needs, and then point out how some present styles of relating to each other fail to satisfy many of those needs.

A First Look

Anthropologists tell us that language developed to meet the needs of early man in his struggle to survive in a hostile environment. Robert Ardrey in his book *The Social Contract* suggests that it was the ability to communicate that made it possible for our distant ancestors to hunt and kill for food, to protect themselves against larger and stronger animals, and to organize their efforts in a manner that made civilization possible. If you think about it for a moment, it becomes apparent that none of these accomplishments would have occurred without the ability to work and plan together, which in turn depends on the ability to communicate.

Today as much as in the past our ability to survive and prosper depends on the same ability. The success of our family, social, and commercial relationships hinges on effective communication. Psychologist Abraham Maslow in his book *Motivation and Personality* identifies five basic types of human needs that each of us must satisfy if we are to live a safe and satisfying life in today's world.

The most fundamental group of needs is *physiological.* We must have sufficient air, food, water, and rest in order to live. As a species, we must reproduce in order to survive. Unless we satisfy these basic physiological needs, we have no future.

The next category of needs involves *safety.* Once assured of nutrition and atmosphere, we have to find shelter and clothing to protect ourselves from the sometimes hostile elements. We must also ensure that we are safe from any forces that threaten our lives or health: these include dangerous animals or people as well as life-threatening diseases.

A third type of need is *social.* Virtually all people have the desire to be accepted, appreciated, or loved by others. We become lonesome in the absence of human company, and thus tend to seek out others even when our physiological and safety needs don't require that we do so.

Maslow's fourth category of needs involves *self-esteem*—the desire to respect ourselves and to be respected by others.

Finally, the last group of needs is concerned with *self-actualization*—the need to fulfill our potential, to become everything we are capable of being.

The order in which these needs are listed is important, for Maslow suggests that we must satisfy the basic ones before moving on to higher categories. For example, a person who is suffocating must find air to breathe before worrying about freezing, and someone who is threatened by a physical attack will seek safety before worrying about being lonesome.

From our standpoint in this book it is significant that each of these levels of needs depends on effective communication for its satisfaction. Physiological survival, safety, social contact, self-esteem, and self-actualization all require the ability to express yourself and understand others. To see how true this is, take a look at some of the activities that might occur in an ordinary day.

Social need	**6:15 a.m.** Your clock radio comes on playing a song which reminds you of a special friend you haven't seen in some time. You make a mental note to phone this person and make plans to get together.
Physiological need	**7:00 a.m.** You are somewhat rushed this morning and ask to have a sandwich made for your lunch. You grab your heavy coat but can't find your gloves. It's cold out so you inquire as to their whereabouts. After a moment of discussion, others at home help you recall where you left the gloves.
Safety need	
Social need	**7:30 a.m.** You're on your way to the college. You stop and pick up your friends. The conversation centers on an exam you will all be taking, and how you are all dreading the ordeal. You make plans to get together for some studying. You feel better now for knowing that you'll be prepared for the test and that you're not facing the experience alone. Misery loves company!
Social need	**8:00 a.m.** You're in class and smile at the interesting, attractive person across the room. The smile is returned, and you drift off into a pleasant daydream. . . . You're not paying attention to the lecture and suddenly realize that the instructor has asked you a question. When you don't know how to respond, the instructor makes a sarcastic remark about students who don't pay attention. Your face suddenly feels hot. You wish you could find the words to apologize to the professor and at the same time request that if he has any complaints about your behavior he share them in a less humiliating way.
Self-esteem need	
Safety need	**12:00 noon** You stop by the auto repair shop to see about an ominous sound coming from one of your car's wheels. Of course, when the service manager goes out for a test drive the noise isn't there. You do your best to describe the problem, stating that it's important you have the problem taken care of before you wind up in an accident. After much discussion the manager begins to decipher the problem and makes an appointment to fix it the next day.
Physiological, safety, and self-esteem needs	**2:00 p.m.** Now you're at work. Today is the day you are going to talk to your boss about a raise. You're convinced that your work has improved enough so that your services are worth more to the company. Finally you get up enough nerve to actually make your request. After considering your reasoning, your boss agrees with you and announces that the raise will be more than you had hoped for. Elated, you phone home to share the good news, receiving congratulations from your family.
Social and self-actualization needs	**8:00 p.m.** During your guitar lesson the teacher praises you for catching on so rapidly. While this pleases you, you believe you could still do a better job, and ask for more help in mastering a new technique.

As you read this account and think about your own daily activities you can see that you are continually communicating. Whether asking for food, smiling at another person, listening to instructions, or requesting help, you're constantly sending and receiving messages in order to satisfy your various needs. How successfully are you communicating to meet your needs?

We in North America do pretty well as far as satisfying our basic physical needs goes. Relatively few people face the danger of starvation. We have some protection against loss of work with unemployment insurance. We have disability and old-age payments for most, and nearly everyone has access to medical care through private, employment, or government programs. It seems that we have few worries about whether or not we can stay alive, but most of us wouldn't call "staying alive" a very satisfying existence.

Our society for the most part is motivated by the human needs on the social, self-esteem, and self-actualization levels. Evidence abounds that a lot of us are not meeting these needs. The figures on divorce in the United States certainly indicate how we're doing at maintaining the marriage relationship. In 1975 there were 2.1 million marriages and 1 million divorces recorded officially. That works out to about one marriage dissolved for every two started. Ten years earlier, in 1965, there was one divorce for every four marriages. In California in 1975 there were 130,000 divorces and 160,000 marriages, or thirteen divorces for every sixteen marriages. Of course, marriage in itself doesn't guarantee social compatibility, increased self-esteem, or self-actualization, but it's fair to assume that many people who are incapable of meeting such needs in one relationship won't do much better in a different one.

1966 Graduates Rate Courses Most Useful

BETHLEHEM, PA. (UPI)—According to a study released by the College Placement Council in cooperation with the National Institute of Education, more than 4,100 college graduates who completed their degrees in 1966 . . . cited communication, administration, interpersonal relations, and mathematical ability as desirable skills. "The implication is that persons with competencies in these areas are better prepared for whatever career they choose," the council said. . .

San Diego Union

Talk for Sale

Even talk isn't cheap any more. In the San Francisco suburb of Kensington, talk is going for $8 an hour in a sadly modern kind of coffeehouse called "Conversation." The café offers a troupe of twenty "conversationalists" for hire at $5 for the first 30 minutes and $3 for each additional half hour, along with fourteen soundproofed booths to chat in. The owners, Dick Braunlich and his wife, Chris, opened Conversation last month. They insist that they are not dispensing therapy, but simply providing the customer with "a nice person to talk to." Says Chris Braunlich: "Most of our patrons want to discuss their philosophy of life. They don't need a psychiatrist."

Indeed, even the hint of therapy is discouraged. When more than 100 applications for the conversationalist job came in, those who stressed guidance and counseling—even those with degrees in psychology—were turned down. "We hired those we felt were good, warm people," says Dick Braunlich. Engel Devendorf, 57, one of the café's more popular professional talkers, recalls a blond divorcée who, stricken with terminal loneliness, wandered in after dropping her children off at a movie matinee. "She was new to California and didn't know anyone here," he says. "She didn't stop talking from the moment she came in." There are many other places—such as churches—where lonely people can find companionship. But, as Chris Braunlich points out, "people think if you're not paying, you're not getting anything."

Newsweek Magazine

Suicide figures are also indicative of our society's ability to meet interpersonal needs. In the United States in 1975 there were 12.6 deaths by suicide for every 100,000 population. A decade before there were 11.6 suicides per 100,000. The increase amounts to a bit more than 8 percent in the ten years. In the last fifteen years there has been a 90 percent increase in suicides among young people between the ages of fifteen and twenty-one. It ranks second to automobile accidents as cause of death now in this age group.

This depressing suicide picture is based on the officially reported figures. The number of suicides disguised as auto accidents, poisonings, and so on will never be known. Moreover, sociologists working in this area estimate that seven to eight times the number who succeed in killing themselves attempt suicide. This means that about 175,000 to 200,000 individuals each year in this country evidently want to give up the struggle to live a satisfying life. It's certainly reasonable to assume that many suicides take their life to escape from loneliness or unhappy relationships. Hence an inability to communicate is again a problem.

put me in your human eye
come taste
the bitter tears
that i cry
touch me
with your human hand
hear me with your ear
but notice me
damn you
notice me
i'm here

Ric Masten

THE DANGLING CONVERSATION

It's a still life water color
On a now late afternoon
And the sun shines through the curtain lace
and the shadows wash the room
And we sit and drink our coffee
cast in our indifference
like shells on the shore
you can hear the ocean roar
In the dangling conversation
and the superficial sighs
the borders of our lives

And you read your Emily Dickinson
and I my Robert Frost
and we note our place with bookmarkers
that measure what we've lost
like a poem poorly written
We are verses out of rhythm
couplets out of rhyme
In syncopated time
And the dangling conversation
and the superficial sighs
are recorders of our lives

Yes we speak of things that matter
with words that must be said
Can analysis be worthwhile?
Is the theater really dead?
and how the room is softly shaded
and our holy kisses shadow

I cannot feel your hand
You're stranger now unto me
lost in the dangling conversation
and the superficial sighs
In the borders of our lives

Paul Simon

Looking at the figures on mental illness we learn that 10 percent of all Americans are considered maladjusted or mentally ill. New laws make it mandatory for teachers and health personnel to report all cases of suspected child abuse to the authorities. A look at any medical text concerned with these problems makes it clear that they are due in great part to unsatisfying relationships in which little effective communication has occurred. It's additionally sad that many people who experience such difficulties are either unwilling or unable to take the step of asking for help.

You don't need to study suicide statistics to see how much people need to learn to communicate more effectively. Another rather recent development that supports this point is the increasing number of groups that focus at least in part on improving the participants' ability to communicate. We have encounter groups, singles groups, support groups for spouses of alcoholics, for child-battering parents, for drug users, for individuals on probation from prison, for widows . . . the list goes on and on, seeming to cover every type of person in the society. Surely the number of people willing to attend such activities suggests a hunger for closeness that just isn't being satisfied through traditional means.

Finally, consider the amount of printed material currently available that is concerned with improving communication. Hardly a week goes by that our local papers don't include a feature article about the subject. Look at the racks of paperback books the next time you visit a drugstore or supermarket. Chances are you'll see several how-to books promising to help the

The more our lives become surrounded by the unfamiliar and uncaring, the more we need authentic communication with a few people significant to us.

Nancy and Ernest Bormann

B.C. by Johnny Hart

© Field Enterprises, Inc., 1972

By permission of John Hart and Field Enterprises, Inc.

A Fuller Brush saleswoman told my mother that lots of elderly people on her route buy things just to make sure she comes back.

Ralph Keyes

reader get along better with others. The current issues of most popular magazines will provide you with several articles aimed at helping you assert yourself, improve your marriage, express your feelings, manage your conflicts, or deal with some other communication-oriented subject. This mass of printed material is both depressing and encouraging. It's sad to think that the need for such information is so great, yet we are encouraged to see how readily people seek it out.

Ralph Keyes in his book *We, the Lonely People* takes a careful look at today's society. He concludes that the loss of community contributes greatly to the difficulty we have in meeting our social, self-esteem, and self-actualizing needs.

> The problem of community, which sociologist Robert Nisbet calls "the single most impressive fact in the twentieth century in Western Society," is relatively modern. For most of man's history, group life was a given, and grew naturally out of the ways we were forced to be with each other—to live, work, wash clothes, and die.

This is no longer true. We have less and less necessity to be together, and fewer ways of knowing each other, while our need for community remains constant. So we're forced back on the only immutable reason for joining hands: the human need for company. Without place, without cause, common work or religion most of us must make that humiliating admission: I can't live alone.

. . . But to join that community, each one of us must take the hard, terrifying first step—saying—even to one other person—"I need you."

Keyes' message comes through loud and clear—we are doomed to disappointment if we can't reestablish community in some way to provide the kind of social intercourse necessary to meet our social needs.

Your Communication Skills Inventory

The purpose of this activity is to inventory your own communication skills. You will do this by determining how satisfied you are with the way you handle your communications in different specific situations. You will proceed as follows:

a. Below you will find fifteen instances that involve communication with others.

b. As you read each item, place yourself in the situation.

c. From this perspective you are to answer this question: *How satisfied am I with my communication skills in this situation and others like it?*

d. Your answer should be expressed by one of the five possible answers provided here.

5 = I'm very satisfied.

4 = I'm usually satisfied, but not always.

3 = I'm satisfied about half the time, and unsatisfied about half the time.

2 = I'm not satisfied very often.

1 = I'm not satisfied at all.

e. Place the number corresponding to the appropriate answer in the space provided by each item.

1 _____ You're considered an adult by others, but a relative still wants to help you make all your decisions. You value your relationship with this person, but you need to be more independent and decide to talk to her about it.

2 _____ You've been asked by a friend who is running for a local elected office to write some spot radio announcements to help her get elected. You need to come up with material that none of the voters will object to.

3 _____ A good friend has just shown you some of his latest poems and asks for your opinion of them. You honestly don't think they are very good. He's waiting for your reply.

4 _____ A friend and you are discussing religion and you want to explain the position you've taken in words that won't cause her to "turn you off."

5 _____ You like to see movies that have lots of action, and your companion can't stand violence on the screen. You both like to go to the movies together. You want to find a solution you can both agree to.

6 _____ A good friend wants to talk to you about a problem you've heard about several times before. You are tired and must finish some homework before you go to bed, and yet you don't want your friend to think you don't care.

7 _____ You ask an acquaintance for help with a problem. She says yes, but the way she says it makes you think she'd rather not. You need the help, but you don't want to impose.

8 _____ A friend comes to you and tells you how angry he is about his girlfriend's behavior. He asks you for advice. You suspect that there is more to the problem than this particular incident. You really want to help your friend.

9 _____ You're asked to join a dance club, but you remember that in junior high you were often embarrassed by your clumsiness. However, you enjoy being associated with those who asked you. They're waiting for your answer.

10 _____ One of your important persons has volunteered to make arrangements for getting concert tickets for you and some friends. He is unable to get the tickets and doesn't let you know until it's too late to do it yourself. Now all your friends are mad at you. You need to "clear the air" with this important person.

11 _____ A person you'd like to have as a close friend asks to borrow two of your favorite tapes. He's anxious to use your tapes, but you know his hi-fi equipment has the reputation of eating tapes.

12 _____ Your roommate always seems to be too busy to do the dishes when it's his turn, and you end up doing them most of the time. Other friends have suggested that you need to stand up for your rights more, but you feel it's more important to get along with others. Even so, you resent being used and want to let your roommate know that.

13 _____ You are the assistant manager in a fast-food franchise. You have been getting along well with your crew, but you have been noticing that they have been neglecting some of their cleanup duties. Your boss is inspecting your area at the end of the week. You want to keep the good rapport you have with your staff, but you have to get the work completed. Time is getting short.

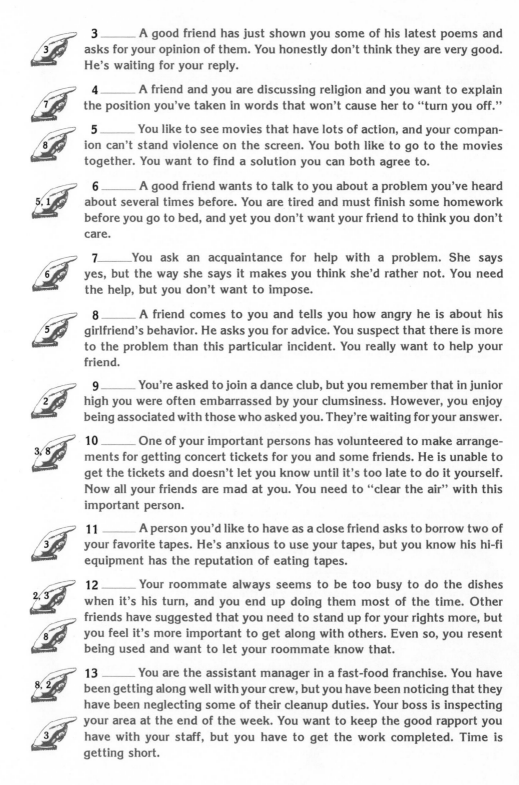

14 _____ You think your history teacher doesn't like being asked questions during class, and you are confused about an assignment that you need to begin working on. You are going to go to your instructor's office to find out just what needs to be done. You're concerned about how you should ask. You don't want to appear stupid, nor do you want to give her the impression that her instructions were inadequate.

15 _____ A new acquaintance has just shared some personal experiences with you that make you think you'd like to develop a closer relationship. You too have experienced some of the same things, but have never revealed these very personal feelings.

Now that you have finished, total up the numbers you've placed beside all fifteen items. If you've scored between 68 and 75, you can conclude that you're highly satisfied with the way you're equipped to deal with these situations. A score of 58 to 67 would suggest that you are usually satisfied with your communication behavior. And 45 to 57 would suggest that you feel dissatisfied with your communication skills nearly half the time. The lower your score, the less satisfied you are, and the more need for improvement is indicated.

At this point let us caution you about concluding that a high score here means you cannot profit from being exposed to the materials in this course. We know of no perfect communicators. We are amazed continually by new learnings, and suspect that improving our communication skills is a lifelong job.

Each of the situations above was designed to focus on one or more of the areas you will be studying as the class proceeds. If you rated yourself low in a particular situation, refer to the adjacent numbered hand, which will direct you to the appropriate chapter.

Another valuable way to use this activity is to return to it at the end of the course and make a final inventory. Have you improved? Are there communication areas you still need to work on?

The Process of Communication

So far we've been talking about communication as if the actions described by this word were perfectly clear. We've found, however, that most people aren't aware of all that goes on whenever two people share ideas. Before going further we want to show you exactly what does happen when one person expresses a thought or feeling to another. By doing so we can introduce you to a common working vocabulary that will be useful as you read on, at the same time previewing some of the activities we'll cover in later chapters.

Since we need to begin somewhere, let's start with you wanting to express an idea. If you think about it for a moment, you'll realize that most ideas you have don't come to you already put into words. Rather, they're more like mental images, often consisting of unverbalized feelings (anger, excitement, etc.), intentions (wants, desires, needs), or even mental pictures (such as how you want a job to look when it is finished). We can represent your mental image like this.

Since people aren't mind readers, you have to translate this mental image into symbols (usually words) that others can understand. No doubt you can recall times when you actually shuffled through a mental list of words to pick exactly the right ones to explain an idea. This process, called *encoding*, goes on every time we speak. Chapter 7 will deal in some detail with the problems and skills of being an effective encoder.

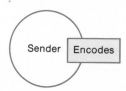

Once you've encoded an idea, the next step is to send it. We call this step the *message* phase of our model. You have a number of ways by which you can send a message. For instance, you might consider expressing yourself in a letter or over the telephone. In this sense writing and speaking words are two of the *channels* through which we send our messages. In addition to these channels we transfer our thoughts and feelings by touch, posture, gestures, distance, clothing, and many other ways as described in Chapter 6. The important thing to realize now is that there are a number of such channels.

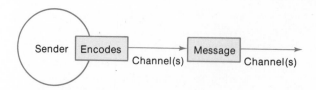

When your message reaches another person, much the same process we described earlier occurs in reverse. The receiver must make some sense out of the symbols you've sent by *decoding* them back into feelings, intentions, or thoughts that mean something to him.

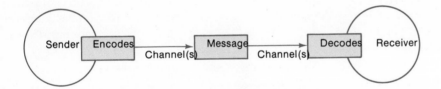

Ideally, at this point the mental images of the sender and receiver ought to match. If this happens, we can say that an act of successful communication has occurred. However, as you know from your own experience, things often go wrong somewhere between sender and receiver. For instance:

your constructive suggestion is taken as criticism

your carefully phrased question is misunderstood

your friendly joke is taken as an insult

your hinted request is missed entirely

And so it often goes. Why do such misunderstandings occur? To answer this question we need to add more detail to our model.

First, it's important to recognize that communication always takes place in an environment. By this term we don't mean simply a physical location, but also the personal history that each person brings to a conversation. The problem here is that each of us has a different environment because of our differing backgrounds. While we certainly have some things in common, we also see each situation in a unique way. For instance, consider how two individuals' environments would differ if

A was well rested and *B* was exhausted

A was rich and *B* was poor

A was rushed and *B* had nowhere special to go

A had lived a long, eventful life and *B* was young and inexperienced

A was passionately concerned with the subject and *B* was indifferent to it

Obviously this list could go on and on. Because the problem of differing environments is so critical to effective communication, Chapter 4 is devoted to showing you the many different ways people can perceive a single event. Even now, though, you can see from just these few items that the world is a different place for sender and receiver. We can represent this idea on our model in this manner.

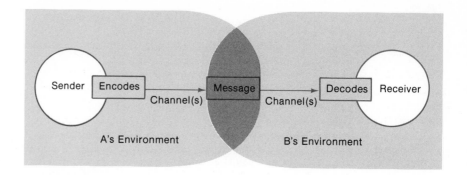

Notice that we've overlapped the environments of *A* and *B*. This overlapping represents those things that our communicators have in common. This is an important point because it is through the knowledge that we share that we are able to communicate. For example, you are able at least partially to understand the messages we are writing on these pages because we share the same language, however imprecise it often may be.

Different environments aren't the only cause of ineffective communication. Communicologists use the term *noise* to label other forces that interfere with the process, and point out that it can occur in every stage.

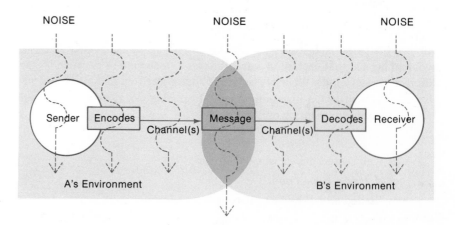

There are two types of noise that can block communication—physical and psychological. Physical noise includes those obvious things that make it difficult to hear, as well as many other kinds of distractions. For instance, too much cigarette smoke in a crowded room might make it hard for you to pay attention to another person, and sitting in the rear of an auditorium might make a speaker's remarks unclear. Physical noise can disrupt communication almost anywhere in our model—in the sender, channel, message, or receiver.

Take some time at this point to list as many different examples of physical noise as you can. Try to come up with examples from each of the different stages in the process.

Psychological noise refers to forces within the sender or receiver that make these people less able to express or understand the message clearly. For instance, an outdoorsman might exaggerate the size and number of fish caught in order to convince himself and others of his talents. In the same way, a student might become so upset upon learning that she failed a test that she would be unable (perhaps unwilling is a better word) to clearly understand where she went wrong. Psychological noise is so important a problem in communication that we have devoted Chapter 3 to investigating its most common form, defensiveness.

So far we've only talked about one-way communication, consisting of a single sender and receiver who never switch roles. There certainly are situations in which this is an accurate picture of what goes on—members of an audience listening to a performance, a congregation hearing a sermon, and a class taking notes from a lecturer. Television, radio, and newspapers also represent one-way communication, as do some unfortunate families where parents expect to do all the talking while their kids are placed in the position of being merely listeners.

At this point you can probably recognize that there are also cases where communication must be *two-way*, with each participant both sending and receiving. Two-way communication is appropriate and important in many situations, not only because it gives us a chance to share our ideas with others, but also because it helps us check and verify our understanding of the messages others have sent. This use of two-way communication for verification is termed *feedback*. To see its role in effective communication, consider the following brief conversations.

Anne: So I'll be by to pick you up as soon as I get off work.
Becca: Good! I'll be in front about six.
Anne: Better make it closer to six-thirty. I've got to stop by the market on my way home.

Charlie: What are you looking at me like that for? I said I was sorry, didn't I?
Dave: Hold it a second! I accepted your apology. What's the problem?
Charlie: Well, it seemed to me that you gave me one of your dirty looks.
Dave: What dirty looks?
Charlie: Well, a lot of the time you kind of smile and shake your head at the same time. It looks to me like you're disagreeing with whatever I've said.

You can see from these examples that if Becca and Charlie had simply accepted their decoding of the sender's message without checking back, a misunderstanding would have occurred. For this reason it's important to realize that being an effective receiver demands that you often use active feedback, and not just passively assume that you understand the sender. We'll cover this essential set of skills in Chapter 5.

So now we have a detailed model of the communication process.

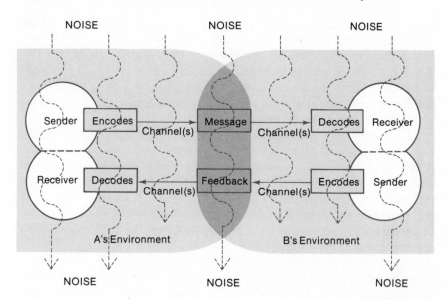

As we said earlier, this picture is probably more complicated than the definition you might have once given. But now you can probably see that every step is important and can't be omitted. Given this model, perhaps you can better understand why effective communication is often so difficult, and why spending some time learning the skills that make it possible can be worth your while.

Make Your Own Model

Check your understanding of the communication model by applying it to your own life.

1   In a group of three, share two important messages you intend to express within the next week.

2   For each message, describe
   a. The idea you want to send and the various ways you could encode it.
   b. Channels by which you could send it.
   c. Problems your receiver might have in decoding it.
   d. Possible differences between your environment and that of the receiver, and how those differences might make it difficult to understand your full message.

e. Likely sources of physical and psychological noise that might make it difficult for you to phrase your message clearly or for your receiver to understand it.

f. Ways you can make sure your receiver uses feedback to verify an accurate understanding of the message.

Elements of a Clear Message

After studying the previous model, you should see that effective communication requires you to express completely and accurately what's happening for you in such a way that the other person receives exactly the message you intended to send.

If you think about it for a moment, you'll recognize that our definition implies that as a sender you must *know* what's happening for you. After all, it's difficult to clearly express an idea that you're not aware of having. Surprisingly, failure to meet this simple requirement of knowing what you want to say is the cause of many communication problems. To put it another way, many communicators aren't aware of some important things about themselves that they must share if others are to fully understand their messages.

In the following pages we will describe several elements of a message that sometimes go ignored, and thus unsent. As we do so, you'll probably see that you often fail to recognize one or more of these elements in yourself, and thus make it hard for others to understand your message.

Sensing Sensing provides the raw material upon which you react. Sense data includes the things you see, hear, touch, smell, and feel with your skin. For instance, a camera records visual sense data and an audio tape recorder picks up and stores sounds.

For our purpose the important thing to recognize about sense data is that it is *objective*. A record of pure sensory information would simply describe an event without interpreting it.

Two examples of purely sensory records of events might look like this:

Example 1
One week ago John promised me that he would ask my permission before smoking in the same room with me. Just a moment ago he lit up a cigarette without asking for my o.k.

Example 2
When I walked into the room, there were about fifteen people there. They were gathered into several groups, all of which were involved in some sort of conversation. As I approached one group the speaker smiled briefly at me and then went on talking. The other members all looked at me and said hello, moved aside, creating space for me to join their circle, and then returned their gaze to the speaker.

Note that in both cases the description records only data that is available through the senses. The observer has not attached any meaning to the behaviors so far. This is the essense of sensing.

Interpreting Interpretation is the process of attaching meaning to sense data. The important thing to realize about interpretations is that they are *subjective.* That is, there is more than one interpretation that we can attach to any set of sense data. For example, look at these two different interpretations of each description above:

Example 1
Interpretation A: "John must have forgotten about our agreement that he wouldn't smoke without asking me first. I'm sure he's too considerate to go back on his word on something he knows I feel strongly about."

Interpretation B: "John is a rude inconsiderate person. After promising not to smoke around me without asking, he's just deliberately done so. This shows that he only cares about himself. In fact, I bet he's deliberately doing this to drive me crazy!"

Example 2
Interpretation A: "I can tell that the people in this group are glad to see me, for they all took a moment out of what was obviously an interesting story to say hello. Naturally they want to hear the speaker through to the end before talking about anything else, so I'll stick around and see what the topic is so I can talk about it when he's finished."

Interpretation B: "The people in the group must think I'm a jerk for butting into their conversation when they already had something going. Oh, they were polite enough to smile at me, but it's obvious that they don't have any interest in an outsider nosing into their private conversation. I'm getting out of here!"

It's clear from these examples that interpretations clearly are made on more than simple sense data. They also grow out of the following:

Our past experience "John has always (never) kept his promises in the past." or "A friend once told me to mind my own business (feel welcome) when I joined what turned out to be a private conversation."

Our assumptions "An unkept promise is a sign of uncaring (forgetfulness)." or "At parties people don't (do) expect to discuss private subjects."

Our expectations "John probably wants (doesn't want) to fight." or "I think these guests will (won't) like me."

Our knowledge "Long-time, habitual cigarette smokers often aren't even aware of lighting up." or "Social psychologists have observed that, as a rule, if members of a group acknowledge a new person by smiling and moving aside to make room, they are willing to have that person join the group."

Once you become aware of the difference between sense data and interpretation, some of the reasons for communication breakdowns become clear. Many problems occur when a sender fails to share the sense data upon which an interpretation is based. For instance, imagine the difference between hearing a friend say

"You are a tightwad!" (No sense data)

. . . and explaining

"When you never offer to pay me back for the coffee and snacks I often buy you, I think you're a tightwad." (Sense data plus interpretation)

The first speaker's failure to specify sense data would probably confuse the receiver, who has no way of knowing what prompted the sender's remarks. This failure to describe sense data also reduces any chance that the receiver will change the offensive behavior, which, after all, is unknown to her.

Just as important as specifying sense data is the need to label an interpretation as such, instead of presenting it as a matter of fact. Consider the difference between saying

"It's obvious that if you cared for me you'd write more often." (Interpretation presented as fact)

. . . and

"When you didn't write, I thought that you didn't care for me." (Interpretation made clear)

As you'll learn in Chapter 3, your comments are much less likely to arouse defensiveness in others when you present them in a tentative, provisional manner.

A third important rule is to avoid making statements that appear to report sense data but are in fact interpretations. For instance, don't mistake these kinds of statements as objective descriptions:

"I see you're tired." (*Tired* is an interpretation. Your sense data might have been "I see your eyes closing and your head nodding.")

"I see you're in a hurry." (*Hurry* is an interpretation. The sense data could have been, "I see you gathering up your books and looking at the clock.")

"I hear that you're hungry." (*Hungry* is an interpretation. The sense data you heard was the sound of your friend's stomach growling.)

"You look eager to get started." *Eager* is an interpretation. What could the sense data be in this case? The short time it took her to answer the doorbell? The outside clothing in which she was already dressed?)

There's nothing wrong with making these interpretations. In fact, this is a necessary step because only by interpreting sense data do you arrive at a meaning. However, we often make inaccurate interpretations, and when we don't separate sense data from our interpretations we fool ourselves into believing that our interpretations are reality—that is, what we *think* is what exists.

Will You Be My Friend?

Will you be my friend?
There are so many reasons why you never should:
I'm sometimes sullen, often shy, acutely sensitive,
My fear erupts as anger, I find it hard to give,
I talk about myself when I'm afraid
And often spend a day without anything to say.
   But I will make you laugh
   And love you quite a bit
   And hold you when you're sad.
I cry a little almost every day
Because I'm more caring than the strangers ever know,
And if at times, I show my tender side
(The soft and warmer part I hide)
   I wonder,
   Will you be my friend?
A friend
   Who far beyond the feebleness of any vow or tie
   Will touch the secret place where I am really I,
   To know the pain of lips that plead and eyes that weep,
   Who will not run away when you find me in the street
   Alone and lying mangled by my quota of defeats
   But will stop and stay—to tell me of another day
   When I was beautiful.

Will you be my friend?
There are so many reasons why you never should:
Often I'm too serious, seldom predictably the same,
Sometimes cold and distant, probably I'll always change.
I bluster and brag, seek attention like a child,
I brood and pout, my anger can be wild,
   But I will make you laugh
   And love you quite a bit
   And be near when you're afraid.

I shake a little almost every day
Because I'm more frightened than the strangers ever know
And if at times I show my trembling side
(The anxious, fearful part I hide)
   I wonder,
   Will you be my friend?
A friend
   Who, when I fear your closeness, feels me push away
   And stubbornly will stay to share what's left on such a day,
   Who, when no one knows my name or calls me on the phone,
   When there's no concern for me—what I have or haven't done—
   And those I've helped and counted on have, oh so deftly, run,
   Who, when there's nothing left but me, stripped of charm and
     subtlety,
   Will nonetheless remain.

  Will you be my friend?
   For no reason that I know
   Except I want you so.

                  James Kavanaugh

Sense Statements

Form a circle with a few other group members. Each person in turn should take one minute to report the sense data he is receiving *as it occurs.* Don't worry about your perceptions being in any logical order—simply describe them as they come to you. Try to be aware of all your senses: seeing, hearing, touching, feeling, and tasting.

A sample report might begin "Now I'm aware of all of you looking at me . . . now I'm aware of a dry taste in my mouth . . . this chair feels uncomfortable . . . and I'm seeing a smile on Kathy's face . . . I feel warm . . . now I'm aware of the hum of the air conditioner. . . ."

Notice how difficult it may be simply to describe what you perceive without attaching interpretations. Does this same problem occur in your everyday life?

Sensing and Interpreting

1 Share with two other group members several interpretations you have recently made about other people in your life. For each interpretation, describe the sense data upon which you based your remarks.

2 With your partners' help, consider some alternate interpretations of your sense data that might be as plausible as your original one.

3 After considering the alternate interpretations, decide
   a. Which one was most reasonable
   b. How you might share that interpretation (along with the sense data) with the other person involved in a tentative, nondogmatic way.

Feelings What emotions can you identify? Without looking at the list on page 36, try to jot down all the feelings you can think of. Go ahead and make your list now, before going on. Many of our readers who try this activity have a hard time coming up with more than a few vague emotions, such as "good" or "bad," "terrible" or "great." Now take a moment and compare your list with the one on page 36, and see if you've been able to recall all the emotions there.

Feelings add an extremely important dimension to a message. For example, consider the difference between saying

"When you kiss me and nibble on my ear while we're watching television (sense data), I think you probably want to make love (interpretation), *and I feel excited.*"

"When you kiss me and nibble on my ear while we're watching television, I think you probably want to make love, *and I feel disgusted.*"

There's quite a difference between these two statements, isn't there? Notice how the expression of different feelings can change the meaning of another message.

"When you laugh at me (sense data), I think you find my comments foolish (interpretation), *and I feel embarrassed.*"

"When you laugh at me, I think you find my comments foolish, *and I feel angry.*"

No doubt you can supply other examples in which different feelings can radically affect a speaker's meaning. Recognizing this, it seems logical to say that we should identify the feelings we're experiencing in our conversations with others. Yet, if you pay attention to the everyday acts of communication you observe, you'll see that no such sharing goes on.*

What prevents people from sharing their feelings? Certainly one cause is that making such statements can bring on a great deal of anxiety. It's often frightening to come right out and say "I'm angry," "I feel embarrassed," or "I love you," and often we aren't willing to take the risks that come with such clear-cut assertions. We'll have more to say about the issue of taking risks in a few pages.

A second reason why people don't express their feelings is simply because they don't recognize them as they occur. If this seems strange to you, take another look at the list of emotions you just recorded. Most likely you'll find that it was much less comprehensive than even the incomplete one we've included in this book. If this was so, you'll begin to see that most of our emotional vocabularies are limited.

Why is it that people sometimes have such trouble recognizing how they feel? This doesn't seem to be a problem we're born with. If you've spent any time with babies or young children, you know that for them there's no gap between feeling and acting. When a one-year-old is happy, she laughs, not just with her face but with her whole body. When she feels pain, she cries; when she's angry, you know it right away. Children this age don't follow the feel-think-act pattern that's so common with grownups; instead it seems that they just *are*.

What happens to get in the way of this easy expression of feelings? Part of the gap between thinking and feeling almost certainly comes from the lessons we learn while growing up. Usually without being aware of it, and almost inevitably, adults send message after message telling a child which emotions are acceptable and which aren't. In a house where angry words are taboo, the child gets the idea that anger is a "not o.k." thing. If sex is never discussed except with great discomfort, then the child will learn to stop talking about—and even stop consciously feeling—emotions that center around the body. If the parents only talk about trivial subjects and never share their deeper feelings, the child's conversation and thinking will tend to follow the same path.

---

*It's important to recognize statements that *seem* as if they're expressing feelings but are really interpretations or statements of intention. For instance, it's incorrect to say "I feel like leaving" (really an intention) or "I feel like you're wrong" (an interpretation). Statements like these obscure the true expression of feelings and should be avoided.

SOME FEELINGS

accepted
afraid
annoyed
anxious
angry
ashamed
bashful
bewildered
bitter
bored
brave
calm
confident
confused *Very*
concerned
defeated
DEFENSIVE
depressed
detached
disappointed
disgusted
disturbed
eager

edgy
elated
embarrassed
enthusiastic
envious
estatic
excited
fearful
foolish
free
frustrated
furious
glum
good
guilty
happy
helpless
high
hopeful
hostile
humiliated
hurt
inadequate
inhibited

intense
intimidated
irritable
jazzed
jealous
joyful
lonely
loving
mean
miserable
needed
neglected
nervous *Perky*
passionate
peaceful
pessimistic
playful
pleased
pressured
protective
puzzled
rejected
relieved
resentful

restless
sad
sensual
sentimental
sexy
shaky
shy
silly
strong
subdued
tender
tense
terrified
tight
tired
trapped
ugly
uneasy
uptight
VULNERABLE
warm
weak
wonderful
worried

Kids don't stop getting angry, having sexual thoughts, or intense feelings; emotions can't be turned off or on at will like water from a faucet. But because we're taught that certain feelings aren't o.k., we learn to push them out of our consciousness so that pretty soon they become hard to recognize.

As we said earlier, this lack of spontaneity in expressing feelings can become a real problem as we grow up. But what can you do if you want to get more closely in touch with your emotions? When you're not sure how you feel, one thing you can do is analyze yourself. Are you really happy in your job, or should you look for a new one? You can list all the reasons for each decision. Do you really love him or her? (It's possible to think this one to death.) Sometimes, after analyzing yourself this way, it's likely that you wind up even more confused than when you began. You start trying to figure out all the ways you *could* be feeling or you ask yourself how you *should* feel, but you never really come up with a satisfying answer.

Fortunately there's another, often better, way to get in touch with those unclear emotions. Unlike the approaches we've been used to, this one relies very little on your intellect. Instead of thinking about how you are, all you need to do with this technique is to listen, to pay attention to your own body. By becoming aware of the messages it sends, you can often find out more clearly what's really going on between you and other people. Try this experience and see what you can learn from your own body.

**to not
be aware
is no aware**
Bernard Gunther

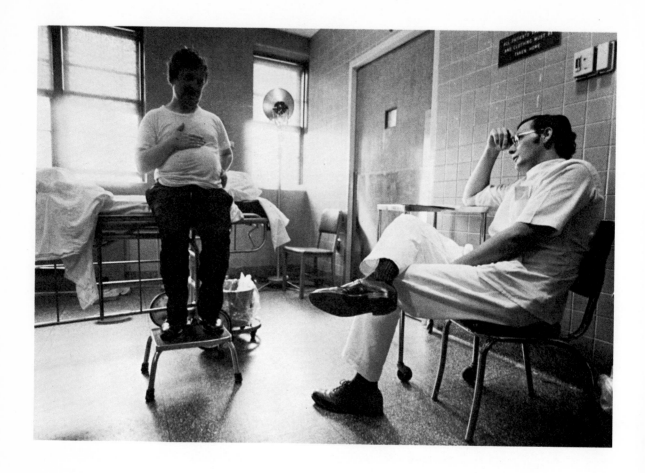

How Does It Feel?

Here's a way to learn more about yourself from your body. You can do this exercise individually outside the classroom. If you do, read all the steps ahead of time so that you can work through the whole experience without interrupting yourself. However, the exercise will have more impact if you do it for the first time in a group because in this way your facilitator can read the instructions for you. Also, in a group your feelings can be shared and compared.

The ellipses (. . .) in the instructions indicate points where you should pause for a moment and examine what you're experiencing.

1 Wherever you are, find yourself a comfortable position, either lying or sitting. You'll need to find a quiet place with no distractions. You'll find the exercise works better if you dim the lights.

2 Close your eyes. The visual sense is so dominant that it's easy to neglect your other senses.

3 Now that your eyes are closed and you're comfortable, take a trip through your body and see how the various parts of it are. As you focus on each part, don't try to change what you find . . . just notice how you are, how you feel.

4 Now let's begin. Start with your feet. How do they feel? Are they comfortable, or do they hurt? Are your toes cold? Do your shoes fit well, or are they too tight?

Now move your attention to your legs. . . . Is there any tension in them, or are they relaxed? . . . Can you feel each muscle and see how it is? . . . Are your legs crossed? Is there pressure where one presses against the other? . . . Are they comfortable?

Now pay attention to your hips and pelvis . . . the area where your legs and backbone join. Do you feel comfortable here or are you not as relaxed as you'd like to be? If you're seated, direct your attention to your buttocks. . . . Can you feel your body's weight pressing against the surface you're sitting on?

Now move on to the trunk of your body. How does your abdomen feel? . . . What are the sensations you can detect there? . . . Is anything moving? . . . Focus on your breathing. . . . Do you breathe off the top of your lungs, or are you taking deep, relaxed breaths? . . . Does the air move in and out through your nose or your mouth? Is your chest tight, or is it comfortable?

Checking out your breathing has probably led you to your throat and neck. Is your throat comfortable, or do you feel a lump there you need to keep swallowing? . . . How about your neck? . . . Can you feel it holding your head in its present position? . . . Perhaps moving your head slowly from side to side will help you feel these muscles doing their work. . . . Is there tension in your neck or shoulders?

Now let's move to your face. . . . What expression are you wearing? . . . Are the muscles of your face tense or relaxed? Which ones? Your mouth . . . brow . . . jaw . . . temples? Take a few moments and see. . . .

Finally, go inside your head and see what's happening there. . . . Is it quiet and dark, or are things happening there? . . . What are they? Does it feel good inside your head, or is there some pressure or aching? . . .

You've made a trip from bottom to top. Try feeling your whole body now. . . . See what new awareness of it you've gained. . . . Are there any special parts of your body that attract your attention now? . . . What are they telling you?

Now there's another very important part of your body to focus on. It's the part of you where you *feel* when you're happy or sad or afraid. Take a moment and find that spot. . . . See how you are now in there. . . . See what happens when you ask yourself "How am I now? How do I feel?" . . . See what happens in that place when you think of a personal problem that's been bothering you lately. . . . Be sure it's something that's important to your life now. . . . Now see if you can get the feel of this problem there in the place where you feel things. . . . Let yourself feel all of it. . . . If the feeling changes as you focus on it, that's o.k. Just stay with the feeling wherever it goes and see how it is. . . . If what you feel now makes a difference to you, see what that difference is. . . . Now, take a few minutes to use in whatever way you like, and then slowly open your eyes.

5   Now think about the following questions. If you're with your group, you may want to discuss them there.

a. Did you find out things about your body that you hadn't noticed before? Did you discover some tensions that you'd been carrying around? How long do you think you've been this way? Did recognizing them make any difference to you?

b. Could you find the part of yourself where you usually feel things? Where was it? Or are there different spots for different feelings? Did focusing on your problem make some kind of difference to you?

Diary of Awareness

Now that you've recognized how your body reflects your feelings, here's a chance to put your new awareness to work.

1   Pay attention to yourself for three days, and see what clues you get from your body that tell you how you're feeling toward other people. See if you experience the following emotions:

a. Happiness   e. Hurt
b. Sadness   f. Loving
c. Fear   g. Liking
d. Anger   h. Any other feelings

Are there any of these emotions that you haven't experienced lately? If so, why do you think this is? Because you don't have them? Because you haven't been recognizing them?

I've got to write about myself. I am my lab.

Fritz Perls

2   Keep a diary of when you experience these feelings and how they show up in your body.

3   For each instance, you should write down:
   a. Where you were when you experienced the feeling—what the situation was (at home with family, at a party with friends, et cetera)
   b. What the emotion is (for example, fear, anger, playfulness)
   c. Where in your body the feeling is located
   d. What you did about it (tried to forget it, shared it with others, made a wisecrack, kept it to yourself)

4   At the end of this second three-day period, see if your survey has made any difference. Are you more aware of your feelings than before you began reading this section? How can you use your new awareness to communicate with others?

Identifying Feelings

1 Divide your group into triads.

2 In turn each person should share with the other two members of the triad a feeling he has experienced in the last few days.

3 Share also the inner and outer physical signs that accompanied your feeling.

4 Explain what you did with the feeling. Did you ignore it, deny it, let it tell you what it could, or deal with it? What happened? Were you satisfied with the outcome?

5 Share feelings for three rounds, trying to introduce as large a variety of feelings as you can.

6 When you have finished sharing a minimum of three feelings each, move into the large group and report the different feelings that were identified in your group. Have someone in the group record all the different feelings mentioned, and post the list so that everyone can see it.

Once you're aware of your feelings, the question is whether or not to share them with the other people involved. While we're convinced that most of us don't express our emotions often enough, we don't want to suggest that you should always share your feelings as soon as they come up. For instance, while you might become angry upon being stopped for speeding by a police officer or after being unfairly criticized by an employer, you might be better off to keep quiet in these situations.

In deciding when to share your emotions, it's a good idea to consider the realistic consequences that would come from speaking out.

1. Ask yourself what might result if you remained quiet. Will your silence encourage the continuation of an unpleasant situation or the end of a satisfying one?

2. Consider the probable result that would occur if you *did* speak out. Would such an action stop the unpleasant behavior or make it worse? Would it help to maintain a pleasant situation or stop it?

3. Whether or not your assertiveness would influence the other person's behavior, decide what impact this sharing would have on yourself. Sometimes the costs of keeping quiet are high enough in terms of psychological wear and tear that simply getting an emotion off your chest is reason enough to speak out.

... Every thought, gesture, muscle tension, feeling, stomach gurgle, nose scratch, fart, hummed tune, slip of the tongue, illness—everything is significant and meaningful and related to the now. It is possible to know and understand oneself on all these levels, and the more one knows the more he is free to determine his own life.

If I know what my body tells me, I know my deepest feelings and I can choose what to do. ... Given a complete knowledge of myself, I can determine my life; lacking that mastery, I am controlled in ways that are often undesirable, unproductive, worrisome, and confusing.

William Schutz,
Here Comes Everybody

i remember
when my body knew
when it was time
to cry
and it was all
right then

to explode
the world
and melt
everything
warm

and start new
washed clean

Bernard Gunther

Intentions We can best identify intentions as statements about where you stand on an issue, what you want, or how you plan to act in the future. Sometimes your intentions involve *making requests of others.*

"When you didn't call last night (sense data) I thought you were mad at me (interpretation), and now I'm worried (feeling). I'd like to know whether you are angry (intention)."

"I really enjoyed (feeling) your visit (sense data), and I'm glad you had a good time too (interpretation). I hope you'll come again (intention)."

In other cases intention statements can describe *how you plan to act* in the future.

"I've asked you to repay the $25 I loaned you three times now (sense data). I'm getting the idea that you've been avoiding me (interpretation), and I'm pretty angry about it (feeling). I want you to know that unless we clear this up now, you shouldn't expect me ever to loan you anything again (intention)."

"I'm glad (feeling) you liked (interpretation) the paper I wrote. I'm thinking about taking your advanced writing class next term (intention)."

Why is it so important to make your intentions clear? Because failing to do so often makes it hard for others to know what you want from them or how you plan to act. Consider how confusing the following statements are because they lack a clear statement of intention.

"Wow! A frozen Snickers. I haven't had one of those in years." (Does the speaker want a bite or is she just making an innocent remark?)

"Thanks for the invitation, but I really should study Saturday night." (Does the speaker want to be asked out again, or is he indirectly suggesting that he doesn't ever want to go out with you?)

"To tell you the truth, I was asleep when you came by, but I should have been up anyway." (Is the speaker saying that it's o.k. to come by in the future, or is she hinting that she doesn't appreciate unannounced visitors?)

You can see from these examples that it's often hard to make a clear interpretation of another person's ideas without a direct statement of intention. Notice how much more direct each of the above statements would be if each speaker had made his or her position clear.

"Wow! A frozen Snickers. I haven't had one of those in years. If I hadn't already eaten, I'd sure ask for a bite."

"Thanks for the invitation, but I really should study Saturday night. I hope you'll ask me again soon."

"To tell you the truth, I was asleep when you came by, but I should have been up anyway. Maybe the next time you should phone before dropping in so I'll be sure to be awake."

As in the above cases we are often motivated by one single intention. Sometimes, however, we act from a combination of intentions, which may even be in conflict with each other. When this happens, your conflicting wants often make it difficult for you to reach decisions.

"I want to be truthful with you, but I don't want you to know where I was last weekend."

"I want to continue to enjoy your friendship and company, but I don't want to get too attached right now."

"I want to have time to study and get good grades, but I also want to have a job with some money coming in too."

While sharing your conflicting intentions isn't a guaranteed way to clear up confusion, there are times when an outright statement such as the ones above can help you come to a decision. Even when you remain mixed up, expressing your contrary wants has the benefit of letting others know where you stand.

Of course, you can't expect others always to make their intentions clear to you, so you'll often have to ask them questions such as "What do you want?" or "What do you intend to do about that?" As long as you ask such questions in a sincere spirit and not in an accusing tone, you'll find that both you and the sender will have a better idea of what's going on between you.

Once you start making your intentions clear and seeking the same clarity from others, you'll be surprised at how much more direct your communication becomes. To see for yourself what a difference this can make, try the following exercise.

What Are Your Intentions?

1   Divide a sheet of paper into three columns. In the first column write the names of five people who play an important role in your life.

2   In the second column write one request you would like to make of each person. Your request might involve asking the person to change a certain behavior, or you might want to have them tell you their opinion of a certain subject.

3 In the third column describe any intentions you suspect the other person might have, but about which you are unclear. Here is the place to ask what they want from you.

4 Now look at your list and imagine how you would actually approach the people on your list to express your intentions. Compare this sort of behavior with the way you usually express yourself to these people. Is there a difference? Which style would be most likely to produce satisfying results?

Now that you understand the importance of sense data, interpretation, feelings, and intentions in a clear message, try your hand at combining all these elements.

Putting Your Message Together

1 Join with two other class members. Each person in turn should share a message they might want to send to another person, being sure to include sensing, interpreting, feeling, and intention statements in the remarks.

2 The others in the group should help the speaker by offering feedback about how the remarks could be made more clear if there is any question about the meaning.

3 Once the speaker has composed a satisfactory message, she should practice actually delivering it by having another group member play the role of the intended receiver. Continue this practice until the speaker is confident that she can deliver the message effectively.

4 Repeat this process until each group member has had a chance to practice delivering a message.

Self-Disclosure and Risk in Communication

You can probably see that the kind of communication that results when you express your sense data, interpretations, feelings and intentions is much more direct and revealing than the messages people typically send and receive. There is certainly risk in sharing yourself so completely; so now we need to talk about the costs and benefits of self-disclosure. How much should you say, and how much should you keep to yourself? When is it appropriate to share your thoughts, feelings, and intentions? What do you stand to gain from being a more open and direct communicator?

One way to look at the important part self-disclosure plays in interpersonal communication is by means of a device called the Johari Window.*

---

*The Johari Window was originated by Drs. Joseph Luft and Harry Ingham during a summer laboratory in group development at UCLA in 1955. The model takes its name from the first names of the two men, Joe and Harry.

Imagine a frame inside which is everything there is to know about you: your likes and dislikes, your goals, your secrets, your needs—everything.

Everything
about
you

Figure 1

Of course, you aren't aware of everything about yourself. Like most people you're probably discovering new things about yourself all the time. To represent this we can divide the frame containing everything about you into two parts: the part you know about and the part you're not aware of, as in Figure 2.

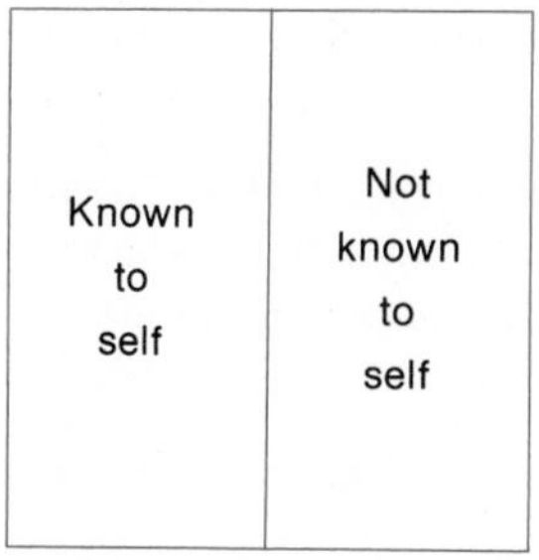

Known to self	Not known to self

Figure 2

We can also divide this frame containing everything about you in another way. In this division one part represents the things about you that others know, and the second part contains the things about you that you keep to yourself. Figure 3 represents this view.

Known
to others

Not known
to others

Figure 3

When we impose these two divided frames one atop the other, we have a Johari Window. By looking at Figure 4 you can see that the Johari divides everything about you into four parts.

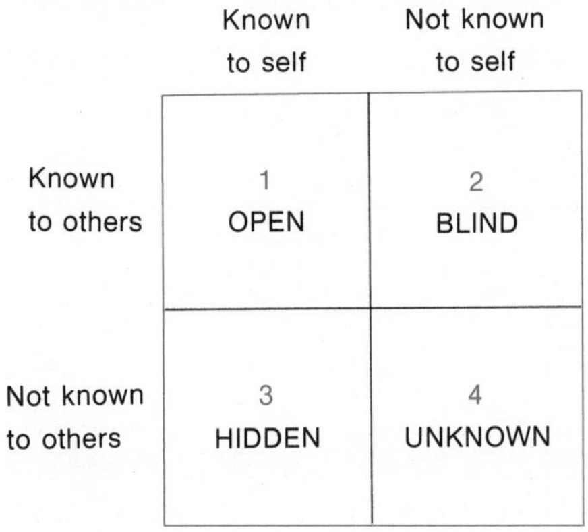

	Known to self	Not known to self
Known to others	1 OPEN	2 BLIND
Not known to others	3 HIDDEN	4 UNKNOWN

Figure 4

Part 1 represents the part of you that both you and others are aware of. This area is labeled your *open* area. Part 2 represents the part of you that you're not aware of but others are. This is called your *blind* area. Part 3 represents your *hidden* area; you're aware of this part of yourself, but you don't allow others to know it. Part 4 represents the part of you that is known neither to you nor to others and is therefore referred to as the *unknown* area.

You can construct a model of your own Johari Window: Draw a square, then locate your boundaries in the positions you think would best fit you. For example, if you think you're an open person, then obviously Part 1 of your window would be larger than the other areas. Such a window would look like the one in Figure 5.

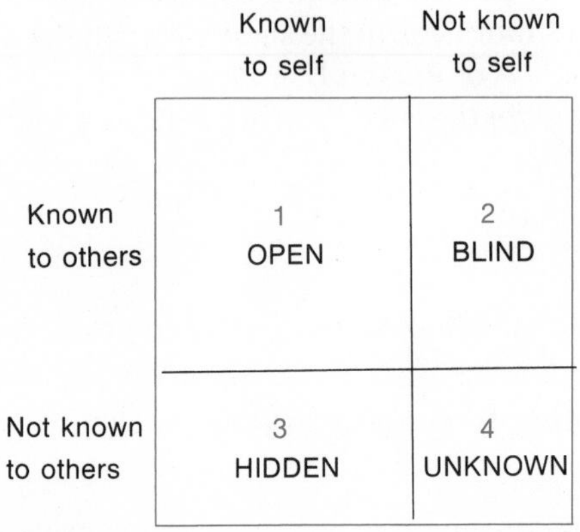

	Known to self	Not known to self
Known to others	1 OPEN	2 BLIND
Not known to others	3 HIDDEN	4 UNKNOWN

Figure 5

Interpersonal communication of any significance is virtually impossible if the individuals involved have little open area. And taking this a step further, you can see that a relationship is limited by the individual who is less open, that is who possesses the smaller open area. Illustrating this situation with Johari Windows, we would have Figure 6.

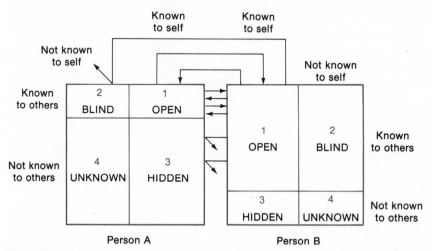

Figure 6

We've set up A's window in reverse so that the number-1 areas of both A and B's Joharis appear next to each other. Note that the amount of successful communication (represented by the arrows connecting the two open areas) is dictated by the size of the *smaller* open area of A. The arrows that are originating from B's open area and being turned aside by A's hidden and blind areas represent unsuccessful attempts to communicate.

Can you put yourself into one of the windows in Figure 6? Have you had the experience of not being able to "really get to know" someone because he or she was too reserved or closed? Or perhaps you've frustrated another person's attempts to build a relationship with you in the same way. Whether you picture yourself as more like Person A or Person B in Figure 6, the fact remains that *self-disclosure is necessary for the success of any interpersonal relationship.*

How Open Are You?

Take out a piece of paper and draw a Johari Window that you feel represents you in relationship to others.

1   First, draw a model of yourself that is directed toward the way you generally relate to people.

2   Next, draw a window for your relationship with someone you consider close to you: a boyfriend, girlfriend, buddy, spouse, or parent. The horizontal

boundary may change from your first model because that line now divides what you feel your "close" person knows or doesn't know about you.

3 So that you might have a model to contrast with the one you just constructed, sketch a Johari window representing the relationship you have with a person who knows very little of you. (Perhaps the professor of one of those large lecture classes would work well here.)

4 Now ask yourself whether there's any relationship between the strength of your friendships and the amount of self-disclosure you have. How would you draw a Johari Window for each of the people you interact with? From these windows, would you say that you're an open or closed person?

The case for self-disclosure seems overwhelming. Why then do we have a problem doing it? Sidney M. Jourard in his book *The Transparent Self* wrote:

> . . . When you permit yourself to be known, you expose yourself not only to a lover's balm, but also to a hater's bombs. When he knows you, he knows just where to plant them for maximum effect.

Jourard's message is clear. There is *risk* involved in self-disclosure: the risk of facing disapproval, being criticized, laughed at, and rejected. Although the thought of these possible consequences often makes self-disclosure pretty frightening, failure to do so is also undesirable. If you don't share yourself with others, you stand little chance of establishing meaningful relationships with others—without sharing yourself, it's difficult for others to help meet your basic social needs of belonging, being accepted, and being loved. Once you understand the connection between sharing knowledge of self and meaningful interpersonal relationships, it becomes apparent that you must take the risk that comes with self-disclosure. The question then becomes, when to open up and when to remain quiet.

MISS PEACH   By Mell Lazarus

One way of deciding when and what to disclose is to consider the risks and benefits involved. The first step here is to ask yourself what you stand to gain by disclosing yourself. Is the other person someone whose friendship, approval, or help is important to you? It might not be wise to share personal information with someone to whom you didn't feel especially close to in the first place. Such openness would be much more worthwhile if the potential for a new and important relationship existed.

You also should take a realistic look at the potential risks of self-disclosure. Even if the probable benefits are great, opening yourself up to almost certain rejection is simply asking for trouble. For instance, it might be foolhardy to share your important feelings with someone you know is likely to betray your confidences or ridicule them. On the other hand, knowing that your partner is trustworthy and supportive makes the prospect of speaking out more reasonable. In anticipating risks, be sure that you are realistic. It's sometimes easy to indulge in catastrophic expectations, in which you begin to imagine all sorts of disastrous consequences of your opening up, when in fact such horrors are very unlikely to occur.

A third point to realize is that there are *degrees* of self-disclosure, so that telling others about yourself isn't an all-or-nothing decision you must make. It's possible to share some facts, opinions, or feelings with one person while reserving riskier ones for others. In the same vein, before sharing very important information with someone who does matter to you, you might consider testing their reactions by disclosing less personal data.

In any case it's important to realize that any information you disclose about yourself should be relevant to your relationship with the person at hand. Self-disclosure isn't a long confession about your past life or current thoughts that is unrelated to the now. On the contrary, it ought to be directly pertinent to your present conversation. It's ludicrous to picture the self-disclosing person as someone who blurts out intimate details of every past experience. Instead, our model is someone who, when the time is appropriate, trusts us enough to share the hidden parts of himself that affect our relationship.

**take a chance
on getting slapped
you might
get kissed**

Bernard Gunther

Please Hear What I'm Not Saying

Don't be fooled by me.
Don't be fooled by the face I wear
For I wear a mask. I wear a thousand masks,
  masks that I'm afraid to take off
  and none of them are me.

Pretending is an art that's second nature with me
But don't be fooled, for God's sake don't be fooled.
I give you the impression that I'm secure
That all is sunny and unruffled with me
  within as well as without,
  that confidence is my name
  and coolness my game,
  that the water's calm
  and I'm in command,
  and that I need no one.
But don't believe me. Please!

My surface may be smooth but my surface is my mask,
My ever-varying and ever-concealing mask.
Beneath lies no smugness, no complacence.
Beneath dwells the real me in confusion, in fear, in alone-
    ness.
  But I hide this.
  I don't want anybody to know it.
  I panic at the thought of my weaknesses
  and fear exposing them.
That's why I frantically create my masks to hide behind.
They're nonchalant, sophisticated facades to help me pre-
    tend,
To shield me from the glance that knows.
But such a glance is precisely my salvation,
  my only salvation,
  and I know it.
That is, if it's followed by acceptance, if it's followed by
    love.

It's the only thing that can liberate me from myself
  from my own self-built prison walls
  from the barriers that I so painstakingly erect.
That glance is the only thing that assures me
  of what I can't assure myself,
  that I'm really worth something.

But I don't tell you this.
  I don't dare.
  I'm afraid to.

I'm afraid you'll think less of me, that you'll laugh
  and your laugh would kill me.
I'm afraid that deep-down I'm nothing, that I'm just no good
  and you will see this
  and reject me.
So I play my game, my desperate, pretending game
With a facade of assurance without
And a trembling child within,
So begins the parade of masks
The glittering but empty parade of masks,
And my life becomes a front.
I idly chatter to you in suave tones of surface talk.
I tell you everything that's nothing
And nothing of what's everything, of what's crying within
    me.
So when I'm going through my routine
Do not be fooled by what I'm saying.
Please listen carefully and try to hear
  what I'm *not* saying.
Hear what I'd like to say
  but what I can not say.

I dislike hiding.
  Honestly.
I dislike the superficial game I'm playing
  the superficial phony game.
I'd really like to be genuine
  and spontaneous
  and me.
But I need your help, your hand to hold
Even though my masks would tell you otherwise.

It will not be easy for you.
Long felt inadequacies make my defenses strong.
The nearer you approach me
The blinder I may strike back.
Despite what books say of men, I am irrational;
I fight against the very thing that I cry out for.

You wonder who I am?
You shouldn't
  For I am everyman
  And everywoman ——— that you meat
  Who wears a mask.
Don't be fooled by me.
At least not by the face I wear.

he stripped
the dark circle
of mystery off
revealed his eyes
and thus
he waited
exposed

and i
did sing the song
around
until i found
the chorus
that speaks
of windows

looking out
means looking in
my friend
and i'm all right
now
i'm fine
i have seen
the beauty
that is mine

you can
watch the sky
for signals
but look
to the eyes
for signs

Ric Masten

A Case for Self-Disclosure

Not long ago Neil began the first meeting of an interpersonal communication class with some of the exercises that you probably used in your group. The class quickly learned each other's names and were then paired for introductions. It was only a moment or two before an attractive, small blonde girl came up to Neil and quietly asked him how she could drop the class.

"What seems to be the problem?" he asked, a bit surprised.

"I can't do these things, so I think I should get out right away," Linda answered in a very quiet voice. She obviously didn't want any of the others to hear her.

"You did a great job with the name exercise. What's the trouble?"

With some effort Linda explained that she was hard of hearing and had to rely on her ability to read lips in order to talk with others. Because she could hear very little in the frequency range of the human voice, she mixed up words that sounded alike to her. This was the cause of what she called "talking funny."

"I don't want all these people to know. I just don't like that."

Neil told Linda that he was sorry to hear that she didn't think she could be comfortable with the other students. He pointed out that the class was run to promote support of each other, but Linda wasn't convinced and repeated that she had probably best get out.

With little to lose, Neil proposed that he and Linda team up for the introduction exercise. He would introduce her to the class, explaining that she had a hearing loss for which she was able to compensate by reading lips. In this way she wouldn't have to go through the usual routine of their finding out because they would all have been told.

Linda thought for a moment and surprised Neil by agreeing, on the condition that if it didn't work, she could drop.

As Linda began sharing information about herself, Neil learned that she worked part time as a waitress and was constantly reminded of her speech problem by customers who unknowingly asked what country she came from with that accent.

The introductions were started, and it was soon Linda's turn to introduce Neil. Now as she put the words together to make her remarks, the whole class became aware of Linda's articulation problem. She had had little trouble with just the names in the first exercise, and so no one had noticed, but now there was no doubt. Linda finished, and Neil began.

"I want you all to know a special and talented person. Linda is special because unlike the rest of us, she has a rather severe hearing loss, and she's talented because she is accomplished at reading lips."

As Neil went on, the room became absolutely quiet. "You see, Linda figured from these first exercises that she couldn't keep her hearing loss a secret, and she has suffered before when people have learned about it. She didn't want to repeat that experience, and so she asked to drop the class.

Researches I have conducted show that a person will permit himself to be known when he believes his audience is a man of goodwill.

Sidney M. Jourard

"I told Linda that when she got to know the individuals in this class, I thought she'd find them pretty supportive. It's been my experience that people who get to know each other tend to care about one another. I therefore asked her to let me introduce her by telling you why she's unique. She agreed and said that she guessed she had nothing to lose. I hope she'll want to stay."

The class's reaction was quick and direct: They applauded! Linda's self-disclosure was just the beginning. Two other students, one female and the other male, disclosed to the class that they were law-enforcement officers. They'd originally decided independently of each other that they would keep quiet about their jobs to avoid being hassled. Linda had changed their minds. they too took the risk that is inherent in self-disclosure and were accepted as individuals rather than stereotyped cops. Like so many other things in communication, self-disclosure is contagious.

We've written in detail about this experience because it was real. We could give literally hundreds of other examples in which self-disclosure in inter-personal communication classes has started lasting relationships. When was the last time you shared something of yourself with another?

i think of my poems as hands
and if i don't
hold them out to you
afraid that you might laugh
and spit on them
i find i won't be touched

if i keep them
in my pocket
i would never get to see you
seeing me
seeing you

and tho i know
from experience
many of you
for a myriad of reasons
will laugh
and spit
and walk away unmoved
still
to meet those of you who are
is well worth
the risk
the pain

so here are my hands
do what you will

Ric Masten

What Is Real?

The Skin Horse had lived longer in the nursery than any of the others. He was so old that his brown coat was bald in patches and showed the seams underneath, and most of the hairs in his tail had been pulled out to string bead necklaces. He was wise, for he had seen a long succession of mechanical toys arrive to boast and swagger, and by-and-by break their mainsprings and pass away, and he knew that they were only toys, and would never turn into anything else. For nursery magic is very strange and wonderful, and only those playthings that are old and wise and experienced like the Skin Horse understand all about it.

"What is REAL?" asked the Rabbit one day, when they were lying side by side near the nursery fender, before Nana came to tidy the room. "Does it mean having things that buzz inside you and a stick-out handle?"

"Real isn't how you are made," said the Skin Horse, "it's a thing that happens to you. When a child loves you for a long, long time, not just to play with, but REALLY loves you, then you become Real."

"Does it hurt?" asked the Rabbit.

"Sometimes," said the Skin Horse, for he was always truthful. "When you are Real you don't mind being hurt."

"Does it happen all at once, like being wound up," he asked. "or bit by bit?"

"It doesn't happen all at once," said the Skin Horse. "You become. It takes a long time. That's why it doesn't often happen to people who break easily, or have sharp edges, or who have to be carefully kept. Generally, by the time you are Real, most of your hair has been loved off, and your eyes drop out and you get loose in the joints and very shabby. But these things don't matter at all, because once you are Real you can't be ugly, except to people who don't understand."

"I suppose *you* are Real?" said the Rabbit. And then he wished he had not said it, for he thought the Skin Horse might be sensitive. But the Skin Horse only smiled.

"The Boy's Uncle made me Real," he said. "That was a great many years ago; but once you are Real you can't become unreal again. It lasts for always."

Margery Williams, *The Velveteen Rabbit*

By this time we hope that you know your classmates pretty well. We hope that the activities you've tried have helped build a comfortable atmosphere for the weeks ahead. In this chapter we've tried to introduce topics and methods you can expect to see throughout the course. Unless we're mistaken, the subjects you'll be exploring in the following chapters will hold considerable interest for you. Each will concern a specific area of interpersonal communication; both the problems that may exist and suggestions for coping with them are presented. If you're willing to apply the ideas you find here to your own life, there's a good chance that this can be a very useful experience for you, not only now but in the years to come.

Roads Not Taken

At the end of each chapter in this book you'll find a list of topics for further investigation. Any book has a limit on how much can be included, and this one is no exception. Therefore, many aspects of human communication are only mentioned here. Our hope is that this list may encourage you to pursue some area that interests you.

1 Explore the history of human communication. When did it begin? Has the human ability to communicate successfully changed from the time of early man to today?

2 How does human communication differ from that of animals?

3 What evidence can you gather that demonstrates the contemporary need for better interpersonal communication?

4 What are the various models of human communication that communicologists have developed?

5 What research exists on risk and trust in interpersonal relationships?

6 Keep a journal that records the degree to which you engage in self-disclosure. Report your opportunities for sharing important information about yourself, the risks and benefits involved, the amount of disclosing you do, and your level of satisfaction.

7 To what degree is the ability to identify and report sense data, make interpretations, experience and share feelings, and state intentions a natural talent, and to what degree is it a learned skill?

8 What are the similarities and differences between interpersonal, group, public, and mass communication?

9 Begin a "Significant Learning Journal." During the term of this course you will be asked to keep a journal in which you record your "significant learnings." We have borrowed this term from Carl Rogers, who defines it in his book, *On Becoming a Person:*

By significant learning I mean learning which is more than an accumulation of facts. It is learning which makes a difference—in the individual's behavior, in the course of action he chooses in the future, in his attitudes and in his personality. It is a pervasive learning which is not just an accretion of knowledge, but which interpenetrates with every portion of his existence.

We want this to be a practical course and we believe this journal can help you focus on what, if anything, you are studying in the classroom that you can apply to the real world.

Your entries should consist of whatever you have learned that has made a difference or will make a difference in the way you relate or communicate with others. *Caution:* Don't pass judgment on what you write in your journal. Even thinking "That's silly" or "Everybody else probably knows that already" will tend to start you censoring those things that you think you want to include. Try to include anything and everything that you consider significant.

Nothing you write will be made available to anyone other than your instructor. The mechanics of how you will handle making entries, how often, and where the journals will be kept should be worked out within your group. It sometimes helps if the journals are kept together and a regular time is allotted each week for writing in them.

I should not talk so
much about myself if there
were anybody else whom
I knew as well.

Henry David Thoreau

More Readings

Harris, Thomas A. *I'm O.K., You're O.K.* New York: Harper & Row, 1967.
The most understandable introduction to transactional analysis we've found. This book may give you another model for looking at the process of interpersonal communication.

Holtzman, Paul D., and Donald Ecroyd. *Communication Concepts and Models.* Skokie, Ill.: National Textbook Co., 1976.
This programmed text gives a thorough treatment of communication models in understandable terms.

Jourard, Sidney M. *The Transparent Self.* New York: Van Nostrand Reinhold, 1971.
This is probably the best-known treatment of self-disclosure in print. Jourard writes well about its role in the helping relationship, particularly the nursing profession.

Kavanaugh, James. *Will You Be My Friend?* Los Angeles: Nash Publishing, 1971.
Kavanaugh's poems speak to many of the rewards and problems contained in this book.

Keyes, Ralph. *We, The Lonely People: Searching For Community.* New York: Harper & Row, 1973.
Keyes makes a strong case for the necessity of community, and describes its absence in contemporary society.

Lazarus, Arnold, and Allen Fay. *I Can If I Want To.* New York: Morrow, 1975.
Lazarus and Fay give a detailed list of the many faulty interpretations people often place on their own behavior and that of others, as well as providing more sensible ways of thinking. We recommend this book highly.

Luft, Joseph. *Of Human Interaction.* Palo Alto, Cal.: National Press Books, 1969.
A clear, detailed introduction to the Johari Window, with an analysis of how various degrees of openness influence communication.

Maslow, Abraham H. *Toward a Psychology of Being.* New York: Van Nostrand Reinhold, 1968.
This is a collection of lectures Maslow has given to explain his humanistic paychology. He carefully works out his hierachy of basic human needs.

Miller, Sherod, Elam Nunnally, and Daniel B. Wackman. *Alive and Aware.* Minneapolis: Interpersonal Communication Programs, Inc., 1975.
This book gives an excellent description of the sensing-interpreting-feeling-intending messages discussed in Chapter 1.

Wood, John. *How Do You Feel? A Guide to Your Emotions.* Englewood Cliffs, N.J.: Prentice-Hall, 1974.

Wood and his friends put into words how they feel when they're experiencing thirty-one different emotions. Many readers find these descriptions helpful in recognizing their own feelings.

Films

Communication Primer. Color. 23 min. 1965. Iowa University.

Animation and other techniques are used to illustrate communications models. Excellent overview and evaluation of the Shannon-Weaver model, the concept of noise, and the utilization of redundancy in language. Good basic film for those unfamiliar with conceptual theories of communication.

Expanding World of Communication. Color. 28 min. 1974. Iowa University.

A fast-paced and contemporary look at the many technologies being used to expand our ability to communicate effectively.

Get the Message. Color. 12 min. Disney. Central Arizona Film Cooperative.

Presents an animated history of human communication. Stresses that in modern times the message is often more complicated than the means of communication.

Process of Communication. Color. 46 min. 1968. Indiana University.

Presents models, theories, and practical examples of various aspects of communication as a process and shows diagrammatic communications models that encompass the concept of noise.

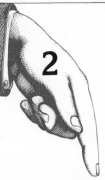

2

The Self-Concept: Key to Communication

Will the Real Me Please Stand Up?

In the beginning, I was one person, knowing nothing but my own experience.

Then I was told things, and I became two people: the little girl who said how terrible it was that the boys had a fire going in the lot next door where they were roasting apples (which was what the women said)—and the little girl who, when the boys were called by their mothers to go to the store, ran out and tended the fire and the apples because she loved doing it.

So then there were two of I.

One I always doing something that the other I disapproved of. Or other I said what I disapproved of. All this argument in me so much.

In the beginning was I, and I was good.

Then came in other I. Outside authority. This was confusing. And then other I became very confused because there were so many different outside authorities.

Sit nicely. Leave the room to blow your nose. Don't do that, that's silly. Why, the poor child doesn't even know how to pick a bone! Flush the toilet at night because if you don't it makes it harder to clean. DON'T FLUSH THE TOILET AT NIGHT—you wake people up! Always be nice to people. Even if you don't like them, you musn't hurt their feelings. Be frank and honest. If you don't tell people what you think of them, that's cowardly. Butter knives. It is important to use butter knives. Butter knives? What foolishness! Speak nicely. Sissy! Kipling is wonderful! Ugh! Kipling (turning away).

The most important thing is to have a career. The most important thing is to get married. The hell with everyone. Be nice to everyone. The most important thing is sex. The most important thing is to have everyone like you. The most important thing is to be sophisticated and say what you don't mean and don't let anyone know what you feel. The most important thing is a black seal coat and china and silver. The most important thing is to be clean. The most important thing is to always pay your debts. The most important thing is not to be taken in by anyone else. The most important thing is to love your parents. The most important thing is to work. The most important thing is to be independent. The most important thing is to speak correct English. The most important thing is to go to the right plays and read the right books. The most important thing is to do what others say. And others say all these things.

All the time, I is saying, live with life. That is what is important.

But when I lives with life, other I says no, that's bad. All the different other I's say this. It's dangerous. It isn't practical. You'll come to a bad end. Of course . . . everyone felt that way once, the way you do, but *you'll learn*.

Out of all the other I's some are chosen as a pattern that is me. But there are all the other possibilities of patterns within what all the others say which come into me and become other I which is not myself, and sometimes these take over. Then who am I?

I does not bother about who am I. I is, and is happy being. But when I is happy being, other I says get to work, do something worthwhile! I is happy doing dishes. "You're weird!" I is happy being with people saying nothing. Other I says talk. Talk, talk, talk. I gets lost.

I know that things are to be played with, not possessed. I likes putting things together, lightly. Taking things apart, lightly. "You'll never have anything!" Making things of things in a way that the things themselves take part in, putting themselves together with surprise and delight to I. "There's no money in that!"

The Self-Concept: Key to Communication

63

I is human. If someone needs, I gives. "You can't do that! You'll never have anything for yourself! We'll have to support you!"

I loves. I loves in a way that other I does not know. I loves. "That's too warm for friends!" "That's too cool for lovers!" "Don't feel so bad, he's just a friend. It's not as though you loved him." "How can you let him go? I thought you loved him?" So cool the warm for friends and hot up the love for lovers, and I gets lost.

So both I's have a house and a husband and children and all that, but both I's are confused because other I says, "You see? You're lucky," while I goes on crying. "What are you crying about? Why are you so ungrateful?" I doesn't know gratitude or ingratitude, and cannot argue. I goes on crying. Other I pushes it out, says "I am happy! I am very lucky to have such a fine family and a nice house and good neighbors and lots of friends who want me to do this, do that." I is not reason-able, either. I goes on crying.

Other I gets tired, and goes on smiling, because that is the thing to do. Smile, and you will be rewarded. Like the seal who gets tossed a piece of fish. Be nice to everyone and you will be rewarded.

People will be nice to you, and you can be happy with that. You know they like you. Like a dog who gets patted on the head for good behavior. Tell funny stories. Be gay. Smile, smile, smile. . . . I is crying. . . . "Don't be sorry for yourself! Go out and do things for people!" "Go out and be with people!" I is still crying, but now, that is not heard and felt so much.

Suddenly: "What am I doing?" "Am I to go through life playing the clown?" "What am I doing, going to parties that I do not enjoy?" "What am I doing, being with people who bore me?" "Why am I so hollow and the hollowness filled with emptiness?" A shell. How has this shell grown around me? Why am I proud of my children and unhappy about their lives which are not good enough? Why am I disappointed? Why do I feel so much waste?

I comes through, a little. In moments. And gets pushed back by other I.

I refuses to play the clown any more. Which I is that? "She used to be fun, but now she thinks too much about herself." I lets friends drop away. Which I is that? "She's being too much by herself. That's bad. She's losing her mind." Which mind?

BARRY STEVENS, *Person to Person*

Who Do You Think You Are?

For each category below, supply the three words or phrases that best describe you. You'll use this list throughout this chapter and beyond, so be sure to complete it now before you go on.

1 What moods or feelings best characterize you? (cheerful, thoughtful, pessimistic, etc.)

a. _____

b. _____

c. _____

2 How would you describe your physical condition and/or your appearance? (tall, handsome, sickly, muscular, etc.)

a. _____

b. _____

c. _____

3 How would you describe your social traits? (friendly, shy, aloof, talkative, etc.)

a. _____

b. _____

c. _____

4 What talents do you possess or lack? (good artist, lousy carpenter, competent swimmer, etc.)

a. _____

b. _____

c. _____

5 How would you describe your intellectual capacity? (curious, poor reader, good mathematician, etc.)

a. _____

b. _____

c. _____

6 What beliefs do you hold strongly? (vegetarian, Christian, pacifist, etc.)

a. _____

b. _____

c. _____

7 What social roles are most important in your life? (brother, student, friend, bank teller, club president, etc.)

a. _____

b. _____

c. _____

8 What other terms haven't you listed so far which describe important things about you?

a. _____

b. _____

c. _____

To be nobody—but—yourself in a world which is doing its best, night and day, to make you everybody—else means to fight the hardest battle which any human being can fight, and never stop fighting.

E. E. Cummings

Have you completed the list above? If not, be sure to do so before going on. Much of what follows in this chapter depends on the information you've recorded here.

... for the love of one's
neighbor is not possible
without the love of
ones-self.

Herman Hesse

Now take a look at what you've written. You'll probably see that the words you've chosen represent a profile of what you now view as your most important characteristics. In other words, if you were required to describe the "real you," this list ought to be a pretty accurate summary.

What you've done in developing this list is to give a partial description of your *self-concept.* There are many different ways of defining this term, but probably the clearest way to think of your self-concept is as the image you hold of yourself. If you could imagine a special mirror that not only reflected physical features, but also allowed you to view other aspects of yourself—emotional states, talents, likes, dislikes, values, roles, and so on—then the reflection you'd see looking back at you in that mirror would be your self-concept.

You probably recognize that the self-concept list you recorded above is only a partial one. To make the description of your self complete you'd have to keep adding items until your list ran into hundreds of words.

Take a moment now to demonstrate the many parts of your self-concept by simply responding to the question "Who am I?" over and over again. Add these responses to the list you started above.

Of course, not every item on your self-concept list is equally important. For example, the most significant part of one person's self-concept might consist of social roles, while for another it might be physical appearance, health, friendships, accomplishments, or skills.

You can discover how much you value each part of your self-concept by rank-ordering the items on the list you've compiled. Try it now: Place number 1 next to the most fundamental thing about you, number 2 next to the second most important term, and continue on in this manner until you've completed your list.

"All right," you say, "now I know pretty clearly what my self-concept is, but what does this have to do with the way I communicate?" We can begin to answer this question by looking at how you came to possess your present self-concept.

How the Self-Concept Develops

You can begin to understand how your self-concept came to be by trying the following exercise.

Uppers and Downers

1 Either by yourself or aloud with a partner, recall someone you know or once knew who was an "upper"—who helped enhance your self-concept by acting in a way that made you feel accepted, worthwhile, important, appreciated, or loved. Your upper needn't have played a crucial role in your life, as long as the role was positive. Often one's self-concept is shaped by many tiny nudges as well as a few giant events.

The Self-Concept: Key to Communication

Some uppers we have known are

a. Sam, who when Ron was six or seven years old treated him to "special days"—a morning spent together exploring the treasures in Sam's jewelry store, followed by a lunch in a restaurant.

b. Marge, a student who recently approached us after completing our class to report her success at a new job and to insist that it wouldn't have been possible without our help.

c. Miss Gardner, Neil's high school history teacher, who invited him to join her in entering a Contemporary History Contest, and repeatedly told him that she was confident he would do an excellent job.

2 After thinking about your upper, take time to recall a "downer" from your life—some person who acted in either a big or small way to diminish your self-esteem.

At this time we can recall downers such as

a. Students who yawn in the middle of our classes. (They may be tired, but it's difficult to avoid the thought that we're not teaching as effectively as we might be.)

b. Ken, a junior high school classmate of Ron's who seemed to enjoy making Ron look bad by challenging him to fight, elbowing him in the ribs constantly in basketball games, and trying to steal away girl-friends, among other things.

c. Joyce, a former girlfriend of Neil's, who shrugged off his romantic overtures by refusing to take them seriously.

3 Now that you've thought about people who were uppers to you, recall the last time you were an upper to someone else. What ways have you acted that helped build others' self-esteem?

Don't merely settle for a recent instance in which you were *nice:* Look for a time when your actions had the effect of letting another know that he was valued, loved, needed, and so on.

For instance, we can recall recently being uppers by

a. Spending time with our children. Taking the time to listen with full attention to their account of a day's events or play a game with them.

b. Buying gifts for our wives for no special occasion.

c. Saying "thanks" to students who have offered valuable comments in class.

4 Finally, recall a recent instance in which you were a downer for someone else. What did you do to diminish another's self-concept?

Some of our recent downers are

a. Yesterday Ron was caught sneaking a look at the clock by a friend who was describing in great detail her recent vacation.

b. Being involved in writing this book, we failed to return the call of a colleague who wanted to talk with us.

c. When Neil questioned his son Steve's explanation, he was asked, "How come you can't ever believe me, Dad?"

25¢ 1ST 1/5 MILE

5¢ EACH 1/2 MILE

Love and the Cabbie

I was in New York the other day and rode with a friend in a taxi. When we got out my friend said to the driver. "Thank you for the ride. You did a superb job of driving."

The taxi driver was stunned for a second. Then he said:

"Are you a wise guy or something?"

"No, my dear man, and I'm not putting you on. I admire the way you keep cool in heavy traffic."

"Yeh," the driver said and drove off.

"What was that all about?" I asked.

"I am trying to bring love back to New York," he said. "I believe it's the only thing that can save the city."

"How can one man save New York?"

"It's not one man. I believe I have made the taxi driver's day. Suppose he has twenty fares. He's going to be nice to those twenty fares because someone was nice to him. Those fares in turn will be kinder to their employees or shop-keepers or waiters or even their own families. Eventually the goodwill could spread to at least 1,000 people. Now that isn't bad, is it?"

"But you're depending on that taxi driver to pass your goodwill to others."

"I'm not depending on it," my friend said. "I'm aware that the system isn't foolproof so I might deal with 10 different people today. If, out of 10, I can make three happy, then eventually I can indirectly influence the attitudes of 3,000 more."

"It sounds good on paper," I admitted, "but I'm not sure it works in practice."

"Nothing is lost if it doesn't. I didn't take any of my time to tell that man he was doing a good job. He neither received a larger tip nor a smaller tip. If it fell on deaf ears, so what? Tomorrow there will be another taxi driver whom I can try to make happy."

"You're some kind of a nut," I said.

"That shows you how cynical you have become. I have made a study of this. The thing that seems to be lacking, besides money of course, for our postal employees, is that no one tells people who work for the post office what a good job they're doing."

"But they're not doing a good job."

"They're not doing a good job because they feel no one cares if they do or not. Why shouldn't someone say a kind word to them?"

We were walking past a structure in the process of being built and passed five workmen eating their lunch. My friend stopped. "That's a magnificent job you men have done. It must be difficult and dangerous work."

The five men eyed my friend suspiciously.

"When will it be finished?"

"June," a man grunted.

"Ah. That really is impressive. You must all be very proud."

We walked away. I said to him, "I haven't seen anyone like you since 'The Man from La Mancha.'"

"When those men digest my words, they will feel better for it. Somehow the city will benefit from their happiness."

"But you can't do this all alone!" I protested. "You're just one man."

"The most important thing is not to get discouraged. Making people in the city become kind again is not an easy job, but if I can enlist other people in my campaign. . ."

"You just winked at a very plain looking woman," I said.

"Yes, I know," he replied. "And if she's a schoolteacher, her class will be in for a fantastic day."

Art Buchwald

After completing the "upper and downer" exercise (you *did* complete it, didn't you?) you should begin to see that everyone's self-concept is shaped by those around him or her. To the extent that you have received upper messages, you have learned to appreciate and value yourself. To the degree that they have communicated downer signals, you are likely to feel less valuable, lovable, and capable. In this sense it's possible to see that the self-concept you partially described in your list on page 64 is a product of the upper and downer messages you've received throughout your life.

To further illustrate this point, let's start at the beginning of life. A newborn child isn't born with any sense of identity: She only learns to judge herself through the way others treat her.

At first the evaluations aren't linguistic. Nonetheless, even the earliest days of life are full of messages that constitute the first uppers and/or downers that start to shape her self-concept. The amount of time parents allow their child to cry before attending to her needs nonverbally communicates over a period of time how important she is to them. Their method of handling her also speaks volumes: Do they affectionately toy with her, joggling her gently and holding her close, or do they treat her like so much baggage, changing diapers, feeding and bathing her in a brusque, business-like manner? Does the tone of voice with which they speak to her express love and enjoyment or disappointment and irritation?

Of course, most of these messages are not intentional ones. It is rare when a parent will deliberately try to tell a child she's not lovable; but whether they're intentional or not doesn't matter—nonverbal statements play a big role in shaping a youngster's feelings of being "o.k." or "not o.k."

As the child learns to speak and understand language, verbal messages also contribute to her developing self-concept. Every day a child is bombarded with scores of messages about herself. Some of these uppers . . .

"You're so cute!"

"I love you."

"What a big girl!"

"It's fun to play with you."

. . . while other messages are downers.

"Can't you do anything right?"

"What's the matter with you?"

"You're a bad girl!"

"Leave me alone. You're driving me crazy!"

As we've said, the evaluations others make of us are the mirrors by which we know ourselves; and since children are trusting souls who have no other way of viewing themselves, they accept at face value both the positive and negative evaluations of the apparently all-knowing and all-powerful adults around them.

The Self-Concept: Key to Communication

Children Learn What They Live

If a child lives with criticism
    he learns to condemn.
If a child lives with hostility
    he learns to fight.
If a child lives with ridicule
    he learns to be shy.
If a child lives with shame
    he learns to feel guilty.
If a child lives with tolerance
    he learns to be patient.
If a child lives with
    encouragement
    he learns confidence.
If a child lives with praise
    he learns to appreciate.
If a child lives with fairness
    he learns justice.
If a child lives with security
    he learns to have faith.
If a child lives with approval
    he learns to like himself.
If a child lives with acceptance
    and friendship
    he learns to find love in the
    world.

Dorothy Law Nolte

These same principles of self-concept formation continue in later life, especially when messages come from what sociologists term "significant others"—those people whose opinions we especially value. A look at the uppers and downers you described in the previous exercise (as well as others you can remember) will show that the evaluations of a few especially important people can have long-range effects. A teacher from long ago, a special friend or relative, or perhaps a barely known acquaintance whom you respected can all leave an imprint on how you view yourself. To see the importance of significant others, ask yourself how you arrived at your opinion of you as a student . . . as a person attractive to the opposite sex . . . as a competent worker . . . and you'll see that these self-evaluations were probably influenced by the way others regarded you.

In addition to specific influential individuals, each of us also formulates a self-concept based on the influence of various reference groups to which we are exposed. A youngster who is interested in ballet and who lives in a setting where such preferences are regarded as weird will start to accept this label if there is no support from significant others. Adults who want to share their feelings but find themselves in a society that discourages such sharing might after a while think of themselves as oddballs, unless they get some reassurance that such a desire is normal. Again, the idea of knowing ourselves through the mirrors of others stands out. To a great degree we judge ourselves by the way others see us.

You might argue that not every part of one's self-concept is shaped by others, insisting there are certain objective facts that are recognizable by self-observation. After all, nobody needs to tell a person that she is taller than others, speaks with an accent, has acne, and so on. These facts are obvious.

While it's true that some features of the self are immediately apparent, the *significance* we attach to them—the rank we assign them in the hierarchy of our list and the interpretation we give them—depends greatly on the opinions of others. After all, there are many of your features that are readily observable, yet you don't find them important at all because nobody has regarded them as significant.

Recently we heard a woman in her eighties describing her youth. "When I was a girl," she declared, "we didn't worry about weight. Some people were skinny and others were plump, and we pretty much accepted the bodies God gave us." In those days it's unlikely that weight would have found its way onto the self-concept list you constructed, since it wasn't considered significant. Compare this attitude with what you find today: It's seldom that you pick up a popular magazine or visit a bookstore without reading about the latest diet fads, and television ads are filled with scenes of slender, happy people. As a result you'll rarely find a person (especially female) who doesn't complain about the need to "lose a few pounds." Obviously the reason for such concern has more to do with the attention paid to slimness these days than with any increase in the number of people in the population who are overweight. Furthermore, the interpretation of characteristics such as weight depends on the way people important to us regard them. We generally see fat as undesirable because others tell us it is. In a society where obesity is the ideal (and there are such societies) a person who regards herself as extremely heavy would be a beauty. In the same way, the fact that one is single or married, solitary or sociable, aggressive or passive takes on meaning depending on the interpretation society attaches to those traits. Thus, the importance of a given characteristic in your self-concept has as much to do with the significance you and others attach to it as with the existence of the characteristic.

By now you might be thinking, "Adler and Towne are telling me it's not my fault that I've always been shy or unconfident. Since I developed a picture of myself as a result of the way others have treated me, I can't help being what I am." While it's true that to a great extent you are a product of your environment, to accept yourself as being forever doomed to possess a poor self-concept would be a big mistake. Having held a poor self-image in the past is no reason for continuing to do so in the future. You *can* change your attitudes and behaviors, as you'll shortly read. So don't despair, and most of all don't use the fact that others have shaped your self-concept as an excuse for self-pity or acting helpless. Now that you know the effect that overly negative evaluations have had on you in the past, you'll be in a better position to revise your perception of yourself more favorably in the future.

"Guess who Miss Price picked to play poison ivy in the class play."

CIPHER IN THE SNOW *

It started with tragedy on a biting cold February morning. I was driving behind the Milford Corners bus as I did most snowy mornings on my way to school. It veered and stopped short at the hotel, which it had no business doing, and I was annoyed as I had to come to an unexpected stop. A boy lurched out of the bus, reeled, stumbled, and collapsed on the snowbank at the curb. The bus driver and I reached him at the same moment. His thin, hollow face was white even against the snow.

"He's dead," the driver whispered.

It didn't register for a minute. I glanced quickly at the scared young faces staring down at us from the school bus. "A doctor! Quick! I'll phone from the hotel. . . ."

"No use, I tell you he's dead." The driver looked down at the boy's still form. "He never even said he felt bad," he muttered. "Just tapped me on the shoulder and said, real quiet, 'I'm sorry. I have to get off at the hotel.' That's all. Polite and apologizing like."

At school, the giggling, shuffling morning noise quieted as the news went down the halls. I passed a huddle of girls. "Who was it? Who dropped dead on the way to school?" I heard one of them half-whisper.

"Don't know his name; some kid from Milford Corners" was the reply.

It was like that in the faculty room and the principal's office. "I'd appreciate your going out to tell the parents," the principal told me. "They haven't a phone and, anyway, somebody from school should go there in person. I'll cover your classes."

"Why me?" I asked. "Wouldn't it be better if you did it?"

"I didn't know the boy," the principal admitted levelly. "And, in last year's sophomore personalities column I note that you were listed as his favorite teacher."

I drove through the snow and cold down the bad canyon road to the Evans place and thought about the boy, Cliff Evans. His favorite teacher! I thought. He hasn't spoken two words to me in two years! I could see him in my mind's eye all right, sitting back there in the last seat in my afternoon literature class. He came in the room by himself and left by himself. "Cliff Evans," I muttered to myself, "a boy who never talked." I thought a minute. "A boy who never smiled. I never saw him smile once."

The big ranch kitchen was clean and warm. I blurted out my news somehow. Mrs. Evans reached blindly toward a chair. "He never said anything about bein' ailing."

His stepfather snorted. "He ain't said nothin' about anything since I moved in here."

Mrs. Evans pushed a pan to the back of the stove and began to untie her apron. "Now hold on," her husband snapped. "I got to have breakfast before I go to town. Nothin' we can do now anyway. If Cliff hadn't been so dumb, he'd have told us he didn't feel good."

After school I sat in the office and stared blankly at the records spread out before me. I was to close the file and write the obituary for the school paper. The almost bare sheets mocked the effort. Cliff Evans, white, never legally adopted by stepfather, five young half-brothers and sisters. These meager strands of information and the list of D grades were all the records had to offer.

Cliff Evans had silently come in the school door in the mornings and gone out the school door in the evenings, and that was all. He had never belonged to a club. He had never played on a team. He had never held an office. As far as I could tell

---

* A true story. "Cipher in the Snow" by Jean Mizer from *Today's Education,* November, 1964. Reprinted by permission of the author and publisher.

he had never done one happy, noisy kid thing. He had never been anybody at all.

How do you go about making a boy into a zero? The grade-school records showed me. The first and second grade teachers' annotations read "sweet, shy child," "timid but eager." Then the third grade note had opened the attack. Some teacher had written in a good, firm hand, "Cliff won't talk. Uncooperative. Slow learner." The other academic sheep had followed with "dull"; "slow-witted"; "low I.Q." They became correct. The boy's I.Q. score in the ninth grade was listed at 83. But his I.Q. in the third grade had been 106. The score didn't go under 100 until the seventh grade. Even shy, timid, sweet children have resilience. It takes time to break them.

I stomped to the typewriter and wrote a savage report pointing out what education had done to Cliff Evans. I slapped a copy on the principal's desk and another in the sad, dog-eared file. I banged the typewriter and slammed the file and crashed the door shut, but I didn't feel much better. A little boy kept walking after me, a little boy with a peaked, pale face; a skinny body in faded jeans; and big eyes that had looked and searched for a long time and then had become veiled.

I could guess how many times he'd been chosen last to play sides in a game, how many whispered child conversations had excluded him, how many times he hadn't been asked. I could see and hear the faces and voices that said over and over, "You're a nothing, Cliff Evans."

A child is a believing creature. Cliff undoubtedly believed them. Suddenly it seemed clear to me: When finally there was nothing left at all for Cliff Evans, he collapsed on a snowbank and went away. The doctor might list "heart failure" as the cause of death, but that wouldn't change my mind.

We couldn't find ten students in the school who had known Cliff well enough to attend the funeral as his friends. So the student body officers and a committee from the junior class went as a group to the church, being politely sad. I attended the services with them, and sat through it with a lump of cold lead in my chest and a big resolve growing through me.

I've never forgotten Cliff Evans nor that resolve. He has been my challenge year after year, class after class. I look for veiled eyes or bodies scrouged into a seat in an alien world. "Look, kids," I say silently, "I may not do anything else for you this year, but not one of you is going to come out of here a nobody. I'll work or fight to the bitter end doing battle with society and the school board, but I won't have one of you coming out of here thinking himself a zero."

Most of the time—not always, but most of the time—I've succeeded.

Jean Mizer

Funny you should mention old Molly Silvester.
She used to,
    in the old days when we were just little shavers
    in grammar school,
Wear brown shoelaces when
    as everyone knew
Everyone was wearing black ones.
We kids used to tease her about that, remember?
    And the way she'd wear
    that short yellow dress.

She'd just sit there and take it, ya know?
Well, just the other day I got the news
That old Molly's in some kind of nut house
    upstate.
We haven't seen her since school
    and she wasn't crazy then.
I can't imagine what could've done it to her.

Karen E. Thomas

Characteristics of the Self-Concept

Now that you have a better idea of how your self-concept has developed, we can take a closer look at some of its characteristics.

The self-concept is not objective The way you see yourself isn't always the same as the way others view you. Sometimes the image you hold of yourself might be more favorable than the way others regard you. You might, for instance, see yourself as a witty joketeller when others can barely tolerate your attempts at humor. You might view yourself as highly intelligent while one or more instructors would see your scholarship as substandard. Perhaps you consider yourself an excellent worker, in contrast to the employer who wants to fire you.

There are several reasons why some people have a self-concept that others would regard as being unrealistically favorable. First, a self-estimation might be based on obsolete information. Perhaps your jokes used to be well received, or your grades were high, or your work was superior, and now the facts have changed. As you'll soon read, people are reluctant to give up a familiar self-image; this principle makes especially good sense when it's possible to avoid the unpleasant truth of the present by staying in the more desirable past.

A self-concept might also be excessively favorable due to distorted feedback from others. A boss may think of himself as an excellent manager because his assistants laving him with false praise in order to keep their jobs. A child's inflated ego may be based on the praise of doting parents.

A third reason for holding what appears to be an unrealistically high self-concept has to do with the expectations of a society that demands too much of its members. Much of the conditioning we receive in our early years implies that anything less than perfection is unsatisfactory, so that admitting one's mistakes is often seen as a sign of weakness. Instructors who fail to admit they don't know everything about a subject are afraid they will lose face with their colleagues and students. Couples whose relationships are beset by occasional problems don't want to admit that they have failed to achieve the "ideal" relationship they've seen portrayed in fiction. Parents who don't want to say, "I'm sorry, I made a mistake," to their children are afraid they'll lose the youngsters' respect. Once you accept such an irrational idea—that to be less than perfect is a character defect—admitting your frailties becomes difficult. Such a confession equates with admitting one is a failure—and failure is not an element of most peoples' self-concept. Rather than label themselves failures, many people engage in self-deception, insisting to themselves and to others that their behavior is more admirable than the circumstances indicate. We'll have more to say about the reasons behind such behavior and its consequences in Chapter 3, when we discuss defense mechanisms.

In contrast to the cases we've just described are times when we view ourselves *more* harshly than the objective facts suggest. You may have known people, for instance, who insist that they are unattractive or incompetent in spite of your honest insistence to the contrary. In fact, you have probably experienced feelings of excessively negative self-evaluation yourself. Recall a time when you woke up with a case of the "uglies," convinced that you looked terrible. Remember how on such days you were unwilling to accept even the most sincere compliments from others, having already decided how wretched you were. While many of us only fall into the trap of being overly critical occasionally, others constantly have an unrealistically low self-concept.

What are the reasons for such excessively negative self-evaluations? As with an unrealistically high self-esteem, one source for an overabundance of self-putdowns is obsolete information. A string of past failures in school or social relations can linger to haunt a communicator long after they have occurred, even though such events don't predict failure in the future. Similarly, we've known slender students who still think of themselves as fat and clear complexioned people who still behave as if they were acne-ridden.

Distorted feedback can also create a self-image that is worse than a more objective observer would see. Having grown up around overly critical parents is one of the most common causes of a negative self-image. In other cases the remarks of cruel friends, uncaring teachers, excessively demanding employers, or even memorable strangers can have a lasting effect. As you read earlier, the impact of significant others and reference groups in forming a self-concept can be great.

A third cause for a very negative self-concept is again the myth of perfection, which is common in our society. From the time most of us learn to understand language we are exposed to models who appear to be perfect at whatever they do. This myth is most clear when we examine the most common stories children are told. In them the hero is wise, brave, talented, and victorious, while the villain is totally evil and doomed to failure. This kind of model is easy for a child to understand, but it hardly paints a realistic picture of the world, in which whatever heroes are identifiable are definitely not faultless. Unfortunately, many parents perpetuate the myth of perfection by refusing to admit that they are ever mistaken or unfair. Kids, of course, accept this perfectionist facade for a long time, not being in any position to dispute the wisdom of such powerful beings. And from the behavior of the adults around them comes the clear message: "A well-adjusted, successful person has no faults." Thus children learn that in order to gain acceptance, it's necessary to pretend to "have it all together," even though they know this isn't the case. Given this naive belief that everyone else is perfect and the knowledge that you aren't, it's easy to see how one's self-concept would suffer.

Don't get the mistaken impression that we're suggesting it's wrong to aim at perfection as an *ideal*. We're only suggesting that achieving this state is usually not possible, and to expect that you should do so is a sure ticket to an inaccurate and unnecessarily low self-concept.

A final reason people often sell themselves short is also connected to social expectations. Curiously, the perfectionistic society to which we belong rewards those people who downplay the strengths we demand they possess (or pretend to possess). We term these people "modest" and find their behavior agreeable. On the other hand, we consider those who honestly appreciate their strengths to be "braggarts" or "egotists," confusing them with the people who boast about accomplishments they do not possess. This convention leads most of us to talk freely about our shortcomings while downplaying our accomplishments. It's all right to proclaim that you're miserable if you have failed to do well on a project, while it's considered boastful to express your pride at a job well done. It's fine to remark that you feel unattractive, but egocentric to say that you think you look good.

After a while we begin to believe the types of statements we repeatedly make. The self-putdowns are viewed as modesty and become part of our self-concept, while the strengths and accomplishments go unmentioned and are thus forgotten. And in the end we see ourselves as much worse than we are.

To contrast this kind of distortion, try the following exercise. It will give you a chance to suspend the rules we've just discussed by letting you appreciate yourself publicly for a change.

Group Bragging

1 Everyone should be seated so they can see each other.

2 Starting at one point of the circle, proceed to your right. In turn, each person should give three brags about herself. These brags needn't be about areas where you are an expert, and they don't have to be concerned with momentous feats. On the contrary, it's perfectly acceptable to brag about some part of yourself or thing you've done about which you're pleased or proud. For instance, you might share the fact that for once you completed a school assignment before the last minute, that you made the final payment on your car, that you bake a fantastic chocolate fudge cake, that you're proud to express your religious faith, or that you frequently drive hitchhikers to their destinations although it's out of your way.

3 If you're at a loss for brags, ask yourself
   a. What are some ways in which you've grown in the past year? How are you wiser, more skillful, or a better person than you previously were?
   b. Why do certain friends or family members care about you? What features do you possess that makes that person appreciate you?

4 If you're at a loss to think of brags, there's a penalty. You must sit and listen without protesting while other group members give you compliments. What a terrible fate!

5 After everyone has finished bragging, discuss the experience. How did you feel as you shared parts of yourself that you feel good about? Was this difficult? Did you have a hard time thinking of things to say? Consider whether you would have found it easier to think of a list of the things that are *wrong* with you. If this would have been less difficult, ask yourself whether this is because you truly are a wretched person or rather because you are in the habit of stressing your defects and ignoring your strengths. Consider the impact of such a habit on your self-concept, and ask yourself whether it wouldn't be wiser to place your self-appreciations and self-putdowns into more balance.

A healthy self-concept is flexible People change. From moment to moment we aren't the same. We wake up in the morning in a jovial mood and turn grumpy before lunch. We find ourselves fascinated in a conversational topic one moment, then suddenly lose interest. One moment's anger often gives way to forgiveness the next. Health turns to illness and back to health. Alertness becomes fatigue, hunger becomes satiation, and confusion becomes clarity.

We also change from situation to situation. You might be a relaxed conversationalist with people you know but at a loss for words with strangers. You might be patient when explaining things on the job and have no tolerance for such things at home. You might be a wizard at solving mathematical problems but have a terribly difficult time putting your thoughts into words.

Over longer stretches of time we also change. We grow older, learn new facts, adopt new attitudes and philosophies, set and reach new goals, and find that others change their way of thinking and acting toward us.

Since we change in these and many other ways, to keep a realistic picture of ourselves our self-concept must also change. Thus an accurate self-portrait of the type described on page 64 would probably not be the same as it would have been a year or a few months ago or even the way it would have been yesterday. This doesn't mean that you will change radically from day to day. There are certainly fundamental characteristics of your personality that will stay the same for years, perhaps for a lifetime. It is likely, however, that in other important ways you are changing—physically, intellectually, emotionally, and spiritually.

The Self-Concept: Key to Communication

"I don't have personal history any more," he said and looked at me probingly. "I dropped it one day when I felt it was no longer necessary."

I stared at him, trying to detect the hidden meanings of his words.

"How can one drop one's personal history?" I asked in an argumentative mood.

"One must first have the desire to drop it," he said. "And then one must proceed harmoniously to chop it off, little by little . . . ."

"It is best to erase all personal history," he said slowly, as if giving me time to write it down in my clumsy way, "because that would make us free from the encumbering thoughts of other people."

I could not believe that he was actually saying that. I had a very confusing moment. He must have read in my face my inner turmoil and used it immediately.

"Take yourself, for instance," he went on saying. "Right now you don't know whether you are coming or going. And that is so, because I have erased my personal history. I have, little by little, created a fog around me and my life. And now nobody knows for sure who I am or what I do."

"But, you yourself know who you are, don't you?" I interjected.

"You bet I . . . don't," he exclaimed and rolled on the floor, laughing at my surprised look.

He had paused long enough to make me believe that he was going to say that he did know, as I was anticipating it. His subterfuge was very threatening to me. I actually became afraid.

"That is the little secret I am going to give you today," he said in a low voice. "Nobody knows my personal history. Nobody knows who I am or what I do. Not even I."

Carlos Castaneda, *Journey to Ixtlan*

HATE YOURSELF?
IT MAY NOT BE THE REAL YOU

Call it gossip, call it character analysis, call it what you will, the demand for private information about public people is running full throttle. We want to know who they *really* are. We want to know what they're *really* like.

We want the warts, and nothing but the warts.

Our reaction, for example, to Joan Mondale is incredulity. She seems to be a bright, friendly, thrifty woman who buys her Christmas presents in July. For which we label her "Too Good to Be True."

That's where we're at. We would never say that someone is Too Bad to Be True these days. We seem to believe wholeheartedly in the bad, and we will only believe that the Real Joan Mondale has stood up when we discover that she rolls burrs into Fritz's socks or kicks cats.

We have come to associate character revelations with Digging Up the Dirt, and we are currently convinced that only the dirt is real. In short, we think the worst of ourselves. We think the worst *is* ourself.

This rampant pessimism comes up in all kinds of little ways. It came up one night when I visited a friend in a state of terminal grubbiness—matched only by the condition of her apartment. She put one hand on her hair rollers, pointed to the laundry with the other hand and grimaced, "Well, now you've seen the Real Me." This woman, who relines her kitchen drawers twice a year, was sure that she had revealed the secret inner soul of a slob.

But why is it that we are all so sure the *real me* is the one with the dirty hair, the one in dire need of a tube of Clearasil, the one screaming at the children, the one harboring thoughts of dismembering the driver behind us?

Why isn't the *real me* the one who remembers birthdays, keeps the scale within the limits of self-hate and plays "Go Fish" with the kids? Doesn't that

count? Why are we so convinced that anything good about us is a civilized shell hiding the *real me*?

The *real me* problem is horribly destructive. If one assumes that the truth about ourselves is too bad to be false, then of course we have to hide it from others. They in turn can't truly love us because they don't know the real us. The unlovable real us. It's a Catch '76 in which we assume the worst of everyone else as well.

Our belief in the bad comes from religion on the right and Freud on the left—original sin and original id. Between psychology and theology we've had a double-whammy that's convinced us that way down deep there in the old subconscious or whatever, we are a mass of grasping, greedy, destructive, angry and rather appalling characteristics.

Abraham Maslow, who was one of the few psychologists to try and help us out of this pessimistic view, once observed that not only do we associate our nature with animal nature, but with the worst of the animals.

"Western civilization has generally believed that the animal in us was a bad animal, and that our most primitive impulses are evil, greedy, selfish and hostile," he said, adding that we have chosen to identify with "wolves, tigers, pigs, vultures or snakes, rather than with at least milder animals like the elephants or chimpanzees."

Maslow was one of those who tried to convince us that the *real me* is no more angry than loving, selfish than generous. He also tried to show us that people are motivated not just by neurotic needs, impulses and fears, but also out of a positive desire to grow, and out of a sense of fun and pleasure.

But we are not yet convinced. The common street-wisdom of the day is that the most successful of us are "compensating" for some lack, and that the happiest-seeming of us are really "repressing" some unhappiness.

Now, I hate to sound like Little Mary Sunshine, and I am not advocating that we accept everyone at face value. We've been plagued by masked men. But maybe we can get off the hook by letting others off it. The things we hate about ourselves, from the roll around the stomach to the bad temper, aren't more real than the things we like about ourselves. The good isn't a fake. Even if we have to dig for it.

Ellen Goodman

"Who are you?" said
the caterpillar.
This was not an encour-
aging opening for a
conversation. Alice
replied rather shyly,
"I hardly know, sir,
just at present—at
least I knew who I
was when I got up
this morning, but I
think I must have
changed several
times since then."

Lewis Carroll
*Alice's Adventures in
Wonderland*

The self-concept resists change In spite of the facts that we change and that a realistic self-concept should reflect this, the tendency to resist revision of our self-perception is strong. When confronted with facts that contradict the mental picture we hold of ourselves, the tendency is to dispute the facts and cling to the outmoded self-perception.

It's understandable why we're reluctant to revise a previously favorable self-concept. As we write these words, we recall how some professional athletes doggedly insist that they can be of value to the team when they are clearly past their prime. It must be tremendously difficult to give up the life of excitement, recognition, and financial rewards that comes with such a talent. Faced with such a tremendous loss, it's easy to see why the athlete would try to play one more season, insisting that the old skills are still there. In the same way a student who did well in earlier years but now has failed to study might be unwilling to admit that the label "good scholar" no longer applies, and a previously industrious worker, pointing to past commendations in a personnel file and insisting that she is a top-notch employee might resent a supervisor's mentioning increased absences and low productivity. (Remember that the people in these and other examples aren't *lying* when they insist that they're doing well in spite of the facts to the contrary; they honestly believe that the old truths still hold precisely because their self-concepts have been so resistant to change.)

Curiously, the tendency to cling to an outmoded self-perception also holds when the new image would be more favorable than the old one. We recall a former student who almost anyone would have regarded as being beautiful, with physical features attractive enough to appear in any glamour magazine. In spite of her appearance, in a class exercise this woman characterized herself as "ordinary" and "unattractive." When questioned by her classmates, she described how as a child her teeth were extremely crooked, and how she had worn braces for several years in her teens to correct this problem. During this time she was often kidded by her friends, who never let her forget her "metal mouth," as she put it. Even though the braces had been off for two years, our student reported that she still saw herself as ugly, and brushed aside our compliments by insisting that we were just saying these things to be nice—she knew how she *really* looked.

Examples like this show one problem that occurs when we resist changing an inaccurate self-concept. Our student denied herself a much happier life by clinging to an obsolete picture of herself. In the same way some

The Self-Concept: Key to Communication

communicators insist that they are less talented or worthy of friendship than others would suggest, thus creating their own miserable world when it needn't exist. These unfortunate souls probably resist changing because they aren't willing to go through the disorientation that comes from redefining themselves, correctly anticipating that it *is* an effort to think of one's self in a new way. Whatever their reasons, it's sad to see people in such an unnecessary state of affairs.

A second problem that comes from trying to perpetrate an inaccurate self-concept is self-delusion and lack of growth. If you hold an unrealistically favorable picture of yourself, you won't see the real need for change that may exist. Instead of learning new talents, working to change a relationship, or improving your physical condition, you'll stay with the familiar and comfortable delusion that everything is all right. As time goes by this delusion becomes more and more difficult to maintain, leading to a third type of problem.

To understand this problem you need to remember that communicators who are presented with information that contradicts their self-perception have two choices: They can either accept the new data and change their perception accordingly, or they can keep their original viewpoint and in some way refute the new information. Since most communicators are reluctant to downgrade a favorable image of themselves, their tendency is to opt for refutation, either by discounting the information and rationalizing it away or by counterattacking the person who shared it. While Chapter 3 will go into details of such defensive communication, it's enough to say now that these sorts of responses are usually quite destructive, and most often lead to increased hard feelings and weakened relationships.

Self-Concept Check

How realistic and up-to-date is your self-concept? You can start to answer this question by trying the following activities.

1   Share the description of your self-concept that you made on page 64 with one or more people who know you well. Ask them to comment on whether they see you in the same way you see yourself. Is their description more favorable than yours in some areas? More critical in others? If so, consider whose characterization is more accurate. Is it true that nobody knows the "real" you, or are you perhaps fooling yourself in some ways?

2   Take another look at your self-concept list. Check how up-to-date it is. Ask yourself how many items would have been there in exactly the same form five years ago, one year ago, or six months ago. Would the items or your ranking of them be different? Probably so. If not, ask yourself whether or not you might be carrying around an obsolete self-image.

"Oh, Little Blue Engine," cried the dolls and toys. "Will you pull us over the mountain? Our engine has broken down and the good boys and girls on the other side won't have any toys to play with or good food to eat, unless you help us. Please, please, help us, Little Blue Engine." . . .

Then she said, "I think I can. I think I can. I think I can." And she hitched herself to the little train.

She tugged and pulled and pulled and tugged and slowly, slowly, slowly they started off.

The toy clown jumped aboard and all the dolls and the toy animals began to smile and cheer.

Puff, puff, chug, chug, went the Little Blue Engine. "I think I can—I think I can—I think I can—I think I can—I think I can—I think I can—I think I can—I think I can—I think I can."

Up, up, up. Faster and faster and faster and faster the little engine climbed, until at last they reached the top of the mountain.

Down in the valley lay the city.

"Hurray, hurray," cried the funny little clown and all the dolls and toys. "The good little boys and girls in the city will be happy because you helped us, kind, Little Blue Engine."

And the Little Blue Engine smiled and seemed to say as she puffed steadily down the mountain.

"I thought I could. I thought I could. I thought I could.

"I thought I could.
  I thought I could
    I thought I could."

Watty Piper,
The Little Engine That Could

The Self-Fulfilling Prophecy and Communication

The self-concept is such a powerful force on the personality that it not only determines how you see yourself in the present, but can actually influence your future behavior and that of others. Such occurrences come about through a phenomenon called the self-fulfilling prophecy.

A self-fulfilling prophecy occurs when a person's expectation of an event makes the outcome more likely to occur than would otherwise have been true. Self-fulfilling prophecies occur all the time, although you might never have given them that label. For example, think of some instances you may have known.

You expected to become nervous and botch a job interview and later did so.

You anticipated having a good (or terrible) time at a social affair and found your expectations being met.

A teacher or boss explained a new task to you, saying that you probably wouldn't do well at first. You did not do well.

A friend described someone you were about to meet, saying that you wouldn't like the person. The prediction turned out to be correct—you didn't like the new acquaintance.

In each of these cases there is a good chance that the event happened because it was predicted to occur. You needn't have botched the interview, the party might have been boring only because you helped make it so, you might have done better on the job if your boss hadn't spoken up, and you might have liked the new acquaintance if your friend hadn't given you preconceptions. In other words, what helped make each event occur was the expectation that it would happen.

There are two types of self-fulfilling prophecies. The first occurs when your own expectations influence your behavior. Like the job interview and the party described above, there are many times when an event that needn't have occurred does happen because you expect it to. In sports you've probably psyched yourself into playing either better or worse than usual, so that the only explanation for your unusual performance was your attitude that you'd behave differently. Similarly, you've probably faced an audience at one time or another with a fearful attitude and forgotten your remarks, not because you were unprepared, but because you said to yourself, "I know I'll blow it."

Certainly you've had the experience of waking up in a cross mood and saying to yourself, "This will be a 'bad day'." Once you made such a decision, you may have acted in ways that made it come true. If you approached a class expecting to be bored, you most probably did lose interest, due partly to a lack of attention on your part. If you avoided the company of others because you expected that they had nothing to offer, your suspicions would

. . . the difference between a lady and a flower girl is not how she behaves, but how she's treated. I shall always be a flower girl to Professor Higgins, because he always treats me as a flower girl, and always will; but I know I can be a lady to you, because you always treat me as a lady, and always will.

G. B. Shaw, *Pygmalion*

have been confirmed—nothing exciting or new did happen to you. On the other hand, if you approached the same day with the idea that it had the potential to be a good one, this expectation probably would also have been met. Smile at people, and they'll probably smile back. Enter a class determined to learn something, and you probably will—even if it's how not to instruct students! Approach many people with the idea that some of them will be good to know, and you'll most likely make some new friends. In these cases and ones like them your attitude has a great deal to do with how you see yourself and how others will see you.

A second type of self-fulfilling prophecy occurs when the expectations of one person govern another's actions. The classic example was demonstrated by Robert Rosenthal and Lenore Jacobson in a study they described in their book, *Pygmalion in the Classroom:*

> 20 percent of the children in a certain elementary school were reported to their teachers as showing unusual potential for intellectual growth. The names of these 20 percent were drawn by means of a table of random numbers, which is to say that the names were drawn out of a hat. Eight months later these unusual or "magic" children showed significantly greater gains in IQ than did the remaining children who had not been singled out for the teachers' attention. The change in the teachers' expectations regardng the intellectual performance of these allegedly "special" children had led to an actual change in the intellectual performance of these randomly selected children.

In other words, some children may do better in school, not because they are any more intelligent than their classmates, but because they learn that their teacher, a significant other, believes they can achieve.

To put this phenomenon in context with the self-concept, we can say that when a teacher communicates to a child the message, "I think you're bright," the child accepts that evaluation and changes her self-concept to include that evaluation. Unfortunately, we can assume that the same principle holds for students whose teachers send the message, "I think you're stupid."

This type of self-fulfilling prophecy has been shown to be a powerful force for shaping the self-concept and thus the behavior of people in a wide range of settings outside the schools. In medicine patients who unknowingly use placebos—substances such as injections of sterile water or doses of sugar pills that have no curative value—often respond just as favorably to treatment as people who actually received a drug. The patients believe they have taken a substance that will help them feel better, and this belief actually brings about a "cure." In psychotherapy Rosenthal and Jacobson describe several studies which suggest that patients who believe that they will benefit from treatment do so, regardless of the type of treatment they receive. In the same vein, when a doctor believes a patient will improve, the patient may do so precisely because of this expectation, while another person for whom the physician has little hope often fails to recover. Apparently the patient's

The Self-Concept: Key to Communication

self-concept as sick or well—as shaped by the doctor—plays an important role in determining the actual state of health.

In business the power of the self-fulfilling prophecy was proved as early as 1890. A new tabulating machine had just been installed at the U.S. Census Bureau in Washington, D.C. In order to use the machine the bureau's staff had to learn a new set of skills that the machine's inventor believed to be quite difficult. He told the clerks that after some practice they could expect to punch about 550 cards per day; to process any more would jeopardize their psychological well-being. Sure enough, after two weeks the clerks were processing the anticipated number of cards, and reported feelings of stress if they attempted to move any faster.

Some time later an additional group of clerks was hired to operate the same machines. These workers knew nothing of the devices, and no one had told them about the upper limit of production. After only three days the new employees were each punching over 2,000 cards per day with no ill effects. Again, the self-fulfilling prophecy seemed to be in operation. The original workers believed themselves capable of punching only 550 cards and so behaved accordingly, while the new clerks had no limiting expectations as part of their self-concepts and so behaved more productively.

The self-fulfilling prophecy operates in families as well. If parents tell a child long enough that she can't do anything right, her self-concept will soon incorporate this idea, and she will fail at many or most of the tasks she attempts. On the other hand, if a child is told she is a capable or lovable or kind person, there is a much greater chance of her behaving accordingly.

There is an old joke about a man who was asked if he could play a violin and answered, "I don't know. I've never tried." This is psychologically a very wise reply. Those who have never tried to play a violin really do not know whether they can or not. Those who say too early in life and too firmly, "No, I'm not at all musical," shut themselves off prematurely from whole areas of life that might have proved rewarding. In each of us there are un-known possibilities, undiscovered potentialities—and one big advantage of having an open self-concept rather than a rigid one is that we shall continue to expose ourselves to new experiences and therefore we shall continue to discover more and more about ourselves as we grow older.

S. I. HAYAKAWA

Margaret

Margaret was the kind of girl whose face you could never remember. It wasn't that she was ugly; in fact, if you took a moment and looked at her closely while she was in the sociology lab you could see that behind her plain clothes and quiet manner she was really quite good looking.

No, it wasn't her looks themself that made Margaret so unmemorable. It was what she did, or rather, *didn't* do with herself. She never approached anybody or offered her opinion on anything. She hardly ever laughed, and when she did it was only a shadow of the real thing. She always seemed so self-conscious and uncomfortable that none of us knew what to say to her.

One day after a lecture on the self-concept, a few of us were talking. "If what they said in there is true," Mark said, "we could change somebody's personality if we wanted to." And that's how our experiment with Margaret got started. A few of us decided that we'd begin treating her as if she was an important person and see if it would help her out.

We started by making it a point to talk to her every chance we got. This wasn't as easy as it sounds, since Margaret was so unused to being approached that she didn't know what to say at first. But we all kept at it, and after three or four weeks she started to loosen up a lot. One afternoon she even asked me what I thought about an idea she had for a paper. This doesn't sound like much, but for Margaret it was something new.

After a while we decided to take turns dating Margaret. We figured that a few dates would really boost her self-esteem. Bill started out by inviting her to lunch after class one day, and Mark took her to a play on campus a week or so later.

After our little plot had gone on for a couple of months, an amazing thing began to happen. Old Margaret began to look better. A few changes were easy to notice, like the way she changed her hair around and started wearing some new clothes. But there were other things about her that changed too. It's hard to say exactly what they were, but she seemed to talk and smile more, and the way she walked made her look a lot better.

Anyhow, after a while it was my turn to ask her out. It's really strange, but I guess I had lost my scientific detachment in the experiment, because I was really looking forward to an evening with her. I had planned a really nice time—a picnic dinner at the beach, and then a drive up to the mountains to hear a bluegrass band I knew about.

Well, to make a long story short, when I ran into her in the library and asked her out, I got the surprise of my life. "Oh, that's really sweet of you Larry, but Mark and I are already busy next Saturday."

I bumbled around and came out with some kind of line about "Maybe some other time," but to tell you the truth I was really disappointed. And what makes matters worse, I've tried two more times to get a date with Margaret and she's been busy both times.

I guess our experiment worked better than we'd planned. Margaret certainly seems much more confident and happy now. But to tell you the truth, my self-concept is a little shaky.

The self-fulfilling prophecy is an important force in interpersonal communication, but we don't want to suggest that it explains all behavior. There are certainly times when the expectation of an event's outcome won't bring about that occurrence. Your hope of drawing an ace in a card game won't in any way affect the chance of that card turning up in an already shuffled deck, and your belief that good weather is coming won't stop the rain from falling. In the same way, believing you'll do well in a job interview when you're clearly not qualified for the position is unrealistic. Similarly, there will probably be people you don't like and occasions you won't enjoy, no matter what your attitude. To connect the self-fulfilling prophecy with the "power of positive thinking" is an oversimplification.

In other cases your expectations will be borne out because you're a good predictor, and not because of the self-fulfilling prophecy. For example, children are not equally well equipped to do well in school, and in such cases it would be wrong to say that the child's performance was shaped by a parent or teacher, even though the behavior did match that which was expected. In the same way, some workers excel and others fail, some patients recover and others don't, all according to our predictions but not because of them.

Keeping these qualifications in mind, it's important to recognize the tremendous influence that self-fulfilling prophecies play in our lives. To a great extent we are what we believe we are. In this sense we and those around us constantly create our self-concepts and thus ourselves. To see just how true this is, try the following exercises.

Your Self-Fulfilling Prophecies

1 Turn to the self-concept list that you have been working with.

2 Decide which of the items you described there exist as self-fulfilling prophecies. In other words, which ideas do you hold about yourself that are true only because you allow them to be? If you're unhappy with any of these items, describe what you can do to change them.

Sample item from self-concept list: "poor student"

Sample analysis: One reason I'm a poor student is that I don't ask questions in class or seek out an instructor when I'm confused. If I did these things, I would probably understand the material better and be more successful in my classes. Therefore, I'm only a poor student because I act in ways that make me one. I can change this if I want to.

Sample item from self-concept list: "unattractive to opposite sex"

Sample analysis: One reason I'm unattractive is because I'm overweight. Although it would be difficult, I *could* lose weight if I chose to work at it. Also, I could pay more attention to the way I dress, and I could also approach people I'm interested in and let them know that I'm an honest, caring person. If I did these things I probably still wouldn't be the most desirable person in town, but I would be a lot more attractive than I am now. I suppose it's my choice to be the way I am.

Changing Your Self-Concept

The previous exercise probably helped you realize that it is possible to change an unsatisfying self-concept. In the next pages we'll discuss some additional methods for accomplishing such a change. The first step in this process is to get a clear idea of the parts of yourself that you hope to modify. You can do this by following the directions.

Discovering My Perceived Self and Ideal Self

1   Below you will find a list of thirty-two items, some of which probably describe you quite well and others that don't fit you at all.

2   Begin by placing these words in the appropriate spaces in Table 1, which describes the way you see yourself. Place the numbers of the two items that *best* describe you in the spaces above the number 1 and the two that *least* characterize you above the number 9. Continue this process until you have placed all thirty-two items. You'll need to keep in mind that the items located to the left of others are more like you, while those placed to the right of other items are less like you. It is most likely that you'll have to move items back and forth before you'll be satisfied with the arrangement. Perhaps the most practical way of working out this arrangement is to transfer the thirty-two items to slips of paper that can be moved easily. Then when you have the items arranged in the form presented in Table 1, note the number of the items in the appropriate spaces.

3   Now repeat the process for Table 2. This time, however, organize the items according to the way *you would like to be,* so that you will have a portrait of your *ideal self* when you have finished. (If you feel that you might be influenced by the way you first arranged the items, allow a few days to pass before you make the second sorting. It will probably help if you do not refer to your first arrangement until you have finished your second.)

4   Now compare your perceived self and ideal self lists, noting the items which moved two or more columns from one sorting to the next. These items will describe the parts of your self-concept you would like to change, so keep them in mind as you read the remainder of this chapter.

5   If you desire, you might want to ask one or more people you know to organize the items according to the way they see you. Do these lists match

your self-perception? In what ways do they differ? Whose description seems the most accurate? What might you have done that makes others view you differently than you see your self? Are you satisfied with this discrepancy?

List of Items to Be Arranged

1. Intelligent
2. Too shy
3. Express my anger construct- ively
4. Give in easily
5. Like other people
6. Feel insecure
7. Talk too much
8. Impulsive
9. Tense
10. Likeable
11. Open-minded
12. Have warm relationship with people important to me
13. Hard to express my temper
14. Basically contented
15. Confused
16. Friendly
17. Emotionally mature
18. Growing in wisdom over time
19. Attractive
20. Selfish
21. Afraid to disagree
22. Willing to stand up for what I believe
23. Unreliable
24. Stand up for my personal rights
25. Don't trust my feelings
26. Honest with myself
27. Honest with others
28. Make lots of excuses
29. Avoid facing things
30. Good student and/or worker
31. Conscientious
32. Comfortable with my sexuality

Table 1   Perceived Self

Most like ... Least like

1   2   3   4   5   6   7   8   9

Table 2   Ideal Self

Most like ... Least like

1   2   3   4   5   6   7   8   9

Now that you have a clearer idea of the parts of your self-concept you'd like to change, let's look at some ways to do so.

Have realistic expectations It's extremely important to realize that some of your dissatisfaction might come from expecting too much of yourself. If you demand that you handle every act of communication perfectly, you're bound to be disappointed. Nobody is able to handle every conflict productively, to be totally relaxed and skillful in conversations, to always ask perceptive questions, or to be 100 percent helpful when others have problems. Expecting yourself to reach such unrealistic goals is to doom yourself to unhappiness at the start.

Sometimes it's easy to be hard on yourself because everyone around you seems to be handling themselves so much better than you. It's important to realize that much of what seems like confidence and skill in others is a front to hide uncertainty. They may be suffering from the same self-imposed demands of perfection that you place on yourself.

Even in cases where others definitely seem more competent than you, it's important to judge yourself in terms of your own growth, and not against the behavior of others. Rather than feeling miserable because you're not as talented as an expert, realize that you probably are a better, wiser, or more skillful person than you used to be and that this is a legitimate source of satisfaction. Perfection is fine as an ideal, but you're being unfair to yourself if you expect actually to reach that state.

Self-Appreciation Exercise

As a means of demonstrating the self-appreciation that can come from recognizing that you're growing, do the following:

1 Form a circle in your group. Your group size may be the group as a whole or several small groups.

2 Each group member in turn should complete the following statement:

"I'm a long way from being perfect at _____,

but I'm slowly getting better by _____."

Here are some examples:

"I'm a long way from being perfect at *my job,* but I'm slowly getting better by *taking on just one task at a time and persisting until I finish.*"

"I'm a long way from being perfect at *approaching strangers,* but I'm slowly getting better by *going to more parties and once in a while actually starting to talk to people I don't know.*"

Have a realistic perception of yourself One source of a poor self-concept is an inaccurate self-perception. As you've already read, such unrealistic pictures sometimes come from being overly harsh on yourself, believing that you're worse than the facts indicate. By sharing the self-concept lists you recorded on pages 64 and 93 with others who know you, it will be possible to see whether you have been selling yourself short. Of course, it would be foolish to deny that you could be a better person than you are, but it's also important to recognize your strengths. A periodic session of bragging such as you tried earlier in this chapter is often a good way to put your strengths and shortcomings into perspective.

An unrealistically poor self-concept can also come from the inaccurate feedback of others. Perhaps you are in an environment where you receive an excessive number of "downer" messages, many of which are undeserved, and a minimum of upper messages. We've known many housewives, for example, who have returned to college after many years spent in home-making where they received virtually no recognition for their intellectual strengths. It's amazing that these women have the courage to come to college at all, so low are their self-concepts; but come they do, and most are thrilled to find that they are much brighter and more competent intellectually than they suspected. In the same way, workers with overly critical supervisors, children with cruel "friends," and students with unsupportive teachers all are prone to suffering from low self-concepts due to excessively negative feedback.

If you fall into this category, it's important to put the unrealistic evaluations you receive into perspective and then to seek out more supportive people who will acknowledge your assets as well as point out your shortcomings. Doing so is often a quick and sure boost to the self-concept.

Have the will to change Often we say we want to change, but aren't willing to do the necessary work. In such cases it's clear that the responsibility for growing rests squarely on your shoulders, as the following example shows.

Reevaluating Your "Can'ts"

1 Choose a partner and for five minutes or so take turns making and listing statements that begin with "I can't . . ." Try to focus your statements on your relationships with family, friends, coworkers and students, and even strangers: whoever you have a hard time communicating with.

Sample statements:

"I can't be myself with strangers I'd like to get to know at parties."

"I can't tell a friend how much I care about her."

"I can't bring myself to ask my supervisor for the raise I think I deserve."

"I can't ask questions in class."

2 Notice the feelings you experience as you make each statement: self-pity, regret, concern, frustration, etc., and share these with your partner.

3 Now go back and repeat aloud each statement you've just made, except this time change each "can't" to a "won't." After each sentence, share with your partner whatever thoughts you have about what you've just said.

4 After you've finished, decide whether "can't" or "won't" is more appropriate for each item, and explain your choice to your partner.

5 Are there any instances of the self-fulfilling prophecy in your list—times when your decision that you "couldn't" do something was the only force keeping you from doing it?

The point of this exercise should be clear. Often we maintain an unrealistic self-concept by claiming that we "can't" be the person we'd like to be, when in fact we're simply not willing to do what's required. You *can* change in many ways, if only you are willing to put out the effort.

Have the skill needed to change Often trying isn't enough. There are some cases where you would change if you knew of a way to do so. To see if this is the case for you, go back to your list of "can'ts" and "won'ts" and see if any items there are more appropriately "don't know how." If so, then the way to change is to learn how. You can do so in two ways.

First, you can seek advice—from books such as this one, the references listed at the end of each chapter, and other printed sources. You can also get advice from instructors, counselors and other experts, as well as friends. Of course, not all the advice you receive will be useful, but if you read widely and talk to enough people, you have a good chance of learning the things you want to know.

A second method of learning how to change is to observe models—people who handle themselves in the ways you would like to master. It's often been said that people learn more from models than in any other way, and by taking advantage of this principle you will find that the world is full of teachers who can show you how to communicate more successfully. Become a careful observer. Watch what people you admire do and say, not so that you can copy them, but so that you can adapt their behavior to fit your own personal style.

At this point you might be overwhelmed at the difficulty of changing the way you think about yourself and the way you act. Remember, we never said that this process would be an easy one (although it sometimes is). But even when change is difficult, you know that it's possible if you are serious. You don't need to be perfect, but you can improve your self-concept if you choose to.

Roads Not Taken

Here is a list of topics or ideas that you might find interesting to investigate further:

1   What implications do recent self-concept studies have for teachers and educators? parents? supervisors?

2   What is the relationship between self-esteem and the process of self-disclosure and feedback?

3   What is meant by the statement that role definition is usually the product of the value system of a society, a group, or an individual?

4   Where does self-concept fit into the explanation of the fact that girls outperform boys in mathematics up to about twelve years of age, after which boys show superior abilities?

5   Can you trace the development of your self-concept, naming persons, places, incidents, and dates?

More Readings on the Self-Concept

Briggs, Dorothy C. *Your Child's Self-Esteem.* Garden City, N.Y.: Doubleday, 1975.

> This is a down-to-earth guide for parents and other adults who work with children. It reminds us of the critical role we play in shaping the self-concept of youngsters.

Campbell, Colin. "Our Many Versions of the Self: An Interview With M. Brewster Smith." *Psychology Today, 9* (February, 1976), 74–79.

> Psychologist Smith discusses the many ways to view the self, and the consequences of each.

Gergen, Kenneth J. "The Healthy, Happy Human Being Wears Many Masks." *Psychology Today 5* (May, 1972), 31–35, 64–66.

> This article makes it clear that the idea of a single "self" may be overly simplistic; perhaps we are different people in different contexts. This article makes a good companion to Campbell's interview with M. Brewster Smith, cited above.

Hayakawa, S. I. *Symbol, Status and Personality.* New York: Harcourt, Brace Jovanovich, Inc., 1953.

> Hayakawa's description of the self-concept in Chapter 4 may have been written over twenty-five years ago, but it is still one of the clearest and most interesting ones around.

Insel, Paul M., and Lenore Jacobson. *What Do You Expect? An Inquiry into Self-Fulfilling Prophecies.* Menlo Park, Cal: Cummings Publishing Co., 1975.

> This collection of essays and research articles describes some of the many ways the self-fulfilling prophecy operates. Especially valuable for educators.

Rosenthal, Robert, and Lenore Jacobson. *Pygmalion in the Classroom.* New York: Holt, Rinehart and Winston, 1968.

> This book contains a fascinating description of how self-fulfilling prophecies operate in education, social science research, medicine, and everyday life.

Films on the Self-Concept

Cipher In The Snow. Color. 24 min. BYU 1970.

> Deals with self-concept and the effect that neglect and unconcern can have on any personality, but particularly on the young.

The Eye of the Storm. Color. 25 min. 1970. Xerox

> Documentary of third graders who learn about racial discrimination firsthand through the tough and tender prodding of a creative teacher. A good look at how uppers and downers can shape children's self-concepts in a short time.

Productivity: The Self-Fulfilling Prophecy. Color. 31 min. 1974.
McGraw-Hill.

A look at how the self-fulfilling prophecy operates both benefically and in business. This film is also useful for general audiences studying the self-concept.

3

Defensiveness: Protecting Our Self-Concept

Surely you know what it's like to be defensive.

After teaching courses in interpersonal communication to thousands of students, we've yet to find a single person who hasn't experienced this feeling. When asked to report the sensations and actions that come with such an attitude, practically everyone describes similar experiences—tense muscles, upset stomach, high-pitched and argumentative tone of voice, a rush of adrenaline, and a temptation either to rush away from the situation at hand or to stay and fight. And just as most people report the same symptoms for defensiveness, they also describe similar consequences—hurt feelings, damaged relationships, personal frustration, and lack of satisfying resolution to the conflicts that brought on the defensiveness in the first place. In fact, defensiveness is such a problem that our students invariably list reducing its occurrence in their lives as one of the major goals of our courses.

What exactly is defensiveness? When and why does it occur? What are you defending? How can you learn to respond less defensively? What can you do to arouse less defensiveness in others? These are the questions we'll try to answer in Chapter 3.

What Is Defensiveness?

The very word defensiveness suggests protecting one's self from attack, but what kind of attack? Surely, few of the times when you become defensive involve a threat to your physical safety; so if you're not threatened by that sort of injury, what can it be that you *are* guarding against? To answer this question we need to talk more about the notion of the self-concept, which we introduced in Chapter 2.

You'll recall that the self-concept consists of your perceptions of yourself, including physical characteristics, personality traits, strengths and weaknesses, as well as a large number of other characteristics and beliefs you see yourself as possessing.

Right now turn to the list you compiled for the exercise in Chapter 2 on page 64. Review the list of terms you used to describe the parts of your self-concept called for.

As you read in Chapter 2, this self-concept is nothing less than the sum of your personal identity, and as such it is extremely important. Consider, for example, the value you attach to the following parts of your self-concept:

Social roles

Intelligence

Ethical standards

Physical appearance

Job-oriented abilities

Of course, not all parts of your self-concept are equally important to you. For example, the fact that you see yourself as a resident of a particular state or having been born in a certain month is probably less important than your identity as a female or male or the kind of friend you are.

Imagine what might happen if someone attacked a part of your self-concept that was particularly important to you. Suppose, for instance, that

> An instructor labeled you as an idiot when you regard yourself as reasonably bright.
>
> A friend accused you of being snobbish when you believe you are a friendly person.
>
> An employer called you lazy, when you see yourself as a hard worker.

What are your choices in such situations? One alternative would be to accept the new information and change your self-concept accordingly, relabeling yourself as stupid, snobbish, or lazy. On the other hand, given the human tendency to perpetuate an existing self-concept, a more likely choice is in some way to discount the critical information in order to maintain your old picture of yourself. You might do so by ignoring this dissonant information (pretending you didn't hear it, forgetting it, avoiding the critic, and so on), or by disputing it (offering evidence to the contrary or counterattacking the critic). In any case, it's important to see that we often act to protect a self-concept that has been threatened.

Testing Your Defensiveness

1 Turn to the self-concept list you recorded on page 64 of Chapter 2 and pick the five items there that are most fundamental to your identity.

2 For each item recall an incident or two in your life in which someone attacked a view you hold of yourself. For example, if you consider yourself to be a good artist, remember how you reacted when someone criticized your work.

3 In recalling these incidents, try to remember
   a. your physical reactions (tensing of muscles, change in tone of voice, and so on)
   b. your communicative response (offering explanations or excuses, counterattacking, agreeing with the critic, and so on)

4 After recalling at least five incidents, decide
   a. whether or not you could label your behavior as "defensive"
   b. what your general style of response is when your self-concept is attacked

Public and private selves So far, then, we've said that people become defensive when they perceive others attacking their self-concept. While this statement explains much defensive behavior, it doesn't account for every case. Often there are times when others offer an evaluation that coincides with your self-concept, and yet you *still* become defensive. For example, consider the many times when you have failed to meet your obligations before the last moment, so that you've had to rush in order to get the job done. Certainly if you are like most people you would probably admit to including the word *procrastinator* in your self-concept. When confronted with this failure to meet deadlines, however, you might not willingly admit your habit of stalling, instead making all sorts of excuses to justify your tardiness. In the same way there are probably other parts of your self-concept that you might not readily own up to when others point them out—perhaps the tendency to tell an occasional lie, a periodic streak of unreasonableness, or tendencies toward selfishness.

To understand what's going on here you need to recognize the existence of two selves, one public and the other private. Your public self is the face you show to the world, while your private self is the person you see in moments of self-honesty. These two selves are similar in many ways. For instance, you might see yourself as a perfectionist or a person who dislikes opera and be perfectly willing to publicly express these attitudes. On the other hand, there are some cases in which the face you show to the world is quite different from the one you see when you stare at yourself in the mirror.

Perhaps you sometimes feel insecure but try to act in a confident manner. Maybe you find yourself feeling angry when you want to appear calm and happy. Or perhaps you sometimes feel stupid but try to look bright to others. Take a few minutes now to explore your public and private selves by completing the following exercise.

Defining My Two Selves

1 Divide a sheet of paper into two halves, top and bottom.

2 On the top half write the ten words that best describe your private self—the person you know yourself to be, although you might or might not share this self with others.

3 Now make some kind of drawing that represents the essential nature of your private self. Don't worry about being an artist: The idea is to put something on paper that captures the feeling of the private you. We've had students draw trees, automobiles, stick people, or even abstract designs. There's no "wrong" way to do this, so use your imagination.

4 Now repeat the process on the bottom half of the paper. This time select ten words and draw something to represent your public self—the person you want others to see. If you find you want to use some of the same terms you used above the line, that's fine.

5 After you have finished, take a moment to notice the relationship between the two halves of your paper. What similarities are there? What differences? In what ways do you act to reflect the public image you've drawn here? How satisfied are you with the selves you've represented? What might you do to change them?

My Two Selves in 3D

1 Another way to illustrate your two selves is by constructing a self-portrait in three dimensions. Perhaps the simplest method is to use a cardboard box, carton, or even a paper bag. The idea is that you've both an outside and an inside to represent the public and private self.

2 Decorate your container in any way you see fit to describe your selves. Clipping pictures or words from magazines and newspapers or attaching or including articles that are meaningful are two possibilities.

3 The style you choose to represent yourself will probably make a statement about you. There's no correct way—any way you choose will be acceptable. You're limited only by your imagination.

4 Before you begin work, decide with your instructor what you'll be doing with your portraits: Should they be kept private, should the owner show his to the group, or should they be collected anonymously with attempts at guessing the artist's identity?

Defensiveness: Protecting Our Self-Concept

Be sure you've completed one of these exercises before reading on. What did you discover about your two selves? Were they mostly similar? In what ways did they differ? Most people find that the face they present to the public is more favorable than their private one. Was this true for you? If so, the reason is probably a social one. From the time most of us are quite young we're taught that certain kinds of behavior are the only way to gain acceptance. In such environments perfection is the model: One should always act in a pleasant manner, be reasonable, selfless, and kind. This stress on perfection is carried on in most forms of entertainment, where the models are characters who are always self-assured, knowledgeable, and socially talented. The message here is that the kind of person who gains the approval of others is *perfect*. Of course, privately each of us knows that we're not perfect, so we are faced with the choices of sharing our private self and risking rejection or putting on a public mask and gaining what we think will be social rewards.

John Powell speaks to the problem of fear and defensiveness with a question that also serves as the title to his book *Why Am I Afraid to Tell You Who I Am?* One of the answers he recorded from an actual conversation says ". . . if I tell you who I am, you may not like who I am, and it is all that I have." So one reason we wear masks is to show the world an acceptable public or "ideal" self, trying to be the kind of person others think we should be instead of the person we truly are.

With this explanation it becomes easy to see why we get defensive at times when a critic makes an evaluation that does match our private image: for the concept that we most strongly defend is our public one. Thus, we can finally say that *defensiveness is the attempt to protect a public image that we perceive is being attacked.*

The extremes we'll go to for the sake of making a "good" appearance are illustrated well in the following account by George Orwell.

my god
it just
occurred to me
underneath
our clothes
everyone
on this bus
is
stark
naked

Ric Masten

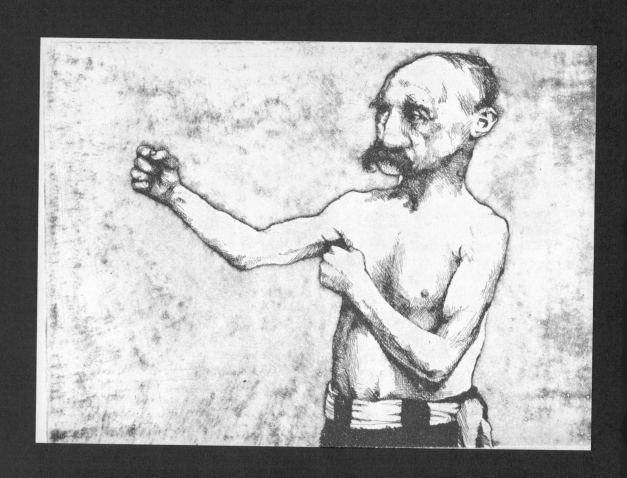

Shooting an Elephant

In Moulmein, in Lower Burma, I was hated by large numbers of people—the only time in my life that I have been important enough for this to happen to me. I was sub-divisional police officer of the town, and in an aimless, petty kind of way anti-European feeling was very bitter. No one had the guts to raise a riot, but if a European woman went through the bazaars alone somebody would probably spit betel juice over her dress. As a police officer I was an obvious target and was baited whenever it seemed safe to do so. When a nimble Burman tripped me up on the football field and the referee (another Burman) looked the other way, the crowd yelled with hideous laughter. This happened more than once. In the end the sneering yellow faces of young men that met me everywhere, the insults hooted after me when I was at a safe distance, got badly on my nerves. The young Buddhist priests were the worst of all. There were several thousands of them in the town and none of them seemed to have anything to do except stand on street corners and jeer at Europeans.

All this was perplexing and upsetting. For at that time I had already made up my mind that imperialism was an evil thing and the sooner I chucked up my job and got out of it the better. Theoretically—and secretly, of course—I was all for the Burmese and all against their oppressors, the British. As for the job I was doing, I hated it more bitterly than I can perhaps make clear. In a job like that you see the dirty work of Empire at close quarters. The wretched prisoners huddling in the stinking cages of the lock-ups, the grey, cowed faces of the long-term convicts, the scarred buttocks of the men who had been flogged with bamboos—all these oppressed me with an intolerable sense of guilt. But I could get nothing into perspective. I was young and ill-educated and I had to think out my problems in the utter silence that is imposed on every Eng-lishman in the East. I did not even know that the British Empire is dying, still less did I know that it is a great deal better than the younger empires that are going to supplant it. All I knew was that I was stuck between my hatred of the empire I served and my rage against the evil-spirited little beasts who tried to make my job impossible. With one part of my mind I thought of the British Raj as an unbreak-able tyranny, as something clamped down, in *saecula saeculorum,* upon the will of prostrate peo-ples; with another part I thought that the greatest joy in the world would be to drive a bayonet into a Buddhist priest's guts. Feelings like these are the normal by-products of imperialism; ask any Anglo-Indian official, if you can catch him off duty.

One day something happened which in a round-about way was enlightening. It was a tiny incident in itself, but it gave me a better glimpse than I had had before of the real nature of imperialism—the real motives for which despotic governments act. Early one morning the sub-inspector at a police station the other end of the town rang me up on the phone and said that an elephant was ravaging the bazaar. Would I please come and do something about it? I did not know what I could do, but I wanted to see what was happening and I got on to a pony and started out. I took my rifle, an old .44 Winchester and much too small to kill an ele-phant, but I thought the noise might be useful *in terrorem.* Various Burmans stopped me on the way and told me about the elephant's doings. It was not, of course, a wild elephant, but a tame one which had gone "must." It had been chained up, as tame elephants always are when their attack of "must" is due, but on the previous night it had broken its chain and escaped. Its mahout, the only person who could manage it when it was in that state, had set out in pursuit, but had taken the wrong direction and was now twelve hours' journey away, and in the morning the elephant had suddenly reappeared in the town. The Burmese population had no weapons and were quite helpless against it. It had already destroyed somebody's bamboo hut, killed a cow and raided some fruit-stalls and devoured the stock; also it had met the municipal rubbish van and, when the driver jumped out and took to his heels, had turned the van over and inflicted violences upon it.

The Burmese sub-inspector and some Indian constables were waiting for me in the quarter where the elephant had been seen. It was a very poor quarter, a labyrinth of squalid bamboo huts, thatched with palm-leaf, winding all over a steep hillside. I remember that it was a cloudy, stuffy morning at the beginning of the rains. We began questioning the people as to where the elephant had gone and, as usual, failed to get any definite information. That is invariably the case in the East; a story always sounds clear enough at a distance, but the nearer you get to the scene of events the vaguer it becomes. Some of the people said that the elephant had gone in one direction, some said that he had gone in another, some professed not even to have heard of any elephant. I had almost made up my mind that the whole story was a pack of lies, when we heard yells a little distance away. There was a loud, scandalized cry of ''Go away, child! Go away, child! Go away this instant!'' and an old woman with a switch in her hand came round the corner of a hut, violently shooing away a crowd of naked children. Some more women followed, clicking their tongues and exclaiming; evidently there was something that the children ought not to have seen. I rounded the hut and saw a man's dead body sprawling in the mud. He was an Indian, a black Dravidian coolie, almost naked, and he could not have been dead many minutes. The people said that the elephant had come suddenly upon him round the corner of the hut, caught him with its trunk, put its foot on his back and ground him into the earth. This was the rainy season and the ground was soft, and his face had scored a trench a foot deep and a couple of yards long. He was lying on his belly with arms crucified and head sharply twisted to one side. His face was coated with mud, the eyes wide open, the teeth bared and grinning with an expression of unendurable agony. (Never tell me, by the way, that the dead look peaceful. Most of the corpses I have seen looked devilish.) The friction of the great beast's foot had stripped the skin from his back as neatly as one skins a rabbit. As soon as I saw the dead man I sent an orderly to a friend's house nearby to borrow an elephant rifle. I had already sent back the pony, not wanting it to go mad with fright and throw me if it smelt the elephant.

The orderly came back in a few minutes with a rifle and five cartridges, and meanwhile some Burmans had arrived and told us that the elephant was in the paddy fields below, only a few hundred yards away. As I started forward practically the whole population of the quarter flocked out of the houses and followed me. They had seen the rifle and were all shouting excitedly that I was going to shoot the elephant. They had not shown much interest in the elephant when he was merely ravaging their homes, but it was different now that he was going to be shot. It was a bit of fun to them, as it would be to an English crowd; besides they wanted the meat. It made me vaguely uneasy. I had no intention of shooting the elephant—I had merely sent for the rifle to defend myself if necessary—and it is always unnerving to have a crowd following you. I marched down the hill, looking and feeling a fool, with the rifle over my shoulder and an ever-growing army of people jostling at my heels. At the bottom, when you got away from the huts, there was a metalled road and beyond that a miry waste of paddy fields a thousand yards across, not yet ploughed but soggy from the first rains and dotted with coarse grass. The elephant was standing eight yards from the road, his left side towards us. He took not the slightest notice of the crowd's approach. He was tearing up bunches of grass, beating them against his knees to clean them and stuffing them into his mouth.

Defensiveness: Protecting Our Self-Concept

I had halted on the road. As soon as I saw the elephant I knew with perfect certainty that I ought not to shoot him. It is a serious matter to shoot a working elephant—it is comparable to destroying a huge and costly piece of machinery—and obviously one ought not to do it if it can possibly be avoided. And at that distance, peacefully eating, the elephant looked no more dangerous than a cow. I thought then and I think now that his attack of "must" was already passing off; in which case he would merely wander harmlessly about until the mahout came back and caught him. Moreover, I did not in the least want to shoot him. I decided that I would watch him for a little while to make sure that he did not turn savage again, and then go home.

But at that moment I glanced round at the crowd that had followed me. It was an immense crowd, two thousand at the least and growing every minute. It blocked the road for a long distance on either side. I looked at the sea of yellow faces above the garish clothes—faces all happy and excited over this bit of fun, all certain that the elephant was going to be shot. They were watching me as they would watch a conjurer about to perform a trick. They did not like me, but with the magical rifle in my hands I was momentarily worth watching. And suddenly I realized that I should have to shoot the elephant after all. The people expected it of me and I had got to do it; I could feel their two thousand wills pressing me forward, irresistibly. And it was at this moment, as I stood there with the rifle in my hands, that I first grasped the hollowness, the futility of the white man's dominion in the East. Here was I, the white man with his gun, standing in front of the unarmed native crowd—seemingly the leading actor of the piece; but in reality I was only an absurd puppet pushed to and fro by the will of those yellow faces behind. I perceived in this moment that when the white man turns tyrant it is his own freedom that he destroys. He becomes a sort of hollow, posing dummy, the conventionalized figure of a sahib. For it is the condition of his rule that he shall spend his life in trying to impress the "natives," and so

in every crisis he has got to do what the "natives" expect of him. He wears a mask, and his face grows to fit it. I had got to shoot the elephant. I had committed myself to doing it when I sent for the rifle. A sahib has got to act like a sahib; he has got to appear resolute, to know his own mind and do definite things. To come all that way, rifle in hand, with two thousand people marching at my heels, and then to trail feebly away, having done nothing —no, that was impossible. The crowd would laugh at me. And my whole life, every white man's life in the East, was one long struggle not to be laughed at.

But I did not want to shoot the elephant. I watched him beating his bunch of grass against his knees, with that preoccupied grandmotherly air that elephants have. It seemed to me that it would be murder to shoot him. At that age I was not squeamish about killing animals, but I had never shot an elephant and never wanted to. (Somehow it always seems worse to kill a *large* animal.) Besides, there was the beast's owner to be considered. Alive, the elephant was worth at least a hundred pounds; dead, he would only be worth the value of his tusks, five pounds, possibly. But I had got to act quickly. I turned to some experienced-looking Burmans who had been there when we arrived, and asked them how the elephant had been behaving. They all said the same thing: he took no notice of you if you left him alone, but he might charge if you went too close to him.

It was perfectly clear to me what I ought to do. I ought to walk up to within, say, twenty-five yards of the elephant and test his behavior. If he charged, I could shoot; if he took no notice of me, it would be safe to leave him until the mahout came back. But also I knew that I was going to do no such thing. I was a poor shot with a rifle and the ground was soft mud into which one would sink at every step. If the elephant charged and I missed him, I should have about as much chance as a toad under a steam-roller. But even then I was not thinking particularly of my own skin, only of the watchful yellow faces behind. For at that moment, with the crowd watching me, I was not afraid in the ordinary sense, as I would have been if I had been alone. A white man mustn't be frightened in front of "natives"; and so, in general, he isn't frightened. The sole thought in my mind was that if anything went wrong those two thousand Burmans would see me pursued, caught, trampled on and reduced to a grinning corpse like that Indian up the hill. And if that happened it was quite probable that some of them would laugh. That would never do. There was only one alternative. I shoved the cartridges into the magazine and lay down on the road to get a better aim.

The crowd grew very still, and a deep, low, happy sigh, as of people who see the theatre curtain go up at last, breathed from innumerable throats. They were going to have their bit of fun after all. The rifle was a beautiful German thing with cross-hair sights. I did not then know that in shooting an elephant one would shoot to cut an imaginary bar running from ear-hole to ear-hole. I ought, therefore, as the elephant was sideways on, to have aimed straight at his ear-hole; actually I aimed several inches in front of this, thinking the brain would be further forward.

When I pulled the trigger I did not hear the bang or feel the kick—one never does when a shot goes home—but I heard the devilish roar of glee that went up from the crowd. In that instant, in too short a time, one would have thought, even for the bullet to get there, a mysterious, terrible change had come over the elephant. He neither stirred nor fell, but every line of his body had altered. He looked suddenly stricken, shrunken, immensely old, as though the frightful impact of the bullet had paralyzed him without knocking him down. At last, after what seemed a long time—it might have been five seconds, I dare say—he sagged flabbily to his knees. His mouth slobbered. An enormous senility seemed to have settled upon him. One could have imagined him thousands of years old. I fired again into the same spot. At the second shot he did not collapse but climbed with desperate slowness to his feet and stood weakly upright, with legs sagging and head dropping. I fired a third time. That was the shot that did for him. You could see the agony of it jolt his whole body and knock the last remnant of strength from his legs. But in falling he seemed for a moment to rise, for as his hind legs collapsed beneath him he seemed to tower upward like a huge rock toppling, his trunk reaching skywards like a tree. He trumpeted, for the first and only time. And then down he came, his belly towards me, with a crash that seemed to shake the ground even where I lay.

I got up. The Burmans were already racing past me across the mud. It was obvious that the elephant would never rise again, but he was not dead. He was breathing very rhythmically with long rattling gasps, his great mound of a side painfully rising and falling. His mouth was wide open—I could see far down into caverns of pale pink throat. I waited a long time for him to die, but his breathing did not weaken. Finally I fired my two remaining shots into the spot where I thought his heart must be. The thick blood welled out of him like red velvet, but still he did not die. His body did not even jerk when the shots hit him, the tortured breathing continued without a pause. He was dying, very slowly and in great agony, but in some world remote from me where not even a bullet could damage him further. I felt that I had got to put an end to that dreadful noise. It seemed dreadful to see the great beast lying there, powerless to move and yet powerless to die, and not even to be able to finish him. I sent back for my small rifle and poured shot after shot into his heart and down his throat. They seemed to make no impression. The tortured gasps continued as steadily as the ticking of a clock.

In the end I could not stand it any longer and went away. I heard later that it took him half an hour to die. Burmans were bringing dahs and baskets even before I left, and I was told they had stripped his body almost to the bones by the afternoon.

Afterwards, of course, there were endless discussions about the shooting of the elephant. The owner was furious, but he was only an Indian and could do nothing. Besides, legally I had done the right thing, for a mad elephant has to be killed, like a mad dog, if its owner fails to control it. Among the Europeans opinion was divided. The older men said I was right, the younger men said it was a damn shame to shoot an elephant for killing a coolie, because an elephant was worth more than any damn Coringhee coolie. And afterwards I was very glad that the coolie had been killed; it put me legally in the right and it gave me a sufficient pretext for shooting the elephant. I often wondered whether any of the others grasped that I had done it solely to avoid looking a fool.

George Orwell

Eleanor Rigby . . .
wearing the face that she keeps in a jar by the door.
Who is it for?

John Lennon and Paul McCartney

Defense Mechanisms

Now you recognize that defensiveness occurs when you try to protect a public (usually ideal) image that you perceive to be under attack. Before going any further it's important to point out that there's usually an element of self-deception in such mask wearing. Much of the time we're misrepresenting ourselves to others, we also want desperately to believe the act we're putting on. It's unpleasant to admit that you're not the person you'd like to be (even if your ideal image is totally unrealistic), and faced with a situation where the truth might hurt, it's tempting to convince yourself that you do fit the superhuman image you've constructed for others.

How do we manage these attempts at deception? In the following pages you'll find a number of devices, generally called defense mechanisms, that enable people to avoid admission to themselves and others of an unpleasant part of the self-concept. Just as the two methods of protecting yourself from physical attack are to flee or fight, the mechanisms for defensive communication fall into the two categories of avoidance and attack. In general, each defense mechanism defines a particular way in which the individual *distorts* reality so that his world will look the way he wants it to be. The fact that these mechanisms become habits we perform unconsciously makes them difficult to recognize, especially in ourselves. Consequently, we don't recognize that we're distorting the reality that makes up our lives, and our communication with others suffers because we're not allowing ourselves to be aware of what's actually happening.

We don't want to suggest that defense mechanisms are always undesirable. There are times when these techniques of protecting your private self are desirable, particularly when such disclosure would be treated cruelly by others. Also, confronting too many unpleasant truths or perceptions of one's self too quickly can be unmanageable, and thus these mechanisms serve as a safety valve for handling the process of self-discovery at a safe rate. However, your own experience will show that, most often, acting in the following defensive ways can damage your relationships with others. We therefore believe that acquainting you with some of the most common defense mechanisms—with the hope of reducing them in your life—is a valuable step in helping you become a better communicator.

© 1964 United Feature Syndicate, Inc.

RATIONALIZATION READER FOR STUDENTS

Situation	What to say
When the course is the lecture type:	We never get a chance to say anything.
When the course is the discussion type:	The professor just sits there. We don't know how to teach the course.
When all aspects of the course are covered in class:	All he does is follow the text.
When you're responsible for covering part of the course outside class:	He never covers half the things we're tested on.
When you're given objective tests:	They don't allow for any individuality for us.
When you're given essay tests:	They're too vague. We never know what's expected.
When the instructor gives no tests:	It isn't fair! He can't tell how much we really know.
When you have a lot of quizzes instead of a midterm and final:	We need major exams. Quizzes don't cover enough to really tell anything.
When you have only two exams for the whole course:	Too much rides on each one. You can just have a bad day.

Rationalization One of the most common ways of avoiding a threat to our self-concept is to *rationalize*, that is, to think up a logical but untrue explanation that protects the unrealistic picture we hold of ourselves.

Have you ever justified cheating in school by saying the information you were tested on wasn't important anyway or that everybody cheats a little? Were those your real reasons, or just excuses? Have you ever shrugged off hurting someone's feelings by saying she'll soon forget what you've done? In cases like these it's often tempting to explain behavior you feel guilty about by justifying it in terms that fit your self-concept.

Compensation This is another technique people use for avoiding what they think is a personal shortcoming. Rather than face a problem head on, compensators stress a strength in some other area of their personality, hoping that it will camouflage what they feel is their fault.

A good example of compensation is the man whose home life is unhappy but refuses to do anything about it; instead, he puts all his energy into becoming successful in his business. Another example, is the girl who can't make friends with other women and compensates by attracting as many boyfriends as she can, rather than working on the real problem.

There are many instances when people try to compensate for the lack of good interpersonal relationships with material things. Parents in broken families may attempt to replace their missing relationships with their children by loading them up with toys, sporting equipment, clothes, and so on. This solution is hardly helpful to either the child or parent. Perhaps even more tragic is today's drug scene. Many individuals attempt to compensate for voids in their lives with alcohol and narcotics. In these cases, compensation keeps the problem covered so that it is never brought into the open, and consequently there is no possibility for a solution.

Reaction formation People who use reaction formation as a defense mechanism are avoiding facing a problem by acting in a way that is an exaggerated opposite of how they truly feel. For example, have you ever known somebody who acts like the life of the party, always laughing and making jokes? In reality this person may be unhappy, but he covers this feeling by acting just the opposite.

A classic example of the reaction formation is the "Don Juan," a person who is insecure about being attractive to members of the opposite sex. He hides this feeling by collecting as many dates and sexual conquests as possible.

Projection In projection you avoid an unpleasant part of yourself by disowning that part and attributing it to others. For instance, on the days when as instructors we aren't as prepared for class as we might be, it's tempting to claim that the hour hasn't gone well because the students didn't do *their* homework. Similarly, you may have found yourself accusing others of being dishonest, lazy, or inconsiderate when in fact such descriptions fit your behavior quite well. In all of these cases we project an unpleasant trait of our own onto another, and in so doing we avoid facing it in ourselves. It doesn't matter whether the accusation you make about others is true or not: In projection the important point is that you are escaping from having to face the truth about yourself.

The mechanism of projection explains the common experience of taking an instant dislike to someone you've just met and realizing later that the traits you found so distasteful in that person are precisely those you dislike in yourself. By criticizing the new acquaintance you can put the undesirable characteristic "out there," and not have to admit it belongs to you.

A surefire test to determine whether you are using projection to fool yourself is to take every attack you make on others and substitute "I" for the words you use to identify the other person. For example, "She talks too much" becomes "I talk too much," or "They're being unfair" is instead "I'm being unfair." When you try this simple experiment and your accusation of another seems to be true of you, you are projecting.

Identification   Sometimes when we're unsure or don't like ourselves, we hide our feelings by imitating someone we admire. The problem with identification of this sort is that it's artificial. We get so involved in "being like" another person that we can't respond to a situation genuinely; instead, we react as we think our "hero" would, often denying our own feelings in the process. Thus, when we use the mechanism of identification, our life becomes an act.

Many families only relate to each other in artificial ways. Without being conscious of it they pick up a mental picture of the "ideal, trouble-free family" from television shows and other clichés. Then when real problems occur—as they're bound to do—nobody is willing to admit it for fear that something is wrong with them. Instead, everyone goes on acting a role, while the problem usually grows because of neglect.

Fantasy   When a person's desires or ambitions are frustrated, he often resorts to a fantasy world to satisfy them. We often daydream ourselves out of our "real" world into one that is more satisfying. A good example of this is the young career woman who finds herself bored with her dull life as a typist. To insulate herself from this unbearable existence she escapes into the excitement of her own fantasies. She becomes the leading lady in the romance magazine stories, the television dramas, and the movies she frequents. No matter how exciting and glamorous these fantasies are, they're not connected to the problem of her reality and therefore can't help her make changes to improve her life.

There is much to be said for the short daydream that lifts the boredom of an unpleasant task, or the fantasies that can be creative tools to help us think up new solutions to problems. But as with all defense mechanisms, the danger of fantasizing is that it keeps us from dealing squarely with what's bothering us by providing a temporary escape which doesn't really solve the problem.

Repression   Sometimes rather than facing up to an unpleasant situation and trying to deal with it, we protect ourselves by denying its existence. Quite simply, we "forget" what would otherwise be painful. Take a couple, for example, who can't seem to agree about how to handle their finances. One partner thinks that money is meant to be spent, while the other believes that it's important to save for the future. Rather than working to solve this important problem, the husband and wife pretend nothing is wrong. This charade may work for a while, but as time goes by each partner will probably begin to feel more and more uncomfortable and will likely begin to build up resentments about the way the other one uses their common money.

. . . I once knew a brilliant and discerning philosopher who spent many hours each week alone in movie houses watching indifferently pictures of a quality far below his actual intellectual tastes. I knew him as an able, friendly, and normal person. Somewhere behind his sunny mask, however, he was in flight, from what, I never knew. Was it job, home, family—or was it rather something lost that he was seeking? Whatever it was, the pictures that passed before his eyes, the sounds, only half-heard, could have meant little except for an occasional face, a voice, a fading bar of music. No, it was the darkness and the isolation he wanted, something in the deep night of himself that called him home.

Loren Eisley

Eventually these resentments are almost sure to leak into other areas of the marriage.

In the same way, we've seen families with serious problems—an alcoholic parent, a teenager into drugs, a conflict between members—try to pretend that everything is perfectly all right, as if acting that way will make it so. Of course, it's unlikely that they'll solve these problems without admitting that they exist.

Dependency or regression   Sometimes rather than admit we *don't want* to do something, we convince ourselves that we *can't* do it. We resort to behavior that is more characteristic of an earlier age, an age when we were more helpless. This behavior is known as *regression* or *dependency*.

The person who says, "Gee, I'd really like to have a relationship with you, but I'm not ready" might really be hiding the truth: that she simply doesn't care enough about the relationship to make it grow. The pitiful soul who says "I'd really like to improve my life, but I can't" could be hiding from the fact that he isn't willing to put in the work necessary to change his present situation.

Emotional insulation and apathy   Often, rather than face an unpleasant situation, people will avoid hurt by not getting involved or pretending they don't care. Probably the most common example of *emotional insulation* is the person who develops a strong attachment to someone only to have the relationship break up. The pain is so great that the sufferer refuses to become involved like this again. At other times people who are hurt in this way defend their feeling of self-worth by becoming *apathetic*, by saying they don't care about whoever hurt them.

I AM A ROCK

A winter's day
In a deep and dark December
I am alone
Gazing from my window
To the streets below
On a freshly fallen silent shroud of snow
I am a rock
I am an island.

I built walls
A fortress deep and mighty
That none may penetrate
I have no need of friendship
Friendship causes pain
Its laughter and its loving I disdain
I am a rock
I am an island.

Don't talk of love
Well, I've heard the word before
It's sleeping in my memory
I won't disturb the slumber
Of feelings that have died
If I'd never loved I never would have cried
I am a rock
I am an island.

I have my books
And my poetry to protect me.
I am shielded in armor
Hiding in my room
Safe within my womb
I touch no one and no one touches me
I am a rock
I am an island

And a rock feels no pain
And an island never cries.

The sad thing about emotional insulation and apathy is that they prevent the person who uses them from doing anything about dealing with the cause of the defensiveness. As long as I say I don't care about dating when I really do, I can't go out with anyone because this would be inconsistent with my artificial self-concept. As long as I don't admit that I care about you, our relationship has little chance of growing.

Displacement This occurs when we vent aggressive or hostile feelings against people or objects that are seen as less dangerous than the person or persons who caused the feelings originally. The child who is reminded that she has to clean up her room before she can play may get rid of some of her hostility by slamming the door to her bedroom or beating up a younger brother or sister. She knows it might cause her more pain if she expressed this hostility against her parents.

A clerk gets angry at his boss because she suggests that he accomplish more than he has. He doesn't want to risk getting fired so he takes it out on his wife and children.

Have you ever had the experience of being in a bad mood or feeling mean? Have you noticed how difficult it seems to get along with others during these times? Chances are something has happened that hasn't been to your liking, and the feelings generated by that "something" are being displaced upon whoever comes along.

Undoing In undoing we make up for an act that doesn't fit with our ideal self-concept by offering a symbolic token of apology, usually to the person we've hurt. For example, the boy who is constantly late picking up his date

Defensiveness: Protecting Our Self-Concept

may bring her gifts to show that he's not so bad after all. A parent who punishes his child and then feels guilty may be "extra" nice to the child for a while to raise his own self-esteem.

We should point out that symbolic gestures that really *do* signal a change in behavior aren't undoing. But these gestures become defense mechanisms when we use them to fool ourselves into thinking we've turned over a new leaf when we really haven't.

Verbal aggression Sometimes, when we can get away with it, the easiest way to avoid facing criticism is to drown it out. Verbal aggression illustrates the old saying "The best defense is a good offense." Counterattacking somebody who threatens our self-concept tends to relieve tension and helps the defensive person feel better because his fireworks probably cover up whatever it was in the original remark that threatened him.

A good example of verbal aggression is the "so are you" defensive maneuver. When a person says something we feel is too critical, we counterattack by telling her all her faults. Our remarks may be true, but they don't answer her criticism and only wind up making her more defensive.

Temper tantrums, hitting below the belt, and bringing up past grievances are some other types of verbal aggression. (For more on these "crazy-makers," see Chapter 8.)

© 1967 Jules Feiffer

It's not all that hard to do the right thing. But it takes so much effort to think of the kid first, especially when you really need to explode. Arthur Wesson sat in my class for a month and never opened his mouth.

One day when I was feeling ugly, I asked him a question about the book we were reading. He didn't say a word. I thought of all the things I should have done, but no—I had to get belligerent. I asked the question again. Then I waited for an interminable length of time. Nothing.

"If you can't answer when you're spoken to, you can leave."

I hated the way I sounded. But I was too wrapped up in my own frustration to cope with anything Arthur might feel. He left. And I had to find out from a far more patient teacher than I that there wasn't anything personal in the kid's apathy. He couldn't read. His mother was insane, and there was no place to send her. The two babies at home hadn't eaten in a couple of days. I was just a very small ugliness in Arthur Wesson's ugly world. At least he'd found someone in school he could cry to. Except for selfishness, it might have been me. Everytime I saw him, I hated myself all over again. I was too ashamed to look him in the eye.

Sunny Decker, *An Empty Spoon*

Now that you've had a look at several ways people defend an unrealistic self-concept, we hope you'll be able to detect the role defense mechanisms play in your life. We want to repeat that these mechanisms aren't usually destructive unless they're practiced to the point where an individual's view of reality becomes distorted. We also hope that you don't instantly become a self-appointed psychiatrist, analyzing the defense mechanisms in others. Rarely will you find an individual's behavior so transparent and uncomplicated that it can be diagnosed from casual observation. What appears on the surface as a defense mechanism in operation may be authentic, honest behavior. Our hope is that you can look at *yourself* with a little more knowledge of how you operate when you detect a threat to your self-concept.

Finally, you'll find defensive mechanisms don't usually appear as simple, clear-cut behaviors. We usually use them in combinaton because it's only natural to protect one's self in as many ways as possible.

Defense Mechanism Journal

For a period of five days keep track of the defense mechanisms you use. You can become more sensitive to your own defensive behavior in three ways. First, you can reread and discuss the material in the preceding pages. Second, learn to pay attention to the messages your body sends you, and in so doing you'll soon recognize that certain things happen when you become defensive—perhaps a tightening of certain muscles, a change in the tone of your voice, or a feeling in the pit of your stomach. Finally, you can share the list of defense mechanisms with the important people in your life and ask

years ago it was there
your beauty
on something as simple
as a square of paper
remember kindergarten
and the yellow spot
the sun
the splash of blue
the sky
the curving
dripping green line
of the hills
and the perfect
red stripe
i remember
how you looked
at your work
and saw
that it was good

what is this
teacher said
questioning the red

why
it's a fire engine
and then you looked
at your work
again
and then you
hurled your brush
into the corner
of the room
and stomped off
defeated

later
out on the playground
you hit barbara jenkins
in the head
with a kickball
and now
you sit
in the barber chair
running figures
through your mind
hating yourself
and the sight of my hair
waiting
for some kind
of good fairy
to come down
and save your ass

but i remember
i wish you did

Ric Masten

them to point out occasions when they perceive that you are using one or more of them.

For each incident you record, describe

a. the time it occurred

b. the person or people involved

c. the subject you were discussing

d. the mechanism or mechanisms you used

e. the part of your self-concept you were trying to protect

f. the consequences of your defensive reaction

g. any alternative ways of behaving that might have been more satisfying

Conclude your journal with a summary of your findings. Include

a. a list of the people with whom you most often become defensive

b. a description of the parts of your self-concept you feel compelled to defend

c. a statement about the usual consequences of your defensiveness

d. a description of more desirable ways you could act in situations like those you encountered here

Defense Mechanism Inventory

List the three defense mechanisms you use most often and describe three recent examples of each. You can arrive at your list both by thinking about your own behavior and by asking others to share their impressions of your behavior. As in the previous journal, conclude your inventory by describing the people with whom you become defensive most often, the parts of your public image that you frequently defend, the usual consequences of using defense mechanisms, and any more satisfying behavior you could promote in the future.

Monday Brings Same Old Things

DEAR ANN LANDERS: What are we coming to when a big airline runs a full-page ad telling people that for $152.00 they can be somebody else for a weekend?

My mother used to tell me, "Be yourself." She emphasized solid values, the wisdom of being a real person—just what you are, nothing more and nothing less. I've tried to raise my three children with that same philosophy. And now I see it's much more desirable to "be somebody else. Laugh and dance barefoot with cordial strangers and fall into the pool."

Have we gone mad? What about it?—

Nobody Else

DEAR N.E.: One of the central problems of our time is that too many people do not like themselves and they deplore the mundane, monotonous quality of their lives. These unfulfilled people respond to an ad that offers them an opportunity to be somebody else, even if only for a weekend at a cost of $152. Sad, of course, because on Monday morning, there they are—the same miserable, inadequate, lonely selves, with the same nagging insecurities they left.

Defensiveness: Protecting Our Self-Concept

A Child's Garden of Defense Mechanisms

dependency-regression

"Childlike behavior" is what I call avoiding a situation by pretending I'm not mature enough to handle it, or that I don't understand it. When there's a homework assignment I'm not particularly thrilled over, I try to convince myself that I'm not smart enough to handle it, thus excusing myself from any guilt feelings over the skipped assignment.

verbal aggression

I was with my boyfriend a few months ago when this man ran a red light and smashed into the side of our van. It was definitely his fault—there were cars stopped in the lane next to him.

Even though this guy must have known he was guilty he jumped out of his car and began yelling at us. He called us "dirty hippies" and "bums."

He let out all that verbal aggression just to cover up the truth—that he was wrong.

repression

Repression is my "favorite" way of facing up to myself and blocking my communication. I'm especially good at repressing my feelings about my parents. It's not that we hate each other or anything—I really dig them and they like me. But there are some problems that keep coming up. The big one is that they want me to go out with girls who are the same religion as we are. I don't think it matters what religion my dates are—I'm not ready to get married or anything.

Anyhow, the problem is that instead of talking the whole thing over, we all try to pretend that there's no problem when there really is. We wind up being so damn polite to each other that it drives us crazy.

projection

I found out I do a lot of projecting. The most classical one I've done was Friday night at my boyfriend's house. His mom fixed tacos (lots of them), the company was good, the beer was plentiful. I had told myself earlier that week that I was going to start cutting down on my food intake for fear of gaining unwanted pounds. I told Joe about it so he was quite aware of it. But that night somehow I couldn't hold to my decision! Beer and tacos taste so-o-oo good together, that somehow it took four and a half to finish off my beer with!! (I was only going to have one). So automatically after Joe commented on the number, I said "Well, you should have told me I couldn't have any more, but you didn't say anything, you just let me go right on eating!!" He seems to always be the one I project upon.

rationalization

A guy I know broke up with his girlfriend not too long ago, and the way he handled the thing really shows how rationalization can hurt communication. The reason he gave her for splitting was that he'd be going away to Europe soon and he didn't want to break off suddenly when he left. But the truth was that he was just tired of her. She knew this, and I think his rationalization hurt her way more than if he'd been honest.

And I know he was only fooling himself because he wants to think he's a great guy who is thinking only of her welfare!

reaction formation

It's really too bad, but I've never gotten along with my husband's mom. Ever since Jim and I met she's acted like I'm not good enough for him. I've always said that I didn't care what she thought about me but the other day I found out that I was kidding myself.

The way I found out was through a reaction formation. You see, neither Jim or I care that much about cooking. We're happy enough eating hamburgers or frozen dinners, but I just realized that everytime Bea (that's his Mom's name) comes over I break my back to fix a fancy dinner. It's almost like I was trying to show her (and myself) that I <u>do</u> take good care of Jim.

displacement

Yesterday at work I used the defense mechanism of displacement. My supervisor had given me a bunch of static about a problem that was really his fault. He's an unrealistic old S.O.B. to begin with, and there's no use arguing with him. So I guess because I was so mad, when one of the guys on my crew asked me if he could take off a little early that afternoon I chewed him out for being a lazy so-and-so. But all it was was my anger at the boss being displaced.

I was really sorry and apologized later, but it'll take a few days for the guy to let the chip melt off his shoulder.

identification

When I was in high school there was always a "popular" group of girls that I wanted to get into but they never seemed to notice me or like me very much, even though I tried to act just the way they did. I always bought the same kinds of clothes and I tried to make the same kinds of jokes that they did. I guess I thought if I could act like them they'd accept me. Now that I'm in college I realize how unhappy I was then and how foolish they seemed, but then I would have given anything to be one of them.

emotional insulation

I think of all the defense mechanisms I can relate to, emotional insulation is the main one.

One example of emotional insulation in all its glory is concerning a friend that <u>was</u> very close but now even though we live in the same house, very little communication goes on between us. Sometimes when I let my pride down, I really feel the full impact of hurt on my part and wonder if she even cares. I've asked myself many times why I can't discuss it with her. And the deep-down reason is because I'm afraid that she won't respond and that would hurt me even worse than it does now; so I've chosen to ignore the situation which has worked only to the degree of convincing myself not to talk it out but so far it hasn't convinced me not to feel.

undoing

I'm terrible about doing chores around the house. My wife has to bug me for weeks before I even change a lightbulb. We were talking about defense mechanisms last night and she suddenly exclaimed "Gordon, every time you don't do a job we end up going out to dinner!"

I always thought I was just being a nice guy by taking us out, but now I see that I've been buying my way back into my wife's good grace!

compensation

The other night I was at a party when the subject turned to politics. I'm really turned off by that whole thing, even though I know it's important to know what's going on in Washington, etc. So when somebody brought up the election I tried to change the subject to motorcycles, which I know a lot about.

I do this a lot. When there's something I don't understand or don't like, I try to change the conversation over to an area where I'm an authority.

fantasy

I've been having troubles at work lately with my boss. I know he thinks I dress too casually, but since no customers ever come into our office I don't see what difference it makes as long as I'm clean. There's been a lot of friction between us because of this dress thing, and it's gotten to the point where I sit at my desk and fantasize having the whole thing out with him. Sometimes I quit, sometimes we become friends—but all this is in my mind, since we never have it out. It's a real bummer.

Many people think they are acting the way they feel when they tell someone off. Someone is critical of me and I answer by calling him an S.O.B. My feeling is not that he is an S.O.B.; my feeling is that he has hurt me: "You have hurt my feelings and now I want to hurt yours." Launching a verbal attack covers up my feeling of being hurt with an appearance of strength. I get angry when I think someone has hurt me in a way I am helpless to do anything about.

Hugh Prather

Defensiveness Ruins Communication

If you've read carefully this far and tried to understand the role defense mechanisms play in your life, you've certainly seen how defensiveness can damage communicaton. If we're lucky, the damage we create in this way is short-lived and heals with time; but in some cases a single defensive outburst can destroy an entire relationship.

What Makes Us Defensive? The Gibb Categories

We've been talking about the defense mechanisms we use to protect our idealized self-concept and the more consciously applied masks we wear to gain acceptance. But what makes us defensive in the first place?

We've already said that the cause of defensiveness is threat to our self-concept; but thanks to the research of Dr. Jack Gibb we can be more specific. After observing groups for eight years, Gibb was able to isolate six defense-causing types of behavior. His work suggests that often when we act in one or more of these six ways, the threat to the other person's self-concept is increased to a degree that defensiveness is likely to result.

But Gibb's work didn't stop here. He identified six contrasting behaviors that when practiced seemed to reduce the level of threat and defensiveness in communication. He termed these ways of responding as supportive behaviors.

In his research Gibb also found that defensiveness is *reciprocal.* That is, when Person *A* in a relationship becomes threatened and begins to use defense mechanisms and masks to protect himself, much of the time his behavior will begin to cause Person *B* to begin putting up his defenses. This in turn threatens Person *A* even more, and so a spiraling defensive cycle is started, making communication more and more difficult.

Fortunately, just the opposite is also true. When Person *A* behaves in a supportive way, *B* has less cause to feel threatened and so usually lowers his defenses; in turn, this openness causes A to become even less defensive. In other words, both defensive and supportive behaviors are cyclical: You get back what you give in a relationship.

In the next few pages we've listed the six pairs of contrasting behaviors that Gibb developed. Each set contains a description of the way people act that's likely to cause defensiveness, and the behavior that tends to reduce it. As you read about these behaviors, keep two things in mind: First, none of the following behaviors will bring on defensive reactions unless the receiver perceives them as threatening. Insecure receivers may be threatened by almost anything that's said to them, but the more secure people are much less easily threatened. You probably know people who seem to take everything in stride. Would you say they tend to be rather secure individuals?

The second thing to keep in mind is that even though we're talking about these behaviors as if they were distinct from one another, in actuality you may run into them in various combinations. The six-part division is made for clarity, but don't be misled by it.

The Gibb Categories of Defensive and Supportive Behaviors

Defensive Behaviors	Supportive Behaviors
1 Evaluation	1 Description
2 Control	2 Problem orientation
3 Strategy	3 Spontaneity
4 Neutrality	4 Empathy
5 Superiority	5 Equality
6 Certainty	6 Provisionalism

Evaluation *vs.* description A message that's received as evaluative or judgmental increases defensiveness in the receiver and is likely to make him behave in a way that will protect his self-concept. Most of us dislike any situation where we will be evaluated—even positively—because there's always the chance that the outcome will be unfavorable. How do you react when you learn that you'll be evaluated . . . in one of your college courses . . . for a driver's license . . . a job promotion? If you've competed in sports, for a scholarship, or for a job, you've probably felt the pressure evaluation by others can place on you. It seems we must be on guard whenever we suspect we're being rated or judged.

Larry has just accidentally upset a glass of milk all over the dinner table. He was reaching for his salad.

Mother: Larry, how old are you anyway? When are you going to be able to go through a meal without spilling your milk?
Father: He can't help it, it looks like he was born clumsy.
Larry: _____

You can certainly fill in an appropriate response for Larry. And in thinking what Larry would say, you've identified with the defensiveness that he felt after his parents' negative evaluations of him as a person.

Sarah has been bothered lately by the pressure of school work and problems with her boyfriend.

Mother: (crossly) You haven't been fit to live with lately. You've been so thoughtless and moody. You'll just have to stop running around with that crowd of friends and get busy on your schoolwork.

Now even if Sarah had been thinking exactly the same things, how do you think she would have responded to these comments? She probably would have acted by arguing and protecting herself because evaluative language is almost certain to whip up hostility between people. This is the problem with all the defense-arousing behaviors we'll discuss here: Even if the sender's ideas are good ones, the way they're phrased blocks communication.

Defensiveness: Protecting Our Self-Concept

Psychologist Thomas Gordon has a good way of recognizing evaluative speech. He calls it "you" language because most of it's prefaced by that word, usually spoken in an accusing tone of voice: "You're wrong," "You're sloppy," "You're stupid," "You're being obnoxious," et cetera. And if you listen to your conversations for a day or so, you'll probably be surprised to find how many of your statements that contain "you are" carry evaluative messages that usually cause defensiveness.

In contrast to evaluative "you" language is what Gibb calls descriptive communication. Gordon labels this style of speaking as "I" language. Instead of putting the emphasis on judging another's behavior, the descriptive speaker simply explains how the other's action affects him. Referring back to our example of Sarah and her mother, imagine how much easier it would have been for Sarah to respond if her mother had said something like

> I don't know what's happening between us lately, but I've been deeply hurt by some things you've said and done. . . .

and then continued to describe what actions of Sarah's she was thinking of and how they made her feel. This kind of approach doesn't put a lot of pressure on Sarah to change; it simply lets her know how her mother feels and allows her to go from there.

Defensiveness: Protecting Our Self-Concept

In interpersonal relationships, I believe first person singular is most appropriate because it places responsibility clearly.

If I say to another person, "I do not like what you did," then no contradiction is possible. No one can correct me because my perception and what I have decided to think about it is mine alone. The other person may, however, suggest that I received only a portion of the information, or that I received it unclearly for one reason or another. In such a case, the meaning of the message may be tentative until it can be negotiated. It also is legitimate for me to perceive the message quite differently from the way the other person perceives it.

On the other hand, if I say "*You* have made me angry," then you may very well contradict me by responding with something such as "No I didn't." In fact, I am eliciting a defensiveness and also inviting "you" to attempt a control of me by your helplessness, suffering, or anger.

Only *I* am responsible for *my* behavior. Only *I* can change what *I* do. However, when I change my behavior, I may give the other person in the relationship the opportunity to evaluate his behavior and perhaps modify it.

John Narciso and David Burkett, *Declare Yourself*

Take a minute to imagine yourself sending "I" and "you" messages to people in your life, and see what difference the two styles of communication would probably make.

Control *vs.* problem orientation   Communication that we sense is aimed at controlling our thoughts or behavior produces defensiveness. We're motivated to react defensively because the speaker seems to be saying that he knows what's best for us.

When was the last time you felt you were being controlled? How do you feel about TV commercials and aggressive salesmen? What about public employees who treat you as if you were some kind of moron? Or how do you react to teachers or parents who lead you into "discussions" when they have the "right" answer all along? All these are examples of controlling behavior in which the sender acts as if his mind is already made up about a course of action before talking takes place.

Needless to say, people who act in controlling ways create a defensive climate. Nobody likes to feel their ideas aren't worth anything and that nothing they say will change the other's determination to have his way—yet this is precisely the attitude a controller communicates. Whether he does it with his words, gestures, tone of voice, or some other channel; whether he controls through his status, insistence on obscure or irrelevent rules, or physical power, the controller generates hostility wherever he goes. The unspoken message his behavior communicates is "I know what's best for you, and if you do as I say we'll get along."

Unlike control, the supportive behavior of problem orientation projects to the listener a willingness to share in the solution of a problem rather than forcing a preconceived idea upon him. The problem-oriented person acts with the attitude "Let's find a solution that works for both of us." As you'll see in Chapter 8, when we talk about the no-lose approach to problem solving, it's often easier than you might think to solve difficulties by finding an answer that's acceptable to everyone. In the end, even if you can't find the perfect solution, the mere fact that you're willing to try can create a far better climate than can the hostility that comes from two people trying to control each other.

If you're in an environment where control is often used (and who isn't!), don't be too surprised if your first attempts at problem orientation meet with some doubt from others. They may suspect that your willingness to look for a mutually satisfactory solution is some kind of trick, just another way to control them. Remember that defensiveness is reciprocal, and keeping your good humor can prevent the start of an ugly upward spiral of mistrust and hostility.

Strategy *vs.* spontaneity   One of the surest ways to make someone defensive is to get caught trying to manipulate her into doing something for you. The fact that you tried to trick her instead of just asking for what you wanted

Defensiveness: Protecting Our Self-Concept

is enough to build mistrust. Nobody likes to be a guinea pig or a sucker, and even well-meant manipulation can cause bad feelings.

A teenager reported that his dad was tricky. It seems that whenever the father wanted to criticize the boy he'd always say something nice first, and then somewhere along the way let the axe fall. This stratagem has been referred to as the "psychological sandwich," two pieces of praise with criticism between.

It didn't take too many repeats of this strategy before the son cringed every time he heard praise from his dad because he learned it was only given to soften criticism. Probably it would have been better for the relationship if the son received honest praise or honest criticism rather than a strategy that seemed a dishonest mixture of both.

Have you ever wanted to go somewhere and not had a way of getting there? Have you ever tried to manipulate a friend, who had transportation, into wanting to go too? Think back to the different relationships you've had. Have any of them ended because you felt you were being used? Do you suppose anyone has stopped his association with you for the same reason?

Spontaneity is the behavior that contrasts with strategy. Spontaneity simply means being honest, reporting that which you're feeling right now rather than planning your words to get the best response. Often the spontaneous response won't get what you want, but in the long run it's usually better to be candid and yourself and perhaps miss out on some small goal than to say all the right things and become a fraud. More than once we've heard people say "I didn't like what he said, but at least I know he was being honest."

Although it sounds paradoxical at first, spontaneity can be a strategy too. Sometimes you'll see people using honesty in a calculating way, being just frank enough to win someone's trust or sympathy. This kind of "leveling" is probably the most defense-arousing strategy of all because once we've learned someone is using frankness as a manipulation there's almost no chance we'll ever trust him again.

While reading this chapter you might get the idea that using supportive behaviors such as description, problem orientation, empathy, et cetera, is a great way to manipulate others. Before going any further we want to say loudly and clearly that if you ever act supportively without being sincere in what you're saying, you've misunderstood the idea behind this chapter, and you're running a risk of causing even more defensiveness than before. None of the ideas we present in this book can go into a "bag of tricks" that can be used to control others: If you ever find yourself using them this way, beware!

Neutrality *vs.* empathy Probably a better word to describe Gibb's idea of the defense-arousing behavior he calls neutrality is *indifference.* Acting with a neutral attitude communicates a lack of concern for the welfare of another and implies that he isn't very important to you. This perceived indifference is likely to promote defensiveness because no one likes to think of himself as worthless, and he'll protect a self-concept that pictures him as worthwhile.

The small child who has urgent things to tell a parent but is met with an indifferent response may be expected to become upset. The physician who seems clinical and detached to his patients may wonder why they find another doctor.

Gibb has found that empathy helps rid communication of the indifferent quality. When someone shows that he cares for the feelings of another there's little chance that a self-concept will be threatened. Empathy means accepting another's feelings, putting yourself in his place. This doesn't mean you need to agree with him; by simply letting someone know you care and respect him, you'll be acting in a supportive way.

In his research Gibb observed the importance of nonverbal messages in communicating empathy. Facial and bodily expressions of concern often are more important to the receiver than the words used.

Defensiveness: Protecting Our Self-Concept

Teens, Parents and Conversation Gap

NEW YORK (UPI)—Expect the communications gap between parent and teen-ager to worsen when you have a confidential talk with son or daughter—then blab contents of same.

The same will happen if every conversation takes on the tone of a courtroom interrogation.

Many of the teen-agers who stand charged with being sparse in the word department on the homefront really long for conversation with parents.

A report in the Christian Herald makes that point, adding that the youngsters keep the exchanges of words on a superficial level for many reasons.

In "How to Talk to a Teen-ager—Maybe," youngsters gave the following reasons for avoiding conversations in depth with adults:

—The youngsters have learned their confidences are not respected. Their parents tell each other, or other relatives, what has been revealed in private, or make jokes, or discuss their opinions with outside friends. Child reacts by clamming up.

—Parents do not accept their children's feelings as real, but attempt to change their moods without sitting down and trying to find out exactly what bothers them.

—Parents substitute advice and orders for real conversation, dodging the issue when it comes to telling their children what they really think about such subjects as petting, cheating on examinations, politics or religion.

—Parents talk pompously, or too knowingly, stressing only what they think without listening to the youngster's ideas. Youngsters find such talks boring.

—Parents pretend to be authorities on subjects about which they really are ignorant. They make fools of themselves especially when parading their ignorance in front of child's friends.

—In the middle of a discussion, parents lose patience yelling at child—"You'd better do what I say" or "I know best." That puts the clamps on the child's tongue, cutting off communication.

Parents who have not lost the word battle with their teen-agers, meanwhile, have certain things in common.

They are patient while trying to catch a teenager's attention. They win their interest before attempting to start a conversation.

One way to bridge the gap, according to the report in the Christian Herald,—arrange for youngsters to help with household chores which give opportunity for normal conversation.

Los Angeles Times

Superiority *vs.* equality How many interpersonal relationships have you dropped because you couldn't stand the superiority that the other person projected? Like the other behaviors we've talked about, an individual who communicates superiority arouses feelings of inadequacy in the recipients. We're not particular as to the type of superiority presented to us; we just become defensive. Money, power, intellectual ability, physical appearance, and athletic prowess are areas in which we learn it's important to excel in our culture. Consequently we often feel a need to express our superiority along these lines.

The individual who acts superior communicates that he doesn't want to relate on equal terms with the other(s) in the relationship. Furthermore, he seems to imply that he doesn't want feedback nor will he need help because the help would be coming from someone inferior to him. This message of superiority alerts the listener to be on guard because the sender is likely to attempt to reduce the receiver's worth, power, or status to maintain or advance his own superiority.

An example you may have come across is the classmate who questions other members of the class to find out their grades. He's delighted each time he discovers another classmate who has received a grade lower than his. His degree of superiority is closely related to the number of fellow students who received marks lower than his. Have you ever been made defensive by this type of person?

Perhaps you've had a professor who continually reminded his students of his superior intellectual ability and position. Remember how delighted you were when you or a classmate caught him making a mistake? Why do you suppose it was so satisfying to let him know of his error? Some might argue that this is a good strategy to keep students awake, but in reality much of the students' effort is directed to defending his own worth rather than pursuing the objectives of the course.

Whenever we detect someone communicating superiority to us we react. We "turn her off," justify ourselves, or argue with her in our minds. Sometimes we choose to verbally change the subject or physically walk away, and of course there is always the counterattack, which includes an attempt to belittle the sender of the superiority message. We'll go to great lengths "to cut her down to size." All these defensive reactions to projected superiority are destructive to an interpersonal relationship.

There are many situations in our lives when we're in relationship with individuals who possess talents greater than ours. But is it necessary for these persons to project superiority? Your own experiences will tell you that it isn't. Gibb has found ample evidence that many people who possess superior skills and talents are capable of projecting feelings of *equality* rather than superiority. Such people communicate that although they may have greater talent in certain areas, they see others as having just as much worth as human beings.

Certainty *vs.* provisionalism Have you run into the person who is certain she's right, certain hers is the only or proper way of doing something, or certain that she has all the facts and needs no additional information? If you have, you've met an individual who projects the defense-arousing behavior Gibb calls *certainty*.

How do you react when you're the target of such certainty? Do you suddenly find your energy directed to proving the dogmatic individual wrong? If you do, you're reacting normally, if not very constructively.

George Smith, a machine operator, was called into his supervisor's office after his third assistant in three weeks had asked for a transfer. When asked

Defensiveness: Protecting Our Self-Concept

by his boss what was happening, George told him that the young guys he was getting couldn't be told anything. Actually all three assistants had given the same reason for having to "get away" from George. George "knew it all," and he was certain his was the only way any job could be done. He'd get mad if they didn't do exactly as he showed them even when they found a method as good or better than his. George made them feel like idiots. The supervisor was successful in getting George to replace his certainty with some provisionalism, and at last report George's latest assistant has been with him more than a year.

What is this provisionalism the supervisor so strongly suggested George practice? George's boss told him he'd have to do something about his attitude that his was the only way a job could be done. He explained that it was possible his assistant could see another method of doing a piece of work, and he should be willing to listen and perhaps even try it out. He needed to stop trying so hard to teach and to treat his assistant as a coworker, not as someone inferior to himself.

Have you noticed that the person who projects certainty is usually more interested in winning an argument than solving a problem? Gibb points out that the individual who works hard at demonstrating his certainty usually communicates inward feelings of inferiority, a reaction formation that we mentioned earlier in the chapter.

When we exhibit provisionalism instead of certainty we communicate an openness to receiving new information and ideas. And this behavior seldom results in making a person defensive. We're not suggesting that you shouldn't express an opinion or take a position on an issue. We're suggesting, however, that when you practice provisionalism you're interested in that which is new or not yet known to you. The provisional attitude encourages participation and communication, whereas certainty discourages them.

Defensiveness, the Great Barrier

It's our feeling that defensiveness is the greatest single barrier to effective interpersonal communication. The sooner you become aware of your part in producing defensiveness or reacting defensively, the sooner you'll find your interpersonal relationships more satisfying. . . . Making another person defensive interferes with interpersonal communication. It may only make communication more difficult, or on the other hand it may make it impossible!

Defensiveness Feedback

1 Approach an important person in your life and request some help in learning more about yourself. Inform the other person that your discussion will probably take at least an hour, and make sure both of you are prepared to invest this amount of time.

2 Begin by explaining all twelve of the Gibb behaviors to your partner. Be sure to give enough examples so that each category is clearly understood.

3 When your explanation is complete and you've answered all your partner's questions, ask her to tell you which of the Gibb categories *you use with her*. Seek specific examples so that you are certain to understand the feedback fully. (Since you are requesting an evaluation, be prepared for a little defensiveness on your own part at this point.) Inform your partner that you are interested in discovering both the defense-arousing and the supportive behaviors you use, and that you are sincerely interested in receiving a candid answer. (Note: If you don't want to hear the truth from your partner, don't try this exercise.)

4 As your partner speaks, record the categories she lists in sufficient detail for both of you to be sure that you have understood her comments.

5 When you have finished your list, show it to your partner. Listen to her reactions and make any corrections that are necessary to reflect an accurate understanding of her comments. When your list is accurate, have your partner sign it to indicate that you have understood her clearly.

6 In a concluding statement note
   a. how you felt as your partner was describing you
   b. whether you agree with the evaluation
   c. what effect your use of the various Gibb categories has on your relationship with your partner

Defensiveness Groups

1 Divide the class into six small groups, keeping the numbers as even as possible.

2 Each group selects one pair of the Gibb defensive and supportive behaviors.

3 Each group should study the explanation of categories given in the text and then compile a list of examples from the members' own experiences. Each group member should share at least one personal experience that illustrates the behavior being studied.

4 The instructor will act as a resource person, answering any questions the groups may have.

5 When each group has understood their particular defensive and supportive behaviors and armed themselves with good, fresh examples, form new groups with six members. This time each group is to contain a member from each of the different behavior groups. You'll probably not be fortunate enough to have this work out evenly, but each of the new groups should have at least one person representing each of the six Gibb categories.

6 Each member of the new group is to acquaint the others in his group with the defensive and supportive behaviors he has studied. They should use the best examples they heard to illustrate them.

7 As the group proceeds they may have questions. Again, the instructor should be considered as a resource member of each group.

8 You may find that you're hearing examples that could fit into other categories. Don't let this bother you. Remember that we prefaced the materials on defensiveness by saying that Gibb's behaviors were categorized for convenience of investigation. An individual may experience these behaviors in many combinations. The important thing is to become aware of defensive behavior as it occurs in our daily communication, not to memorize the textbook terminology.

9 When each group has finished there should be a chance for anyone who has questions to throw them out to the group as a whole for possible answers.

A Defensiveness Diary

1 For one week (seven days) keep a journal or diary of your encounters with defensiveness. Your objective is to see what part defensiveness plays in your relationships with others.

2 Keep track of the following:
  a. Times you're made defensive by others.
  b. Times you cause others to be defensive.

3 Identify these areas of each incident
  a. The persons involved, labeled by their relationship to you—give names (for example, brother, mother, friend, teacher).
  b. The situation—very briefly, what happened.
  c. The cause of the defensiveness according to Gibb labels. Remember, a combination of behaviors may be observed.
  d. How the situation came out.

4 Keep your notes to a minimum—jot down a word or two as soon after the incident happens as you can, and then write it up at the end of the day.

5 Don't wait and try to write your journal the hour before you're due to hand it in. This defeats the whole purpose of the assignment.

6 Place your name in the upper right-hand corner of the first page only so that it may be cut off. The papers can then be used in class anonymously.

7 After finishing your log answer these questions:
  a. Did you find you identified defensiveness more quickly and more often as the week passed?
  b. Did you find it easier to recognize defensiveness when you initiated it or when someone else did?

c. Were there any times when someone's defensive behavior was caused by a remark you originally made?

d. Has this exercise affected you in any way?

By now we hope you've a clearer idea of the role defensiveness plays in your life. We've tried to help you become aware of the times you consciously wear masks to protect the self you fear others won't accept. We've pointed out some of the defense mechanisms you probably use unconsciously to protect an unrealistic self-concept from attack; and finally, we've shown how defensiveness is caused by certain kinds of behaviors and reduced by others.

Even if you've tried long and hard, you've almost certainly found that it isn't easy to strip away defenses. On the other hand, the people who make the greatest strides in improving their communication are those who will accept the risk involved in discarding their defenses. We feel strongly that this willingness is the key to more satisfying communication. We hope you can begin to look at your own defensiveness and start the process of opening yourself to those with whom you communicate.

"This all sounds fine" you say, "but let the other guy drop his defenses first!" This attitude would probably please an instructor teaching classes in a war college, but it's hardly growth promoting in the area of interpersonal communication. We've already written about the self-fulfilling prophecy in connection with our self-concept; now we can apply the same principle to dropping our defenses. If you're open and supportive in your behavior toward others, they'll tend to respond in a like manner. If you decide to wait for your partner to lower his defenses first, you can expect that again he'll respond in the same fashion; the defensive behavior spiral is set in motion.

Behold the turtle who makes progress only when he sticks his neck out.

Cecil Parker

Roads Not Taken

1   Make a study of the level of defensive communication in a particular part of your life—on the job, at school, at home, and so on. In your observations note

a. which attacking and supporting categories as described by Gibb each person uses

b. the response that each person gives in response to the behaviors described in step a above

c. the consequences that come from the behaviors you have described in steps a and b.

2   Based on your knowledge gained in this chapter, describe in specific terms the ways you must act to arouse less defensiveness in others and to be less defensive yourself. Keep a record of your successes in using these behaviors and note the benefits of your doing so.

3   Observe models in your life who are rarely defensive and observe how they behave when attacked by others. How might you learn from their actions?

4 Read *I Can If I Want To* (described in this chapter's readings section) and comment on which of the mistaken ideas listed there you have been living by, noting the defensive consequences that can come from accepting such ideas.

5 Expand your knowledge of defense mechanisms by doing a thorough investigation of the subject in your library.

More Readings on Defensiveness

Adler, Ronald B. *Confidence in Communication: A Guide to Assertive and Social Skills.* New York: Holt, Rinehart and Winston, 1977.

Chapter 7 deals extensively with nondefensive ways of coping with criticism. In it you'll find detailed, step-by-step instructions for including these skills in your everyday life. Students often find that once they've learned these coping skills, they welcome and enjoy criticism, even when it's totally unfair and mistaken!

Gergen, Kenneth J. "Multiple Identity: The Healthy, Happy Human Being Wears Many Masks." *Psychology Today* (May 1972).

This article suggests that we wear a series of masks; instead of a single identity there are a whole series of "you's" which emerge in various situations. Although the ideas suggested in this article don't totally agree with the ones presented in this book, we recommend you consider them.

Gibb, Jack R. "Defensive Communication." *The Journal of Communication* 11:3 (September 1961).

This is the original article in which the six categories of defensive and supportive behaviors discussed in this book appeared.

Lazarus, Arnold, and Allen Fay. *I Can If I Want To.* New York: Morrow, 1975.

This brief, extremely readable book lists many mistaken ideas by which people try to run their lives and in so doing create tremendous potential for becoming defensive. We're positive that recognizing these mistaken ideas and eliminating them from your public image can lead to a great decrease in your own defensive behavior.

Powell, John. *Why Am I Afraid To Tell You Who I Am?* Chicago: Argus Communications, 1969.

Powell's brief, attractive book attempts to answer the question its title proposes. This is a simple but effective introduction to many issues discussed in this book, including defensiveness.

Shostrom, Everett L. *Man, the Manipulator.* New York: Bantam Books, 1968.

A description of the whys and hows of many masks people wear as well as an argument about the reasons for dropping them.

Films on Defensiveness

The Emperor's New Armor. Color. 6 min. 1970. Pyramid Films.
A short cartoon that demonstrates how too much armor (defensiveness) can have tragic results. The final words of this film never fail to stimulate considerable discussion.

The Fence. Color. 7 min. 1969. B.S.A. Educational Materials.
This clever film shows the reciprocity of our actions toward another, and how these behaviors tend to escalate when allowed to continue. It also shows how supportive behaviors enhance relationships.

Neighbors. Color. 9 min. 1952. National Film Board of Canada.
Nonverbal study of two people who have lived happily side by side for some time, but who come to blows over a flower growing on their property line. An Academy Award winner.

Twelve Angry Men. B/W. 95 min. 1957. United Artists.
Among many things this film demonstrates about human relationships you will find many fine examples of defensiveness. The film can be referred to for examples of conflict resolution and group decision-making as well.

4

Perception: What You See Is What You Get

Study the drawing on the opposite page. What does it look like to you? Do you see a half view of an old woman with a big nose? Or do you see a young woman looking away from you to the left? If you can't see them both, let us help you. The long vertical line that makes up the old lady's nose is the cheek and jaw of the girl; the old woman's mouth is the girl's neckband, and her left eye is the girl's ear. Can you see them both now?

Suppose you saw only one picture at first, the way most people do. What would you have thought about someone who said she saw the other one? If you weren't familiar with this type of experiment, if you didn't particularly like the person, or if you happened to be feeling impatient that day, you might be tempted to call her wrong or even crazy. It's possible that you could end up in a nasty argument over who was right, with each of you pushing your own view, never recognizing or admitting that both interpretations are correct.

We think that a lot of communication problems follow this pattern. We tend to ignore the fact that all of us are different and that these differences equip us to view the world from our very own vantage point. Usually we spend more energy defending our position than understanding another's.

In this chapter we want to help you deal with these problems by giving you some practice in empathy—seeing the world through other people's eyes as well as your own. We'll take a look at some of the reasons things look different to each of us. In our survey we'll explore several areas: the physiological factors that shape our perception; the role culture plays in creating our world view; and, finally, how our personal needs, interests, and biases cause us to see things differently. In so doing we'll cover many of the types of physiological and psychological noise described in the communication model you studied in Chapter 1.

□ □ □

Taste

We'll start our survey of perception by looking at some physiological factors that influence the way we experience the world. To see how your sense of taste differs from others', try this experiment:

Taste Test

1 From your biology department or a chemical supply house, obtain strips of litmus paper treated with the chemical phenyl-thio-carbamide (PTC). (They're very inexpensive.)

2 Give one strip to each member of your group, and have everyone taste their paper at the same time.

3 Now immediately conduct a survey:
   a. How many people found the paper salty?
   b. How many found it sweet?
   c. How many found it bitter?
   d. How many found no taste at all?
   e. Did anyone find a different taste?

> If, to Man, the cricket seems to hear with his legs, it is possible that to the cricket Man seems to walk on his ears.
>
> Anonymous Nineteenth-Century Saying

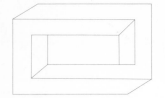

Chances are that to some people the paper tasted bitter, while to others it was sweet, sour, or salty. Somewhat less than half your group probably didn't taste anything at all. The reason for this is hereditary. If you've inherited a dominant "taster" gene from someone in your family, you'll get one taste or another. Otherwise, the treated paper won't seem any different from the untreated type.

The fact that the paper has different tastes for different people is interesting in itself, but it also has important implications for communication. You can imagine that something similar is true for our taste in foods. Do you ever remember having a conversation that went something like

"Eat your liver, dear, it tastes so good."
"But Ma! I hate liver! It tastes horrible!"
"Don't be foolish, dear. I spent a lot of time in the kitchen fixing it. It's delicious."
"But every time I eat it, it makes me choke! I don't want any."
"You listen to me. This is the best liver money can buy. Now be quiet and eat your dinner. All this 'not liking' is just in your mind."

This kind of dialog probably sounds familiar to you. In view of the litmus-paper experiment you can see its flaw: Both mother and child are arguing as if liver tastes the same to everyone. Either the food tastes good or it doesn't—somebody's right and somebody's wrong. But when you think about the litmus-paper experiment, you begin to get the idea that maybe it just tastes *different.*

When was the last time you told someone he was "crazy" for not liking a food? How did this kind of remark affect your communication?

Odor

What's true for taste is also true for your sense of smell. Most people can easily agree about what odors they like the least (burnt rubber or vomit, for example), and to a lesser degree the ones they especially like (fresh strawberries, honeysuckle), but there's no real consistency about whether most smells are good or bad. For example, in one study people ranked their preferences among 132 different odors. Bay leaf (a spice commonly used in cooking) ranged from 9th to 98th; peppermint from 1st to 76th; and raw onion from 5th to 110th. Age and sex seem to play some part in people's odor preferences. Children and men generally like sweeter fruit odors, while women prefer them less sweet; men ranked musky-smelling perfumes higher than women did; and children tolerate odors such as those from feces more than adults do.

Differences like these demonstrate that smells or tastes pleasing to one person can be repulsive to somebody else. So whether it's your perfume, ladies, or your aftershave lotion, men, that provokes the comment "What stinks?" don't be upset—the other person may only be perceiving the odor differently than you do.

Perception: What You See Is What You Get

Try your own odor test. Conduct a survey in class of the odors that people like and dislike most. For many smells you'll probably find agreement, but in a few cases you might be quite surprised.

Temperature

Like the other senses, sensitivity to temperature varies from person to person; forgetting this can block communication. For example, think of the times you've called someone "chicken" who thought the water was too cold for swimming or gotten angry at someone for turning the heat up or down when you were comfortable.

Again, the root of the problem may be biological. People's sensitivity to temperature varies greatly. Thus, if you're less sensitive to cold, it might be that sixty-five degrees to you feels like fifty-five to somebody else. If people could keep this in mind, they'd have less reason to disagree over who's right about the temperature. Rather than fighting, they could figure out alternative behaviors that would suit everyone involved. (That's why electric blankets with dual controls are so popular.)

If your room is equipped with a thermostat, take turns letting different people regulate the temperature each day to suit their taste. You might even chart the variations.

Hearing

Let's continue our study of the senses by examining hearing. We'll try to give you some feeling for how the world sounds to people who hear differently than you do, and then we'll examine the implications this has for communication.

Suppose you have normal hearing. You can represent this visually by holding your book at arm's length and reading what's written below:

LOUDNESS

You should have no trouble reading this comfortably, just as the person with normal hearing has no difficulty understanding others in a conversation. However, it's possible to have a hearing loss without ever knowing it; in fact, it's likely that you know someone who does. To these people the same sounds you hear so easily would be difficult to understand. You can represent how a person with the most common type of loss might hear a word by again holding your book at arm's length and reading this word:

LOU IIE⦚ ⦚

You probably had to magnify these letters or move closer and also mentally fill in the blanks to understand the word. Likewise, hard-of-hearing

people try to understand sounds by magnifying the volume (often with a hearing aid) or by getting closer to the source; they utilize clues in the situation and context to "fill in" sounds they can't hear or are unable to read on a speaker's lips.

The increased noise of our civilization has caused permanent damage to the ears of many people, especially those who spend much of their time in noisy environments—factories, war zones, rock bands, and so on. These people with hearing losses are usually the ones who may have to turn up the television or radio to a level that's uncomfortable for the rest of us.

Forgetting the difference between people's sensitivity to sound can lead to sad consequences. Audiologists and physicians report many cases of children being held back in school for being "slow learners" and punished at home for "not paying attention" when the real problem was that they simply couldn't hear what was going on.

Spend a day experiencing a hearing loss. Put a wad of cotton in each ear (don't push it in too deeply), and notice the difference this makes to your communication. Do you find your mind wandering when you can't follow a conversation clearly? Do you develop the annoying habit of needing to have everything repeated? Do you turn up the radio and TV to a "normal" level and blast others out of the room?

Have you ever wondered how many people you know may have some degree of hearing loss?

Vision

It's obvious that people with uncorrected visual problems see differently than the rest of us. Let Sherri, Ron's wife, tell you how poor vision can affect communication.

I started wearing glasses when I was eight years old, and my eyesight continued to deteriorate until I was about seventeen. So practically all my life I've had to account for communication difficulties because of my very poor vision. (In my last eye test I couldn't even read the big "E" at the top of the chart without my contact lenses!)

When I was young I went through the embarrassment of having "four eyes" and would only put my glasses on to sneak a look at the blackboard. Asking the teacher if I could sit closer to the front would have solved part of the problem, but also would have singled me out again as a glasses-wearer. I stayed quiet, and my grades declined.

I used to love swimming, having grown up with a swimming pool and then moving to the ocean. As my vision became worse I swam less and less, though my friends and family would spend whole summers on the beach. I just recently discovered that by wearing a face mask and my contacts I could swim again! Those weird, dark things floating in the water really are seaweed! No more explanations to people who just couldn't understand that it's scary to swim when you can hardly see!

Since I've known Ron we've had some experiences that have caused communication problems because of our differences in vision: He has perfect eyesight, and even when I'm wearing contacts he can see better than I.

Last summer we drove to Colorado. I would get angry (and frightened) when he continuously passed cars on narrow two-lane roads, and he would get mad at me for following slow-moving cars for thirty minutes without passing. When I explained that I just couldn't see as far up the road as he could, he realized that we didn't see things the same way and that our safety would be threatened if I was to drive the way he wanted me to.

This same problem occurs with freeway and street signs. I can't plan ahead when to turn because I can't see the signs until I'm practically on top of them! Because of this I'm a rather poor navigator, and Ron and I have to be careful to avoid fights when driving together.

I have to sit in the front half of a movie theater to be able to see well. Ron has adjusted to this, but he says he always sat in the back before he met me.

On a camping trip, lying in sleeping bags outdoors:
    Ron:"Aren't the stars fantastic?"
    Me: "What stars?"

We were camping in Mexico, and Ron had constructed a makeshift shelter with a tarp to cover our sleeping bags in case of bad weather. In the middle of the night it started to pour, and our shelter soon had a puddle of water overflowing onto us. Ron told me to get out, keep dry, get our clothes so they wouldn't get wet, put something on so I wouldn't get wet, help with the tarp, find the flashlight . . . . While he was wet and angry at me for being so slow, I was practically in tears trying to explain I couldn't move that fast because I couldn't see!

Sex

So far we've taken a look at how your five senses can make the world seem a different place to you and other people. Now we want to talk about another physiological factor that causes you to perceive things differently and show you how it can affect your communication.

At one time or another every man is puzzled at the changeability of the females in his life. Before his very eyes women who were gentle, smiling friends turn into irritable, moody strangers. At times like these it's easy to mutter chauvinistically something about "that time of the month," and go bowling or take a walk. But to do this is to underestimate the tremendously powerful influence that a woman's menstrual cycle plays in her feelings and her communication.

For many women nothing different happens during their menstrual cycle, but for many others and their friends and families it's a difficult time. Besides the physical symptoms of premenstrual tension—headache, backache, fatigue, pelvic discomfort, and temporary weight gain—the woman goes through all sorts of emotional lows. She's often depressed for no apparent reason, and tears come more easily. She's more likely to lose her temper over little things and sometimes can't seem to keep from eating more than she should.

If you don't know from your own experience, you can certainly imagine how these symptoms can hurt communication between the woman who is undergoing them and those around her. Arguments start more quickly, and feelings get hurt more easily. Little things that would have gone unnoticed any other time become major problems. And the really sad thing is that many times neither the woman who's suffering from the premenstrual tension nor those around her are aware of what's causing the problem.

Women aren't the only ones whose communication is affected by periodic changes in mood. Men, too, go through recognizable mood cycles, even though they aren't marked by physical changes. Although they may not be

GORDO   **By GUS ARRIOLA**

More than 40 years ago, the late Dr. Rex Hersey believed that male factory workers were incorrectly thought to be stable and unchanging in their daily capabilities. For a year, he observed both management and workers, concentrating on a group of men who seemed particularly well-adjusted and at ease in their jobs. Through a combination of four-times-a-day interviews with the workers, regular physical examinations, and a supplementary set of interviews with their families, he arrived at charts for each individual, showing that emotions varied predictably within the rhythm of 24 hours, and within the larger rhythm of a near-monthly cycle of four to six weeks. Low periods were characterized by apathy, indifference, or a tendency to magnify minor problems out of all proportion. High periods were often marked by a feeling of well-being, energy, a lower body weight, and a decreased need for sleep.

Each man tended to deny that he was more or less irritable, more or less amiable, at different points in his cycle, but standardized psychological tests established clearly that he responded very differently to the same life stresses at different times of his cycle. This denial by men of a cyclicity traditionally accepted by women may be an important factor: a two-edged sword for both men and women.

ESTELLE RAMEY, Ph.D., *Ms. Magazine*

aware of it, all men seem to go through biologically regulated periods of good spirits that are followed by equally predictable times of depression. The average length of this cycle is about five weeks, although in some cases it's as short as sixteen days or as long as two months. However long it may be, this cycle of ups and downs is quite regular.

If you were to ask most men why they were feeling so bad during the low part of their cycle, you'd get plenty of reasons: troubles with the family or at work, the state of the economy, the cussedness of politicians, or a million other explanations. However reasonable these woes may sound, they're often rationalizations and not the real cause of the problem. Although extremely good or bad events can alter our feelings, more often they're governed by the internal clock everyone carries around inside.

Although neither men nor women can change these emotional cycles, simply learning to expect them can be a big help in improving communications. When you understand that the cause of a bad mood is predictable and caused by physiological causes, you can plan for it. You'll know that every few weeks your patience will be shorter, and you'll be less likely to blame your bad moods on innocent bystanders. The people around you can also learn to expect your periodic lows and attribute them to biology instead of getting angry at you.

Social Roles

So far you've seen how everyone's physiological makeup varies and how these variations can block communication if we're not careful. But besides our physical makeup there's another set of perceptual factors that can lead to communication breakdowns. From almost the time we're born, each of us is indirectly taught a whole set of roles that we'll be expected to play. In one sense this collection of prescribed parts is necessary because it enables a society to function smoothly and provides the security that comes from knowing what's expected of you. But in another way having roles defined in advance can lead to wide gaps in understanding. When roles become unquestioned and rigid, people tend to see the world from their own viewpoint, having no experiences that show them how other people view it. Naturally, in such a situation communication suffers.

In every society one of the most important factors in determining roles is sex. How should a woman act? What kinds of behavior go with being a man? Until recently most of us never questioned the answers our society gave to these questions. Boys are made of "snips and snails and puppy-dog tails" and grow up to be the breadwinners of families; little girls are "sugar and spice and everything nice," and their mothers are irrational, intuitive, and temperamental. Not everyone fits into these patterns, but in the past the patterns became well established and were mainly unquestioned by most people.

But in recent years many men and women have found that following these roles caused them to live in different worlds that only partially meet, and they've found this kind of life unsatisfying. The following article describes how one couple overcame the restriction of their roles and in doing so improved their relationship.

"You're wrong" means "I don't understand you"—I'm not seeing what you're seeing. But there is nothing **wrong** with you, you are simply not me and that's not wrong.

Hugh Prather

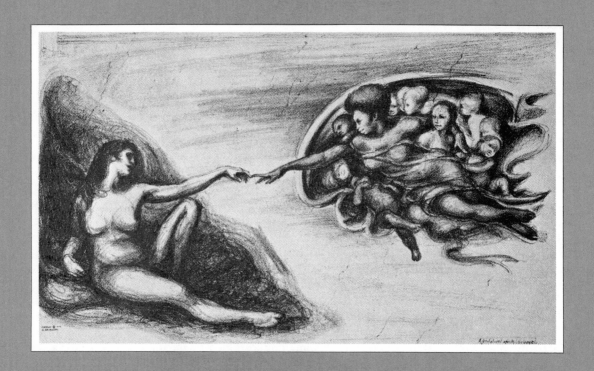

Mother Went to Work and Father Stayed Home

A poster on the wall of the living room where Steve Everett is relaxing as he knits on a bulky ski sweater reads, "Love is the hardest lesson."

That lesson is one Steve and Marge Everett are determined to learn, so determined that they recently devoted a year to a brave experiment: Marge went to work and paid the bills while Steve stayed at home in Chicago's Oak Park suburb to take care of their two children and the domestic chores. The experience revolutionized their attitudes and their whole approach to life. It also quite possibly saved their marriage.

In the early months of their marriage Marge willingly filled the traditional role of housekeeper with one exception—she continued to teach. Since she had more experience than Steve, she also made more money, and this bothered him. When Steve decided to go on to graduate school, Marge paid all the bills and took care of their tiny, two-room apartment. "I thought it was my duty as a woman to help him get ahead at a sacrifice to myself. Later I resented the fact that he got his Master's and there was no thought of my going for one."

By the time the Everetts celebrated their sixth wedding anniversary, Marge was thoroughly dissatisfied with her life. "I had to take care of the kids all day and most of the night too. I had to clean the house just to see it get dirty again. I had to get all the meals." But worse than the physical work was the psychological isolation. "My world grew so small. For four years I lived through Steve's life." Steve's homecoming was the highlight of her day, and she often jumped him at the door for news of the outside world. It was a greeting Steve didn't relish.

"I hated it," he says. "I didn't always feel like rehashing every little thing I'd done during the day."

The situation was brought into sharp focus on a camping trip they took that summer with some friends. Three times during the evening one of the Everett children cried, and each time it was Marge —not Steve—who left the party of adults to check on them. "I didn't say anything to Steve, but I was so angry that by the third time I hated his guts."

Finally, the other couples got after Steve for letting Marge do all the work. "Don't you take any responsibility within your own family?" they asked and began discussing it.

Marge was so relieved she started crying and walked away from the group. "That was such a feeling—that other people understood! I'd felt resentments so many times before and held them in. Now someone else was drawing his attention to the unfairness."

Steve's first reaction was puzzlement. "At the time I thought all the criticism was unjustified. Now, looking back, I think it was pretty mild." But it did strike a chord, and the Everetts regard the camping trip as a major turning point.

After a lot of talk and study, the Everetts came up with an idea that most men (including Steve a few years earlier) would automatically reject. It involved changing places with each other for a full school year. In a practical sense, the Everetts were in an ideal situation for a role switch. Since both were teachers, their earning power was roughly comparable. Steve was due for a year's sabbatical, so the timing was perfect. They did have some qualms about the psychological effects of a role reversal. They wondered what would happen to a male ego cut off from the competitive jungle and left at home to file recipes. Does a woman who becomes a provider also become an emasculator? And what about Andy and Anne, then at the impressionable ages of four and two? How would a little boy identify with a father who cooked breakfast while Mommy paid the bills? And who would be the female model for a little girl—a bread-baking father or a breadwinning mother? "At first we were afraid to take the risk, but then we decided we had to take it."

In the fall of 1969, Marge went back to work teaching first grade, and Steve stayed home with the children. When Marge got home from school at 4:30, she did the things most people do after a day of work. "Sometimes I'd read the paper or flop on the couch. Usually I played with the kids, too. It was so nice to see them! I wasn't bitchy and I didn't take things out on them the way I did when I was home all day." Still, it was a little while before she got over feeling guilty about leaving the children. "As a woman, I was brought up to believe it was my role to stay home and take care of the children. It's really pretty hard to shove off all that conditioning."

As the experiment progressed, Steve found himself looking forward to Marge's homecoming more and more each evening. "One night she was late getting home and I caught myself running back and forth and looking out the window for the car and worrying about dinner spoiling. And all of a sudden it just shook me—realizing that Marge had been doing the same thing and going through these same feelings. But when she'd gotten angry at me for coming home late, I thought there was something wrong with her."

Again and again, the Everetts found themselves having the same experiences and conversations they'd had before—with the roles and dialogue reversed. Before the switch, Marge had complained when Steve came home too tired for conversation. More than one argument started when he turned on the news and fell asleep in front of the television set. "One night," says Marge, "I came home from work and flopped down on the couch. And Steve said, 'Do you have to do that? I'd like some time to talk.' Well," Marge continues, "I could only laugh and cry at the same time, because the same thing he wanted, I had wanted so many times before."

Meanwhile, Marge was having a marvelous time. "Being home for four years had given me the feeling

that I wasn't too worthwhile, that I had nothing to offer. What could I do besides fold diapers? Not that it's not important to fold diapers and do housework—it's just different when you're doing something outside. What I did for my students and people on the outside brought me alive. I was receiving praise for what I could do as a person. I wasn't being taken for granted. I began to feel like someone."

The experiment is over now. Steve is teaching again and Marge is back at home. But things aren't the same as they were before. Both have become more sensitive to the other's feelings, and more able to express their own.

Marge notices that she's less apt to have attacks of "my nasties"—sniping at Steve about personal gripes in the company of other people. And now that they're verbalizing and ventilating their feelings, the snide gestures have decreased, too. "Steve used to come into the house and look around kind of checking to see if I'd done my thing—once I even caught myself doing that when I came home from work."

Although it might seem that a year of being housebound would prompt Steve to get out and stay away as much as possible, he comes home earlier and spends more time with the family than ever before. "I have more of a feeling now that I belong," he says.

Also Marge doesn't jump him the second he walks in the door these days. "Now I have my own life, too," she says. "There's more meaning to my life than just what Steve's doing." In turn, this relieves Steve of a burden.

"Marge isn't getting all her status from me any more. She's getting it from her own people, her own world."

The Everetts believe their children have benefited from the experiment. Although Anne and Andy were a little confused during the first weeks—they kept calling Steve "Mommy"—adjustment was quick, and they had the great advantage of getting to know their father better than most youngsters do. They now turn to Steve as often as Marge—much to her relief. "I love them," she says, "but it's so much better when somebody shares the responsibility."

But the Everetts believe the main change wrought by the experiment was in themselves. As Steve puts it, "The home is a functional situation and all the duties of the house can be shared by all the members of the family. This leaves time for them to enjoy each other, react to each other spontaneously and also frees them to grow in the way they want to grow."

The future promises an even bigger change. This fall—eight years after Marge put Steve through graduate school—he's going to do the same for her. But in a very real sense, both Everetts have already undertaken "advanced studies" in responding to the challenge on their poster: Love is the hardest lesson.

Jorie Lueloff

Cross-Cultural Differences

So far you've seen how both physiological factors and social roles can make the world a different place for each of us. But there's another kind of perceptual gap that often blocks communication—the gap between people from different backgrounds. Every culture has its own view, its own way of looking at the world, which is unique. When we remember these differing cultural perspectives, they can be a great way of learning more about both ourselves and others. But at times it's easy to forget that people everywhere don't see things the way we do; as the following story shows, at such times this cultural barrier can lead to trouble.

"I don't understand it. Why didn't he marry both of them?"

Beware of a Crocodile Bag

There was a girl they all said later was American. She went stepping down the street ahead of me, young, with a good figure, well covered. She was well dressed too, and she had a way of working her haunches as she walked that rather singled her out. I had been specially conscious of her for the past hundred yards or so because there was a man following along close behind her who found her irresistible—it was clear to see in the way he was jockeying for position, sidling up on her right, whipping over to the left again, only to be foiled each time by some clumsy interfering pedestrian or a lamp-standard or whatever it might be. I knew what he planned to do, too.

This was in Athens and the three of us—first the girl, next the man I speak of, and then myself bringing up the rear—were walking across the top of Constitution Square along with a whole crowd of others. On we went, the girl wiggling, the man set on his little plan, head held rigid and a bit to one side, one arm behind his back—she must surely have been aware of him as over the road she wobbled and on to the further pavement, down the side of the Hotel Grande Bretagne. The man was most certainly Greek and I guessed that the girl could not be. He was coming right up alongside her now, very close . . . and then suddenly, without warning, the girl spun on her heel in a ninety-degree turn and the next moment she would be in at the Grande Bretagne side-entrance, safe in one of the little segments of those revolving doors. It all but caught the man off-balance: but the Greek mind is very quick and he reacted instantly. He had to move before she could slip away for ever. So his arm shot out and he pinched her smartly on the behind.

What should a girl do when this happens in the public street? In Athens it is an occupational risk all girls run and I have had talks with several of them about it. They mostly give the same answer. Noth-

ing. They are very sensible about it: they realize that if they dress provocatively and walk provocatively, someone is likely to be provoked into pinching them. An Athenian girl can recognize a pincher a block distant. He is quite easy to identify, it seems —the slightly furtive sideways advance, the hand behind the back symbolically out of sight, as it were, the manoeuvring—girls quickly learn to take evasive action, such as keeping away from shop-windows or points where they could get cornered, and the nervous ones certainly welcomed the full flaring skirts with the layers of stiff frilly petticoat underneath when that fashion came in. But those narrow, hobbling skirts. . . . I have questioned several Athenians. They say it is better to come up from behind if you can. I can see the sense in that. "A mezedaki," they are apt to call it: a little *hors d'oeuvre*. It is a game, really: a game for two persons, whether the second person wishes to play or not. And once the pincher has got his pinch in, or else the girl has outwitted him and escaped, he does not follow her up. He is content with his pinch, just as a picador is content with his pic, or the banderillero with banderillas. Most girls say there is only one rule—if she loses she must do so with grace. No shrieks, no angry cries. She must just walk on as if nothing whatever had happened. The game is over. She has lost.

The game is not always very well understood by foreign ladies visiting Athens. The case of the American girl who had fled to the safety of the Grande Bretagne underlines my point. Her thinking was confused. She was not in the wrong, maybe, but she reacted wrongly. When the man landed his pinch and won, she lost her head as well as the game. She went black in the face and did something very shocking. Everyone present gasped. She was carrying a big crocodile travel-bag—a splendid thing with metal clasps and buckles, and so on. She swung this bag of hers in a great arc and caught the man over the head with it. He went to the ground instantly. She tossed her head furiously and as she turned to wobble through the revolving doors to refuge, the man was rising to his feet again and wagging his head in his bewilderment.

"I only pinched her. . . ." he said plaintively, looking round at us.

We were quite a little crowd by now—the hotel doorman, taxi-drivers, other passersby, a policeman.

"Tch-tch! . . ." the people went, wagging their heads too and staring through the big plate-glass windows at the girl's retreating back. What sort of girl could she be? A taxi-driver helped the poor man up, brushing him down.

"Did she hurt you, then?" he asked with great solicitude.

Peter Mayne

An innocent pinch on the behind led to one cultural misunderstanding. A student described another one, which he swears is true.

He was visiting Lagos, Nigeria, and while walking down the street one afternoon he came upon two men, one a Nigerian and the other an American. The men were fighting wildly and cursing at each other, each in his own language. The police had come and seemed to be ready to take both fighters away when an English-speaking taxi driver saved the day.

After talking to both men, he explained the story: It seems that the American was hitchhiking through town, signaling for a ride the only way he knew—standing at the roadside with his thumb sticking out where the drivers could easily see it. Unfortunately for him, in Nigeria this gesture doesn't mean the same thing as in the United States. In fact, its closest equivalent in our terms is what we call "the finger." So, although the American meant to politely ask for a ride, instead he had insulted the Nigerian's honor.

Thanks to the taxi driver, who ought to be working for the U.N., the last time our student saw the two former enemies they were heading arm in arm into a bar. They'd learned by experience that to members of different cultures even little differences can have big consequences when you're not aware of them.

Subcultural Differences

After looking at these examples, you can see that different cultures have customs that can cause trouble for the unaware foreigner. But you don't have to go this far from home to come across people with differing cultural perspectives. Within this country there are many subcultures, and the members of each one have backgrounds that cause them to see things in unique ways.

Probably the clearest example of these differing perceptions is the gap between white and black men in America. Even to people of goodwill it seems that there's a barrier which makes understanding difficult; there just seem to be too many different experiences that separate us. If this is true, how can we possibly understand each other?

BLACK LIKE ME

Writer John Howard Griffin found one way to bridge the gulf that separates whites and blacks. Realizing the impossibility of truly understanding the black experience by simply reading or talking about it, he decided to go one big step further. "How else except by becoming a Negro could a white man hope to learn the truth?" he wrote. "The only way I could see to bridge the gap was to become a Negro."

And this he did. Through a series of treatments that included doses of skin-darkening drugs, applications of stain, and shaving off the hair on his head, Griffin transformed himself into a black man—or at least a man with black skin.

In the following selections from his book you'll read some of Griffin's experiences as a black man in the southern United States in 1959. The narrative begins as he takes the first steps into a new world.

November 8

. . . I caught the bus into town, choosing a seat halfway to the rear. As we neared Canal, the car began to fill with whites. Unless they could find a place to themselves or beside another white, they stood in the aisle.

A middle-aged woman with stringy gray hair stood near my seat. She wore a clean but faded print house dress that was hoisted to one side as

she clung to an overhead pendant support. Her face looked tired and I felt uncomfortable. As she staggered with the bus's movement my lack of gallantry tormented me. I half rose from my seat to give it to her, but Negroes behind me frowned disapproval. I realized I was "going against the race" and the subtle tug-of-war became instantly clear. If the whites would not sit with us, let them stand. When they became tired enough or uncomfortable enough, they would eventually take seats beside us and soon see that it was not so poisonous after all. But to give them your seat was to let them win. I slumped back under the intensity of their stares.

But my movement had attracted the white woman's attention. For an instant our eyes met. I felt sympathy for her, and thought I detected sympathy in her glance. The exchange blurred the barriers of race (so new to me) long enough for me to smile and vaguely indicate the empty seat beside me, letting her know she was welcome to accept it.

Her blue eyes, so pale before, sharpened and she spat out, "What're you looking at me like *that* for?"

I felt myself flush. Other white passengers craned to look at me. The silent onrush of hostility frightened me.

"I'm sorry," I said, staring at my knees. "I'm not from here." The pattern of her skirt turned abruptly as she faced the front.

"They're getting sassier every day," she said loudly. Another woman agreed and the two fell into conversation. . . .

I learned a strange thing—that in a jumble of unintelligible talk, the word "nigger" leaps out with electric clarity. You always hear it and always it stings. And always it casts the person using it into a category of brute ignorance. I thought with some amusement that if these two women only knew what they were revealing about themselves to every Negro on that bus, they would have been outraged.

November 10–12

Two days of incessant walking, mostly looking for jobs. I wanted to discover what sort of work an educated Negro, nicely dressed, could find. I met

no rebuffs, only gentleness when they informed me they could not use my services as typist, bookkeeper, etc.

November 14

My money was running low so I decided to cash some travelers checks before leaving for Mississippi. The banks were closed, since it was past noon on Saturday, but I felt I would have no difficulty with travelers checks in any of the larger stores, especially those on Dryades where I had traded and was known as a customer.

I took the bus to Dryades and walked down it, stopping at the dime store where I'd made most of my purchases. The young white girl came forward to wait on me.

"I need to cash a travelers check," I said, smiling.

"We don't cash any checks of any kind," she said firmly.

"But a travelers check is perfectly safe," I said.

"We just don't cash checks," she said and turned away.

"Look, you know me. You've waited on me. I need some money."

"You should have gone to the bank."

"I didn't know I needed the money until after the banks closed," I said.

I knew I was making a pest of myself, but I could scarcely believe this nice young lady could be so unsympathetic, so insolent when she discovered I did not come in to buy something.

"I'll be glad to buy a few things," I said.

She called up to the bookkeeping department on an open mezzanine. "Hey! Do we cash travelers ch____"

"No!" the white woman shouted back.

"Thank you for your kindness," I said and walked out.

I went into one store after the other along Dryades and Rampart Streets. In every store their smiles turned to grimaces when they saw I meant not to buy but to cash a check. It was not their refusal—I could understand that. It was the bad manners they displayed. I began to feel desperate and resentful. They would have cashed a travelers check without hesitation for a white man. Each time they refused me, they implied clearly that I had probably come by these checks dishonestly and they wanted nothing to do with them or me. . . .

[Later that day Griffin takes a bus to Hattiesburg, Mississippi, which he has been told is the most oppressive part of the South for the black man.]

My room was upstairs in a wooden shanty structure that had never known paint. From the tavern below a man improvised a ballad about "poor Mack Parker . . . overcome with passion . . . his body in the creek."

"Oh Lord," a woman said in the quiet that followed, her voice full of sadness and awe.

"Lordy . . . Lordy . . ." a man said in a hushed voice, as though there were nothing more he could say.

Canned jazz blared through the street with a monstrous high-strutting rhythm that pulled at the viscera. The board floor squeaked under my footsteps. I switched on the light and looked into a cracked piece of mirror bradded with bent nails to the wall. The bald Negro stared back at me from its mottled sheen. I knew I was in hell. Hell could be no more lonely or hopeless, no more agonizingly estranged from the world of order and harmony.

The music consumed in its blatant rhythm all other rhythms, even that of the heartbeat. I wondered how all of this would look to the casual observer, or to the whites in their homes. "The niggers are whooping it up over on Mobile Street tonight," they might say. "They're happy." Or, as one scholar put it, "Despite their lowly status, they are capable of living jubilantly." Would they see the immense melancholy that hung over the quarter, so oppressive that men had to dull their sensibilities in noise or wine or sex or gluttony in order to escape it? The laughter had to be gross or it would turn to sobs, and to sob would be to realize, and to realize would be to despair. So the noise poured forth like a jazzed-up fugue, louder and louder to cover the whisper in every man's soul, "You are black. You are condemned." This is what the white man mis-

took for "jubilant living" and called "whooping it up."

Words of the state song hummed through my memory:

"Way down South in Mississippi,
  Cotton blossoms white in
  the sun,
We all love our Mississippi, Here
  we'll stay where livin' is fun.
The evening stars shine brighter,
  And glad is every dewy morn,
For way down South in Mississippi,
  Folks are happy they have been
  born."

December 1

I developed the technique of zigzagging back and forth. In my bag I kept a damp sponge, dyes, cleansing cream and Kleenex. It was hazardous, but it was the only way to traverse an area both as Negro and white. As I traveled, I would find an isolated spot, perhaps an alley at night or the brush beside a highway, and quickly apply the dye to face, hands and legs, then rub off and reapply until it was firmly anchored in my pores. I would go through the area as a Negro and then, usually at night, remove the dyes with cleansing cream and tissues and pass through the same area as a white man.

I was the same man, whether white or black. Yet when I was white, I received the brotherly-love smiles and the privileges from whites and the hate stares or obsequiousness from the Negroes. And when I was a Negro, the whites judged me fit for the junk heap, while the Negroes treated me with great warmth.

As the Negro Griffin, I walked up the steep hill to the bus station in Montgomery to get the schedule for buses to Tuskegee. I received the information from a polite clerk and turned away from the counter.

"Boy!" I heard a woman's voice, harsh and loud.

I glanced toward the door to see a large, matriarchal woman, elderly and impatient. Her pinched face grimaced and she waved me to her.

"Boy, come here. Hurry!"

Astonished, I obeyed.

"Get those bags out of the cab," she ordered testily, seeming outraged with my lack of speed.

Without thinking, I allowed my face to spread to a grin as though overjoyed to serve her. I carried her bags to the bus and received three haughty dimes. I thanked her profusely. Her eyebrows knitted with irritation and she finally waved me away. . . .

Suddenly I had had enough. Suddenly I could stomach no more of this degradation—not of myself but of all men who were black like me. Abruptly I turned and walked away. The large bus station was crowded with humanity. In the men's room, I entered one of the cubicles and locked the door. For a time I was safe, isolated; for a time I owned the space around me, though it was scarcely more than that of a coffin. In medieval times, men sought sanctuary in churches. Nowadays, for a nickel, I could find sanctuary in a colored restroom. Then, sanctuary had the smell of incense-permeated walls. Now it had the odor of disinfectant.

The irony of it hit me. I was back in the land of my forefathers, Georgia. The town of Griffin was named for one of them. Too, I, a Negro, carried the name hated by all Negroes, for former Governor Griffin (no kin that I would care to discover) devoted himself heroically to the task of keeping Negroes "in their place." Thanks in part to his efforts, this John Griffin celebrated a triumphant return to the land from which his people had sprung by seeking sanctuary in a toilet cubicle at the bus station.

John Howard Griffin

How valid do you think Griffin's experiences are in terms of your own life? His experiment took place in the Deep South of 1959, and times have certainly changed since then. But to what extent is the world still a different place to whites and blacks today? How about other groups—Mexican-Americans, Orientals, Native Americans, old people, longhairs, military men and women. Do you ever find yourself prejudging or being prejudged before getting acquainted with someone from a different sector of society?

Perhaps by sharing the personal experiences of others in your group you can gain a more personal insight into how people from different subcultures view life in your community, not only in terms of discrimination, but also in terms of values, behavioral norms, and political and economic issues. How would life be different if you were of a different race or religion, social or economic class? See if you can imagine.

But talking can enable us to understand another person's viewpoint only to a certain degree. To comprehend what it's truly like to be someone else you have to almost become that person the way Griffin did. Have you ever read Mark Twain's famous story of *The Prince and the Pauper?* If you have, you'll remember what an education the young prince had when he was mistaken for a young peasant and treated accordingly. In the same way, think of the huge growth in tolerance that would result if the rich could become poor for a bit, if teachers could recall their student days, if whites could become black.

Total role reversals aren't likely to happen, but it's possible to create experiences that give a good picture of another's perspective. The story of one Iowa schoolteacher and her class illustrates the point. Shortly after Martin Luther King's assassination in 1968, Mrs. Jane Elliott wanted to make sure her third graders never became prone to the sickness that caused such events. But how could she do this? Everyone in the small town of Riceville was white, and most of her eight-year-olds had never really known blacks. How could she bring home to them the nature of prejudice?

Her solution was to divide the class into two groups: one containing all the children with blue eyes, and the other made up of the brown-eyed students. Then for the next few days she treated the brown-eyes as better people. They all sat in the front of the room, had second helpings at lunch, got five extra minutes of recess, and received extra praise for their work from Mrs. Elliott. At the same time the blue-eyes were the butt of both subtle and obvious discrimination. Besides the back-row seats, skimpy meals, and other such practices, the blue-eyes never received praise for their schoolwork from Mrs. Elliott, who seemed to find something wrong with everything they did. "What can you expect from a blue-eyed person?" was her attitude. The level of the blue-eyed children's schoolwork dropped almost immediately.

At first the children treated the experiment as a game. But shortly they changed from cooperative, thoughtful people into small but very prejudiced

O great spirit! Let me not judge another man without first walking a mile in his moccasins.

Sioux Prayer

bigots. Classmates who had always been best friends stopped playing with each other and even quit walking to school together.

After the level of intolerance had grown painfully high, Mrs. Elliott changed the rules. Now the blue-eyed people were on top and the brown-eyes were inferior. And soon the tables were turned, with children who had only days before been the object of discrimination now being bigots themselves.

Finally Mrs. Elliott ended the experiment. When she asked the children if they wanted to go back to the old days, where everyone was the same, the class answered with a resounding "Yes!" Now they really knew what discrimination was, and they didn't like it.

Role Reversal

Walk a mile in another man's moccasins. Find a group that is foreign to you, and try to become a member of it for a while.

If you're down on the police, see if your local department has a ride-along program where you can spend several hours on patrol with one or two officers.

If you think the present state of education is a mess, become a teacher yourself. Maybe an instructor will give you the chance to plan one or more classes.

Perception: What You See Is What You Get

23 Judges Shaken by Night in Nevada Prison

RENO (UPI)—More than one of the 23 shaken judges from across the country who spent the night at the Nevada State Prison said Thursday it should be torn down along with others in the country.

"Appalling."

"My conscience is scarred."

"Am I glad to get out of there. I didn't get five minutes sleep."

These were typical comments from the judges as they climbed off the bus in the morning after returning to Reno from the state prison in Carson City.

The judges, all attending a graduate seminar at the University of Nevada in Reno, volunteered to spend the night in prison to learn more about the prisoners' point of view.

"After that experience I'm going to work for total reform of our prisons," vowed Tom Lee of Miami.

"I was in a cage like an animal," said Newton Vickers of Topeka, who complained the prisoners "screamed and rattled cans against the wall all night and I couldn't sleep."

"Ten years in there is like 100 or maybe 200," he said. "They should take two bulldozers out there and tear it down."

If you're adventuresome, follow the example of the men in the following article and become a bum for a day. See how you're treated.

If you're a political conservative, try getting involved in a radical organization; if you're a radical, check out the conservatives.

Whatever group you join, try to become part of it as best you can. Don't just observe. Get *into* the philosophy of your new role and see how it feels. You may find that all those weird people aren't so strange after all.

Race isn't the only barrier that separates people in our culture. Another problem involves the enforcement of laws. On one hand, many people—especially members of minority races, the poor, and politically radical—claim police harassment and prison brutality; on the other hand, government officials claim they're doing a difficult job as fairly as possible.

The usual behavior in this debate is to take one side or the other. People either defend law-enforcement agencies and criticize the people who "get in trouble," or they sympathize with the lawbreakers and blame police and prison officials for brutality in their job. Again it's the either-or philosophy: One side has to be right and the other wrong. Do you ever find yourself thinking that way?

Fortunately, many police officers realize that the world isn't made up of "good guys" and "bad guys." In some departments part of a recruit's training gives him a perspective of law enforcement very different from the one he usually sees, as the following account describes.

''Relatively.'' Here we have three forces of gravity working perpendicularly to one another. Three earth-planes cut across each other at right-angles, and human beings are living on each of them. It is impossible for the inhabitants of different worlds to walk or sit or stand on the same floor, because they have differing conceptions of what is horizontal and what is vertical. Yet they may well share the use of the same staircase. On the top staircase illustrated here, two people are moving side by side and in the same direction, and yet one of them is going downstairs and the other upstairs. Contact between them is out of the question, because they live in different worlds and therefore can have no knowledge of each other's existence.

M. C. Escher

Field Experiments: Preparation for the Changing Police Role

We are all aware that it is extremely difficult to immerse the average policeman into situations that will reveal the feelings of the down-and-outer, the social outcast, the have-nots, and show us their perspective of normal law-enforcement procedures. Obviously the officer, in his police role, would not fit into a ghetto of any kind. But suppose he were a man with a great deal of courage, willing for the sake of experimentation to become a bum, a skid row habitant.

Our Covina officers who were willing to become skid row habitants were carefully selected and conditioned for the role they were about to play. Each man was given three dollars with which to purchase a complete outfit of pawn shop clothing. The only new article of attire he was allowed was footwear —reject tennis shoes purchased for a few small coins. Among his other props were such items as a shopping bag filled with collected junk, and a wine bottle camouflaged with a brown paper sack.

Conditioned and ready, our men, assigned in pairs, moved into the Los Angeles skid row district. They soon discovered that when they tried to leave the area, walking a few blocks into the legitimate retail sections, they were told, "Go back where you belong!" Our men knew in reality they were not "bums," but they found that other citizens quickly categorized them and treated them accordingly. Some women, when approached on the sidewalk and asked for a match, stepped out into the street rather than offer a reply, much less a light for a smoke.

During the skid row experiment, our men ate in the rescue missions, and sat through the prayer services with other outcasts and derelicts. They roamed the streets and the alleys, and discovered many leveling experiences. Some were anticipated, others were not. Perhaps the most meaningful experience of the skid row exercise occurred to Tom Courtney, a young juvenile officer with five years' police service.

It was dusk, and Tom and his partner were sauntering back to a prearranged gathering place. Feeling a little sporty, the pair decided to "polish off" the bottle of wine. They paused in a convenient parking lot and Tom tipped the bottle up. As if from nowhere, two uniformed policemen materialized before the surprised pair. Tom and his partner were spread-eagled against a building and searched. Forgetting the admonishment not to reveal identities and purpose unless absolutely necessary, Tom panicked and identified himself.

Later, Tom found it difficult to explain why he was so quick in his revelation. "You wouldn't understand," he told me; then blurted out that he "thought he might get shot."

I found it difficult to receive this as a rational explanation, especially since Tom stated that the officers, while firm, were courteous at all times. With some additional prodding, Tom admitted that as he was being searched, he suddenly thought of every negative thing he had ever heard about a policeman. He even perceived a mental flash of a newspaper headline: "Police Officer Erroneously Shot While on Field Experiment."

"I know better now," Tom continued, "but when you feel that way about yourself, you believe—you believe."

I attempted to rationalize with Tom his reason for fear. I asked if he was certain that the officers were courteous. He replied in the affirmative, but added, "They didn't smile, or tell me what they were going to do next." Tom had discovered a new emotional reaction within his own personal make-up, and it left a telling impression.

Today, Tom Courtney is still telling our department personnel, "For God's sake, smile when you can. And above all, tell the man you're shaking down what you are going to do. Take the personal threat out of the encounter, if you can.''

Equally important as Tom's experience, I believe, is the lesson we learned about personal judgments. Our men in the "Operation Empathy" experiment found they were adjudged by the so-called normal population as "being like" all the other inmates of skid row, simply because their appearance was representative.

Perhaps we would all do well to heed the lesson, for now, more than at any other time in our history, policemen must guard against the natural tendency to lump people into categories simply because they look alike.

The invisible barrier that stands between the law enforcer and the law breaker is being bridged through experimentation. Human beings are dealing with human beings, and successful field experiments, conducted by law enforcement, have shown that empathy, understanding another's emotions and feelings, can, in some potentially volatile situations, play an important role towards nonviolence in police-involved situations.

R. Fred Ferguson, Chief of Police, Riverside Police Department, Riverside, California. Formerly Chief, Covina Police Department, Covina, California.

Selective Perception

Getting beyond the one-sided view of life that our environment imposes on us isn't easy. The Covina policemen, Mrs. Elliott's third graders, and John Howard Griffin have provided examples of how it can be done.

But other times it's a personal bias or need that keeps us from being open to other people. All the information in the world wouldn't cause us to change our minds. When someone wants to believe something badly enough, he'll go to amazing lengths to support his position. Social scientists call this tendency *selective perception.*

To understand how selective perception works, think back to the discussion of self-concept in Chapter 3. You'll remember that we described the tendency people have to behave in ways that support the image they hold of themselves. If I see myself as a good student or musician, then an instructor who gives me a poor grade or a critic who doesn't appreciate my music *must* be wrong, and I'll find evidence to show it. If I've committed myself to support the government in what I believe is a moral cause, and someone tells me about illegal or immoral acts, I'll find a way to prove that no such thing happened. If I want to think of myself as a good sport, and someone shows me that the athletic team I've identified with all season plays dirty, I'll do everything I can to contradict this evidence.

As you can imagine, this tendency to protect our self-concept sometimes leads us to distort the facts. You only need recall the long list of defense mechanisms in Chapter 3 to see how inventive people can be when a threatened self-concept is at stake. And needless to say, when two or more people perceive the same event differently, communication between them suffers.

Selective perception is especially great when the subject turns to politics. Several years ago, at the height of the Vietnam War, we decided to show our students how their own political bias distorts their thinking and causes them to see incidents in a way that's favorable to their own philosophy. We decided that the best way to make our point would be to catch them redhanded at selective perception, and so we set up this incident:

One evening, just after class had begun, a student entered the room and asked if he could have a few minutes to make an announcement. Unknown to the class, he was a drama major who was part of our plot. We'd carefully chosen his costume and manner of speaking in advance: He was wearing Levis, a T-shirt, and an Army field jacket (he was a veteran, though we didn't let the class know this), and he spoke in a polite manner. This experiment took place right before a large antiwar demonstration, and our actor-visitor encouraged the class members to go to express their sentiments to the President.

After these remarks one student (who was also in on our plot) asked the visitor whether the demonstration was really in the best interests of the country. We'd carefully coached him to be polite, just like the visitor, so at this point the discussion was very low-key.

A discussion about the merits of the protest followed, mostly conducted by our two actors. As we'd planned, after a few minutes they gradually began to act more excited, but they escalated their behavior evenly so that it was nearly impossible to say who was responsible for changing the tone of the discussion. After about ten minutes this had become *very* heated, with both actors yelling at the top of their voices. Then, just as we'd planned, things began to happen fast: The visitor reacted to a really insulting remark from the student by calling him a "pig" and stalking out. The student shouted, "I don't have to take that!" and ran out of the room, slamming the door behind him. The two actors made a great deal of noise, which sounded like a fight, just outside the classroom. Ron immediately ran outside as if to quiet things down, and he came back in after a short time, followed by the student, who was breathing heavily and muttering to himself.

Ron then announced that "When things like this happen (never saying *what* happened), I have to turn in a report to the administration." He then asked each student to write exactly what had taken place, making sure to be impartial.

Take a look at some of the responses and you'll see just how objective people can be:

> This guy came into our class and interrupted what we were talking about. He invited us to a "demonstration-protest" against the war this weekend, and started going on about how Nixon is a liar and how writing letters to him is a waste of time. When one of the students in the class disagreed with him, he told the guy he should "go be counted with the pigs," and left. When our student went outside, the other guy started a fight. Personally, I think he was a pig.

APART FROM ABSTRACT PROPOSITIONS OF COMPARISON (SUCH AS TWO AND TWO MAKE FOUR), PROPOSITIONS WHICH TELL US NOTHING BY THEMSELVES ABOUT CONCRETE REALITY, WE FIND NO PROPOSITION EVER REGARDED BY ANY ONE AS EVIDENTLY CERTAIN THAT HAS NOT EITHER BEEN CALLED A FALSEHOOD, OR AT LEAST HAD ITS TRUTH SINCERELY QUESTIONED BY SOME ONE ELSE.

William James,
The Will to Believe

A man entered our room and asked to say something about the war, and was allowed by the instructor. He then told us about the demonstration to be held Saturday, and encouraged us to attend. Then a member of our class started questioning him. (I think he was trying to rile the announcer.) The guy talking was trying to be very calm and not to raise a fuss, but the man in the class followed him out of the room, where a fight was started. Neither Ron Adler nor the announcer should be blamed for the incident.

A young man came into the room to tell us about the moratorium demonstration, and Ron Adler gave him permission (somewhat reluctantly) to do this. The man was a very poor speaker and did not put his point across well. A member of the class took some offense at the speaker's remarks and asked questions relating to why it was necessary to attend such gatherings. The speaker then became very offensive and said something to the effect that the student was a pig. The member of the class stood up and said, "Oh, yeah," and then proceeded outside where a fight ensued.

Too much! A guy comes in to talk about the peace movement and a certain man in the class started really hassling him and telling this guy (who was doing a good thing) that it was bad to have these movements and really hassled the guy to death. The guy saw he was getting nowhere and began to leave and this man in the class started following him and started a fight. The teacher, Mr. Adler, of course, the fine teacher that he is, stopped the fight immediately. I myself thought that this man should not have opened his big fat mouth and hassled this guy who was telling the class about this *great movement.*

By now you have the picture: No two people experienced this event in the same way, even though they were asked to describe it only a few minutes after it happened. Their accounts were incredibly different: The visitor was described as everything from a "gentleman" to a "punk" and his behavior from "wild" to "very calm"; the student-actor's response was seen ranging from "logically questioning" to "trying to rile the visitor"; and people described what occurred outside as "running outside to start a fight," "the visitor started a fight," "the student started a fight," and "trouble was averted."

After we'd collected these descriptions, but before we let the class in on the secret, we handed out a questionnaire designed to test each person's political views, particularly in relation to foreign policy. Over the next week we matched these responses with the student's descriptions. What turned up was a perfect illustration of how selective perception works.

In practically every case the description of the fake fight fitted with the person's political views. That is, someone opposed to the war was sympathetic to the visitor who publicized the moratorium, while people who favored the government's position blamed him and supported the class member.

When we finally told the class what we'd done, they were angry at first and then embarrassed at letting their bias distort their judgment so much. But as a result of the experience, at least there are thirty or so people who'll think twice before they give another "impartial" account.

Of course this kind of selective perception isn't limited to politics. The same principle operates in other areas: criminal trials, where supposedly impartial eyewitness accounts can be distorted by the attitude of the witness toward the defendant; in religious discussions, where each person chooses evidence to support one side and ignores information that argues against it; and, perhaps most commonly, in our personal evaluations of others. If, for instance, you describe an acquaintance of yours whom you'll soon be introducing to me by claiming that he is a terrific person, my expectations and my subsequent impression of him will probably be different than if you described the same person as an obnoxious fool.

Two Views

1 Choose a disagreement you presently have with another person or group. The disagreement might be a personal one—such as an argument about how to settle a financial problem or who is to blame for a present state of affairs—or it might be a dispute over a contemporary public issue, such as the right of women to obtain abortions on demand or the value of capital punishment.

2 In 300 words or so describe your side of the issue. State why you believe as you do, just as if you were presenting your position to an impartial jury.

3 Now take 300 words or so to describe in the first-person singular how the *other* person sees the same issue. For instance, if you are a religious person, write this section as if you were an atheist: For a short while get in touch with how the other person feels and thinks.

4 Now show the description you wrote in step 3 to your "opponent," the person whose beliefs are different from yours. Have that person read your account and correct any statements that don't reflect his position accurately. Remember, you're doing this so that you can more clearly understand how the issue looks to the other person.

5 Make any necessary corrections in the account you wrote in step 3, and again show it to your partner. When he agrees that you understand his position, have him sign your paper to indicate this.

6 Now record your conclusions to this experiment. Has this perceptual shift made any difference in how you view the issue or how you feel about your partner?

It was six men of Indostan
   To learning much inclined,
Who went to see the elephant
   Though all of them were blind
That each by observation
   Might satisfy his mind.

The first approached the elephant
   And, happening to fall
Against the broad and sturdy side,
   At once began to bawl:
"Why, bless me! But the elephant
   Is very much like a wall!"

The second, feeling of the tusk,
   Cried: "Ho! What have we here
So very round and smooth and sharp?
   To me, 'tis very clear,
This wonder of an elephant
   Is very like a spear!"

The third approached the animal,
   And, happening to take
The squirming trunk within his hands
   Thus boldly up he spake:
"I see," quoth he, "the elephant
   Is very like a snake!"

The fourth reached out his eager hand
   And felt about the knee:
"What most this wondrous beast is like
   Is very plain," quoth he:
'Tis clear enough the elephant
   Is very like a tree!"

The fifth who chanced to touch the ear
   Said: "E'en the blindest man
Can tell what this resembles most—
   Deny the fact who can:
This marvel of an elephant
   Is very like a fan!"

The sixth no sooner had begun
   About the beast to grope
Than, seizing on the swinging tail
   That fell within his scope,
"I see," quoth he, "the elephant
   Is very like a rope!"

And so these men of Indostan
   Disputed loud and long,
Each in his own opinion
   Exceeding stiff and strong;
Though each was partly in the right,
   And all were in the wrong.

                 John G. Saxe

I've always admired those reporters who can descend on an area, talk to key people, ask key questions, take samplings of opinions, and then set down an orderly report very much like a road map. I envy this technique and at the same time do not trust it as a mirror of reality. I feel that there are too many realities. What I set down here is true until someone else passes that way and rearranges the world in his own style. In literary criticism the critic has no choice but to make over the victim of his attention into something the size and shape of himself. . . .

So much there is to see, but our morning eyes describe a different world than do our afternoon eyes, and surely our wearied evening eyes can only report a weary evening world.

John Steinbeck, *Travels with Charley*

Rumor Clinic

One way to see how individual perceptions can distort the reporting of an event is to conduct a rumor clinic. Here's how to go about it:

1 Pick six volunteers. Their task will be to describe a simple picture.

2 Send five of the volunteers out of the room, making sure they can't see or hear what's going on inside.

3 Show the remaining volunteer a Rumor Clinic photograph. The photo should be of a subject liable to be distorted—police and demonstrators, people arguing, wartime scenes. Let the volunteer examine the picture for two minutes, and then show it to the audience.

4 Now hide the photograph, bring a second volunteer into the room, and have the first volunteer describe the picture to him. Appoint a timer to clock the length of each description that will follow. (It's important that there be no coaching or reaction from the audience during the description.)

5 Continue this process until all six participants have described the picture, one at a time.

6 Now show the picture to the last volunteer, and note how it compares with the description he just gave.

7 Now answer the following questions:

a. How close was the final volunteer's description to the actual photo?

b. In what ways did the descriptions change? Were any of these changes due to selective perception?

c. Did you find that each description became progressively shorter, omitting some important details and stressing others?

d. Do you think distortions such as this occur in your life? How might you distort the following accounts as you retold them:

A date you had last Saturday night

Your role on a high school athletic team

The behavior of a person you dislike

The height of a mountain you climbed

The width of a river you swam

The length of a fish you caught.

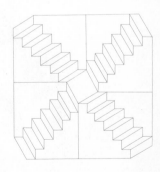

So far we've talked about the many ways that differing perceptions can block communication. We've tried to show you that even though we all inhabit separate worlds, understanding each other isn't a hopeless task. You've seen how many people have learned to experience perspectives different from their own and in doing so have grown closer to others.

But empathy isn't easy, especially when it's most needed. Your own experience almost certainly shows you that the times when you disagree most strongly with someone are the times when it's hardest to see the other side. The tendency is to dig in and defend your side, to show that you're right and your opponent is wrong.

We want to close this chapter on perception with a selection that shows one way to go beyond this either-or, two-valued orientation. The method that Paul Reps describes is a paradoxical tool because on the one hand it seems too simple really to work, and on the other, making the effort to try it can be difficult. As you read about these simple Japanese children, think about how you can apply their method to your lives.

Pillow Education in Rural Japan

How do you solve your problems?

In growing up, as much as we do grow up mentally, each of us has personal difficulties and social problems in relation with those about us.

In rural Japan a group of children are meeting their difficulties in a splendid way and even teaching their parents how to do so.

They are using a method of thinking for themselves that works. If someone has done a child an injustice, if his feelings have been hurt, if he is in pain, if his or her father is quarreling—anything becomes the subject of the study. They have no name for it, but since it is done with a pillow it might be called pillow education.

A pillow has four sides and a middle. A problem has four approaches and a middle.

For example: A child is slow in his school work. It is his turn to show the group how he is thinking through this situation. He sits before the pillow, placing his hand at 1.

"Suppose I can't think quickly," he says. "If I place here at 1, 'I can't think quickly,' then this may change at some time."

"Here at 2," he continues, placing his hand in the 2 position, "is the place where I can think quickly and easily."

In doing this, the child has objectified a handicap. He takes a look at it instead of letting it corrode inside. He also has imagined the possibility of his difficulty resolving.

He continues: "If 1 is where I can't think quickly and 2 is the place where I can, then I will say that here, 3, is a situation where I can think both slowly and quickly, where 1 and 2 are together."

This third step (the 3 place on the pillow) merges the opposites 1 and 2, just as 2 reverses the problem originally placed at 1. This is education in action done by the individual for himself or herself. There are as many girls as boys in the group.

It is a fact that most adults can only think to 2: white 1, black 2; right 1, wrong 2. "If I am right as I am, 1, you are wrong, 2." Entire lives are lived with this kind of thinking. Such dichotomy, either-or, right-wrong, often results in private and public unresolved differences.

When we consider the millions of dead in recent wars from a few leaders not being able to think beyond 2, we see how urgently such education is needed.

"You say you are right, father, and our neighbor is wrong," the child tells his father who is in a property dispute. "But may there not also be a place where you are wrong and he is right. And both of you may be wrong and both right. And at still another place, 4, all this may be forgotten."

"What are you talking about?" asks the father.

The child gets out a pillow. In a few weeks the father, considerably interested, has visited the school.

Such sharp thinking came from a very young child. He had a method of thinking. If he finds no difficulty to solve for himself during the week, he begins looking for one. When called on in class, he doesn't like to be without a subject he has worked on.

The child reasons not in numbers but in a relational sequence of four steps: wrong, 1; right, 2; both wrong and right, 3; and neither wrong nor right, 4. He does this as if walking a 4-step figure with his hand and with his mind.

In conclusion each child summarizes his presentation by cupping his hands in the middle of the pillow ( ), affirming an unnamed center from which 1, 2, 3, 4 emerge. It is as if he holds the complete problem in his own hands at the center of the pillow.

He then places the hand at 4, 3, 2, 1 and concludes by saying, "All these are gloriously affirmed," or "Each of these steps is good."

It is a tremendous relief to the child to be able to reverse his thinking and not be continually held in one viewpoint. In such kind of problem-solving, "nothing is the matter," their mentor says. A rebellious child joining the others invariably becomes gentle in a few weeks.

The number of students has grown from 3 to more than 30. The meetings are a happy time. Students are entirely unhesitant about making personal problems public.

All kinds of subjects come before the pillow: Hunger and not hungry, beauty and ugliness, environment and mood, a bucket of water and a sea of water, blood of Orientals and blood of Occidentals, after my death the world will be and will not be—anything that troubles or concerns the child.

Even the pillow itself is treated as a subject: "When 1, I first heard of this study, I grasped it easily. But 2, since I understand it, it never finishes in me."

Another child offers: "Here 1, I will say that American culture surpasses Japanese culture. But here 2, I will say Japanese culture surpasses American culture. And here 3, I will say that both American culture surpassing Japanese and Japanese culture surpassing American are correct. And here 4, actually neither does any such surpassing.

Moreover since all these spring from center ( ), in such a view 4, 3, 2, 1, each is fully affirmed by me."

The students' building is inadequate. They are poor. They share clothes and food with those still poorer. But they have declined publicity for the group, thinking it might only bring more problems.

"Someone else must tell others about our method, we don't know how," they say. They are too busy using it in their own lives.

Have you something troubling you? Have you a pillow? If so, you may join these children in their wide way of thinking. It is not easy to translate the feeling of one person into the language of another and to convey in words the sensible delight of gentle hands on a pillow showing parents how to think.

Paul Reps, *Square Sun, Square Moon*

Pillow Talk

Try using the pillow method in your life. It isn't easy, but once you begin to understand it, the payoff in increased understanding is great.

1   Pick a person or viewpoint with which you strongly disagree. If you've chosen a person, it's best to have him there with you; but if that's not possible, you can do it alone.

2   What disagreement should you choose? No doubt there are many in your life:

    parent-child
    teacher-student
    employer-employee
    brother-sister
    friend-friend
    nation-nation
    Republican-Democrat

3 For each problem you choose, really place yourself in each position on the pillow as you encounter it:

    a. Your position is correct and your opponent's is wrong.
    b. Your opponent's position is correct and yours is wrong.
    c. Both your positions are correct and both are wrong.
    d. It isn't important which side is right or wrong. Finally, affirm the fact that all four positions are true.

4 The more important the problem is to you, the harder you'll find it to accept positions 2, 3, and 4 as having any validity. But the exercise will work only if you can suspend your present position and imagine how it would feel to hold the other ones.

5 How can you tell if you've been successful with the pillow method? The answer is simple: If after going over the four steps you can understand—not necessarily *accept* but just *understand*—the other person's position, you've done it. After you've reached this understanding, do you notice any change in how you feel about the other person?

Now we've reached the end of our look at the role perception plays in communication. Before we move to the subject of listening, we want to say one final thing about the chapter.

Lest you misunderstand, in all our talk about empathy we've never suggested that it means giving up your opinion in favor of someone else's. There's a big difference between understanding someone and agreeing with her; we've been advocating the first approach, not the latter.

The world would be a very dull place if everybody agreed on everything. The attitude we've suggested here is quite different from this tame, falsely accommodating one. We're convinced that the ability to empathize, to understand another's viewpoint without necessarily accepting it for your own, is a big key to effective interpersonal communication. The German poet and dramatist Goethe expressed this point most clearly when he said, "All sects seem to me to be right in what they assert and wrong in what they deny." If each of us could develop this attitude, the world (to borrow an old phrase) would be a better place to live.

Roads Not Taken

1 Find someone who is color-blind and interview him. Try to find out how you and he differ in the way you see the world.

2 Interview someone who has grown up in a culture unlike yours. Before your talk select several different topics to ask about that might bring out differences in the way you each view your environments. For example, you might discuss food, women's place in society, education, religion, dating habits, and so on.

3   Check with your local police department to see if they have a program of public education whereby citizens may ride with an officer while he is on duty. If you are fortunate enough to have this experience, share with your class any changes the experience made in your views of police work and law enforcement.

4   Try to locate some establishment that deals with the public. If possible, make arrangements to observe what a person who meets and works with the public or customer goes through. Try to physically position yourself on the worker's side of the desk or counter. Places that might serve well for this experience would be Department of Motor Vehicles, License Bureau at City Hall, the post office, the returns desk of a local store, or the registrar's office of your college. If you can arrange this, share with your group any changes the experience makes in the way you view the activity you monitored.

5   Attempt to create an experiment that will point up how susceptible we are to selective perception. Can you devise an experience that individuals with different occupations, religions, philosophical beliefs, levels of knowledge, or nationalities would view differently?

6   Select a current topic of controversy. Create several questions pertinent to this topic and interview a number of people who you suspect would see the topic from different viewpoints. How do their answers agree and disagree with each other? What factors caused these variations?

7   For a one-week period apply the pillow method to issues in your life.

8   Write an account of a single event that is perceived differently by two or more people. Whether your account is fictional or based on events that actually occurred, be sure to write it in the first-person singular for each person.

More Readings in Perception

Bohannon, Laura. "Shakespeare in the Bush." *Natural History* 75 (August–September 1966): 28–33.

> A woman who believes that Shakespeare's *Hamlet* has a universal theme gets a shock when she tries to describe it to a remote African tribe. A great example of culturally influenced perception.

Brown, Esther L. *Newer Dimensions of Patient Care* (part I). New York: Russell Sage, 1961.

> Written for nurses, this book emphasizes the importance of empathizing with the patient in providing good care.

Buckhout, Robert. "Eyewitness Testimony." *Scientific American* 231: 6 (December, 1974).
An excellent account of the manner in which perceptual factors distort eyewitness testimony in criminal trials.

Burke, Kenneth. *Permanence and Change.* Indianapolis: Bobbs-Merrill, 1965.
Probably the best description we've read of the process of selective perception. We wish we could write as clearly as Burke does here!

Fairlie, Henry. "The Unreal World of Television News." *Reader's Digest,* August 1967.
Warns the viewer how television inherently distorts events and thus gives viewers an unrealistic picture of the world.

Hammer, Richard. "Role Playing: A Judge Is a Con, A Con Is a Judge." *New York Times Magazine,* September 14, 1969.
The account of a role-reversal workshop that gave some judges and police a new perspective on what it means to be a prisoner.

Hastrof, Albert, David Schneider, and Judith Polefka. *Person Perception.* Reading, Mass.: Addison-Wesley, 1970.
A survey of research in the field.

Hastrof, Albert H., and Hadley Cantril. "They Saw a Game: A Case Study." *Journal of Abnormal and Social Psychology* 49 (January 1954).
This study clearly illustrates Goethe's remark that we quoted in our conclusion to this chapter: Shows how football fans view their home team as saints and the opposition as monsters.

Ramey, Estelle. "Men's Cycles." *Ms.,* Spring 1972.
A description of men's emotional, physical, and sexual cycles as well as the daily rhythms that both men and women undergo.

Tyler, Leona. *The Psychology of Human Differences.* New York: Appleton-Century-Crofts, 1965.
A survey of the psychological differences between people. Covers intelligence, personality, sex, age, race, class.

Wilentz, Joan S. *The Senses of Man.* New York: Thomas Y. Crowell, 1968.
This book provides a good bridge between overly simple and technical work in perception.

Films and Recordings on Perception

The Eye of the Beholder. B/W. 25 min. 1955. Indiana University.
The "classic" film on perception. Extremely well produced. Although it is dated, there is not a contemporary film to replace it. Dramatizes a twelve-hour period in the life of an artist, with audience perceptions of the incidents based upon mistaken impressions of five persons. The second half of the film reviews the incidents, but with emphasis on what "really" happened. Three of the five incorrect perceptions are caused by the defense mechanism projection, the other two by faulty generalization.

The Outrage. B/W. 97 min. 1964. Films Inc.
The American version of *Rashomon,* the award-winning Japanese film. Artistically it is not as good, but because it is in English it's easier to follow. The viewer sees the same incident through the eyes of different characters. Each person's perception is very believable.

Perception and Communication. Color. 34 min. 1968. Iowa University.
Explains the manner in which human perceptions affect the process of communication, specifically in the teaching–learning area. Introduces two theories of perception, cognitive and transactional, and illustrates each in a number of sequences.

Person to Person Communication. B/W. 14 min. 1956. Iowa University.
A boss is so preoccupied he doesn't hear why a man wants time off. A replay of the incident permits the audience to see and hear the unvoiced thinking of each participant. It is apparent that what we hear may differ markedly from what is said.

Rashomon. B/W. 83 min. 1950. Janus Films.
An excellent film that illustrates the nature of selective perception by telling the story of a sexual assault through the eyes of the different characters involved. Subtitles.

A World to Perceive. B/W. 29 min. NET. 1965.
The role of perception in handling and processing information from the environment and the way in which our personalities affect that perception.

How They Hear: Simulated Sounds of Abnormal Hearing.
Through the use of filters this record simulates the world as people with various hearing defects perceive it. Includes a brief discussion of the physiology involved.
Available from Gordon N. Stowe and Associates, P.O. Box 233, Northbrook, Ill. 60062.

Getting Through: A Guide to Better Understanding of the Hard of Hearing.
   This record is similar to *How They Hear.*
   Available from Zenith Radio Corp., 6501 W. Grand Ave., Chicago, Ill.
   60635.

5

Listening
vs.
Really Hearing

i have just
wandered back
into our conversation
and find
that you
are still
rattling on
about something
or other
i think i must
have been gone
at least
twenty minutes
and you
never missed me

now this might say
something
about my
acting ability
or it might say
something about
your sensitivity

one thing
troubles me tho
when it
is my turn
to rattle on
for twenty minutes
which i
have been known to do
have you
been missing too

Ric Masten

There's more to listening than gazing politely at a speaker and nodding your head every so often. All of us know the frustration of not being heard, and unfortunately all of us are guilty of not listening to others at times. In fact, as you'll find out for yourself shortly, it's likely that more than half the things you say every day might as well have never been spoken because they're not understood clearly.

Maybe the reason most people listen so poorly is that they were never taught this skill. Is this true for you? Think back on your own education. You spent twelve years in classes learning how to read and write, yet you probably never had any instruction in how to listen.

In this chapter we'll introduce you to some skills that can make you a better listener. First we'll talk about poor listening. You'll see just how often you truly listen to others and how often you simply pretend—the results may surprise you. You'll learn why we don't listen much of the time and you'll see some of the bad habits we've developed in this area. After looking at this rather gloomy picture, you'll learn some ways of improving your listening skills, making sure that you understand others and that they understand you. And finally we'll show you the technique of active listening, which not only lets you understand others better but can actually show you how to help them solve their own problems.

Before we start talking about better ways of listening, here's an exercise that may remind you of some bad habits in this area.

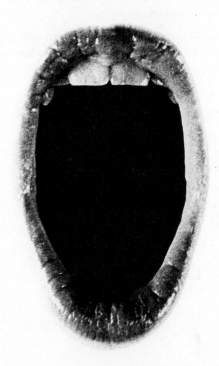

Not Listening

1 Divide the class into groups of four or five people.

2 Each person in turn should take two minutes to discuss with the group his ideas about a current issue (abortion, capital punishment, et cetera) that is important to him. *But,* as the talker shares his ideas, the other group members should think about the unfinished business in their lives—incomplete assignments, on-the-job work, things to discuss with the family. They should try to decide what they're going to do about these situations. The group members shouldn't be rude, they should respond politely every so often to the speaker, putting on a good appearance of paying close attention to him. But they should keep their mind on their personal concerns, not the speaker's remarks.

3 After everyone in your group completes step 2, spend some time sharing the feelings you experienced when you were talking and being listened to by the others. Also discuss how you felt as you thought about your problems instead of listening to the speaker.

4 For five minutes try to have a discussion in which each member of your group shares one personal communication problem she hopes to solve. Try to be as sincere and open with your feelings as you can. But as you all talk, try to keep the discussion focused on *your* problem. Every time someone shares an idea or experience of hers, try to turn it around to relate to your situation. Don't get sidetracked by her comments. Your task is to tell the others about your communication problem.

5 After your discussion, take a few minutes to talk about how you felt during the conversation—when others ignored your message and when you ignored theirs.

WE HAVE BEEN GIVEN
TWO EARS
AND BUT A SINGLE MOUTH,
IN ORDER THAT
WE MAY HEAR MORE
AND TALK LESS.

ZENO OF CITIUM

Is Anyone Listening?

America has better means of communication than any nation on earth. We are constantly developing splendid new techniques for the dissemination of sound, pictures, and print. The only problem is that on the most basic level of communication—person-to-person, live, mouth-to-ear, low-frequency conversation—we're still in the dark ages; for everyone sends well enough, but very few of us are receiving.

Last week in the elevator of my mother's apartment house, a man asked her, "How are you?"

Since Mother had just spent three hours with a tax collector, she smiled graciously and said, "Lousy, thank you."

The man returned the smile and said, "That's nice."

Mother suspected that he either had misunderstood her or was simply a sadist. However, later the same day, she passed a woman who said, "How are you?"

"Suicidally distraught," said Mother.

"Fine," said the woman. "Hope the family's well, too."

This second exchange gave Mother the kind of revelation that only scientists have known when discovering great truths. Because that man and woman weren't people who would have wanted to see Mother out of the way (neither is in her will), she reached a profound conclusion: if you are well enough to be talking, people consider your condition superb, even if you colorfully describe an internal hemorrhage.

Mother's pioneering experimentation in the amenities has so inspired me that I have dedicated myself to continuing her work. Yesterday, I made real progress.

"How are you?" asked a man in front of my house.

"I'll be dead in a week," I said.

"Glad to hear it. Take care now."

There is no known way to shake the composure of the man who makes a perfunctory inquiry about your health; he loves his lines so well that the grimmest truth can't make him revise them. Never is human communication so defeated as when someone asks casually about your condition.

Some day, perhaps when I'm under a bus getting the last rites, I expect such a man to throw me a breezy, "How are you?"

"As well as can be expected," I'll say.

"Good. And the kids?"

"The older one goes to the chair tomorrow. The little one was lost on a Scout hike."

"Swell. The wife okay?"

"She just ran off with the milkman."

"Glad to hear it. You'll have to bring the whole family over one night soon."

Ralph Schoenstein, *Time Lurches On*

Types of Nonlistening

The preceding exercise demonstrated some of the most common types of poor listening. As you read on, you'll begin to recognize them as behaviors that you and those around you probably use quite often. While you'll soon learn that a certain amount of inaccurate listening is understandable, and sometimes even desirable, it's important to be aware of these styles so that you can avoid them when understanding others is important to you.

Pseudolistening Pseudolistening is an imitation of the real thing. Good pseudolisteners give the appearance of being attentive: They look you in the eye, nod and smile at the right times, and even may answer you occasionally. Behind that appearance of interest, however, something entirely different is going on, for pseudolisteners use a polite facade to mask thoughts that have nothing to do with what the speaker is saying. Often pseudolisteners ignore you because of something on their mind that's more important to them than your remarks. Other times they may simply be bored, or think that they've heard what you have to say before, and so tune out your remarks. Whatever the reasons, the significant fact is that pseudolistening is really counterfeit communication.

Stage hogging The Stage hogs are only interested in expressing their ideas and don't care about what anyone else has to say. These people will allow you to speak from time to time, but only so they can catch their breath, use your remarks as a basis for their own babbling, or to keep you from running away. Stage hogs really aren't having a conversation when they dominate others with their talk; they're making a speech and at the same time probably making an enemy.

• Listening vs. *Really* Hearing

Selective listening Selective listeners respond only to the parts of our remarks that interest them, rejecting everything else. All of us are selective listeners from time to time, as for instance when we screen out radio commercials and music as we keep an ear cocked for a weather report or an announcement of the time. In other cases selective listening occurs in conversations with people who expect a thorough hearing, but only get their partner's attention when the subject turns to their favorite topic—perhaps money, sex, a hobby, or some particular person. Unless and until you bring up one of these pet subjects, you might as well talk to a tree.

Insulated listening Insulated listeners are almost the opposite of their selective cousins just mentioned. Instead of looking for something, these people avoid it. Whenever a topic arises which they'd rather not deal with, insulated listeners simply fail to hear, or rather acknowledge it. You remind them about a problem, perhaps—an unfinished job, poor grades, or the like—and they'll nod or answer you and then promptly forget what you've just said.

Defensive listening Defensive listeners take things you intended as innocent comments as personal attacks. The teenager who perceives her parents' questions about her friends and activities as distrustful snooping is a defensive listener, as is the insecure breadwinner who explodes any time his mate mentions money or the touchy parent who views any questioning by her children as a threat to her authority and parental wisdom. As your reading in Chapter 3 suggests, it's fair to assume that many defensive listeners are suffering from shaky public images, and avoid admitting this by projecting their own insecurities onto others.

Ambushing Ambushers listen carefully to you, but only because they're collecting information that they'll use to attack what you have to say. The cross-examining prosecution attorney is a good example of an ambusher. Needless to say, using this kind of strategy will justifiably initiate defensiveness on the other's behalf.

Insensitive listening Insensitive listeners offer the final example of people who don't receive another person's messages clearly. As we've said before, people often don't express their thoughts or feelings openly but instead communicate them through subtle and unconscious choice of words and/or nonverbal clues. Insensitive listeners aren't able to look beyond the words and behavior to understand their hidden meanings. Instead, they take a speaker's remarks at face value. The kind of companions Ralph Schoenstein described on page 193 were insensitive listeners.

My grandmother was a great Monologuist. In nothing flat, she could bring even the most well-channeled conversation around to the subject of the Old West. I remember one afternoon when she was serving tea to two elderly Monologuist contemporaries, a Mr. McDillip and his wife. My grandmother started off by saying what a cold winter it was, and Mr. McDillip said Yes, it was almost as cold as the winter of '81 when his house burned in Maine. My grandmother said she guessed she had been out in the Old West that year; and Mrs. McDillip said her rheumatism was bothering her again; it always did in cold weather. Mr. McDillip said it was 20 below zero when his house caught fire in Maine. At around 11 p.m. he had smelled smoke and had yelled like an Indian. My grandmother said she had got pretty accustomed to Indians out in the Old West, although she had to admit she'd been a bit leery of them when the Colonel first married her and took her to Fort Laramie. Sometimes, she was left alone in the house with Annie the cook and an orderly who was too crippled to be of much use. Mrs. McDillip sympathized with the crippled orderly. Some mornings she could scarcely move, she said. Of course, she had her new heating pad, but it was hard to regulate the heat. Heat! said Mr. McDillip. Nobody ever felt anything like the heat from the burning kitchen the night he and his parents and two younger brothers hurried through the hallway in their bathrobes out into the freezing weather. . . . And so it went, all afternoon, the three of them carrying on their monologues quite amicably in the naive belief that they were communicating with one another.

Kaye Starbird, *Caution! Conversation Being Demolished*

Why We Don't Listen

After thinking about the styles of nonlistening described in the previous pages, most people begin to see that they listen carefully only a small percentage of the time they're with others. It's pretty discouraging to realize that much of the time you aren't hearing others and they aren't getting your messages, but this is a fact of life. Sad as it may be, it's impossible to listen *all* the time, for several reasons, each of which has to do with a type of physiological or psychological noise, such as you read about in Chapter 1.

First, the amount of speech most of us encounter everyday makes careful listening to everything we hear impossible. According to one study, many of us spend as much as one-third of the time we're awake listening to verbal messages—from teachers, coworkers, friends, family, salesmen, and total strangers. This means we often spend five hours or more a day listening to people talk. If you add this to the amount of time we tune in radio and television, you can see that it's impossible for us to keep our attention totally focused for this amount of time. Therefore we have to let our attention wander at times.

A second reason we don't always listen carefully is that we're often wrapped up in personal concerns that are of more immediate importance to us than the messages others are sending. It's hard to pay attention to someone else when you're anticipating an upcoming test or thinking about the wonderful time you had last night with good friends. Yet we still feel we have to "listen" politely to others, and so we continue with our charade.

Listening carefully is also difficult for a physiological reason. Although we're capable of understanding speech at rates up to 600 words per minute,

Bore, *n.* A person who talks when you wish him to listen.

Conversation, *n.* A fair for the display of the minor mental commodities, each exhibitor being too intent upon arrangement of his own wares to observe those of his neighbor.

Egotist, *n.* A person of low taste more interested in himself than me.

Heaven, *n.* A place where the wicked cease from troubling you with talk of their personal affairs, and the good listen with attention while you expound your own.

Ambrose Bierce,
The Devil's Dictionary

the average person speaks between 100 and 140 words per minute. Thus we have a lot of "spare time" to spend with our minds while someone is talking. And the temptation is to use this time in ways that don't relate to the speaker's ideas, such as thinking about personal interests, daydreaming, planning a rebuttal, and so on. The trick is to use this spare time to understand the speaker's ideas better, rather than letting your attention wander.

Finally, the physical world in which we live often presents distractions that make it hard to pay attention to others. The sound of traffic, music, others' speech, and the like interfere with our ability to hear well. Also, fatigue or other forms of discomfort can distract us from paying attention to a speaker's remarks. Consider, for example, how the efficiency of your listening decreases when you are seated in a crowded, hot, stuffy room that is surrounded by traffic and other noises. In such circumstances even the best intentions aren't enough to ensure clear understanding.

Before going any further we want to make it clear that we aren't suggesting that it's always desirable to listen intently, even when the circumstances permit. Given the number of messages to which we're exposed, it's impractical to expect yourself to listen well 100 percent of the time. This fact becomes even more true when you consider how many of the messages sent at us aren't especially worthwhile: boring stories, deceitful commercials, remarks we've heard many times before, and so on. Given this deluge of relatively worthless information, it's important for you to realize that behaviors such as insulated listening, stage hogging, and pseudolistening are often reasonable. Our only concern is that you have the ability to be an accurate receiver when it really does matter. To see how to do so, read on.

At a Lecture—Only 12% Listen

Bright-eyed college students in lecture halls aren't necessarily listening to the professor, the American Psychological Association was told yesterday.

If you shot off a gun at sporadic intervals and asked the students to encode their thoughts and moods at that moment, you would discover that:

• About 20 percent of the students, men and women, are pursuing erotic thoughts.

• Another 20 percent are reminiscing about something.

• Only 20 percent are actually paying attention to the lecture; 12 percent are actively listening.

• The others are worrying, daydreaming, thinking about lunch or—surprise—religion (8 percent).

This confirmation of the lecturer's worst fears was reported by Paul Cameron, 28, an assistant professor at Wayne State University in Detroit. The annual convention, which ends Tuesday, includes about 2000 such reports to 10,000 psychologists in a variety of meetings.

Cameron's results were based on a nine-week course in introductory psychology for 85 college sophomores. A gun was fired 21 times at random intervals, usually when Cameron was in the middle of a sentence.

San Francisco Sunday Examiner and Chronicle

Listening vs. *Really* Hearing

AT THE PARTY

Unrhymed, unrhythmical, the chatter goes:
Yet no one hears his own remarks as prose.

Beneath each topic tunelessly discussed
The ground-bass is reciprocal mistrust.

The names in fashion shuttling to and fro
Yield, when deciphered, messages of woe.

You cannot read me like an open book.

I'm more myself than you will ever look.

Will no one listen to my little song?

Perhaps I shan't be with you very long.

A howl for recognition, shrill with fear,
Shakes the jam-packed apartment, but each ear
Is listening to its hearing, so none hear.

                                        W. H. Auden

THE ART OF NOT LISTENING

Everybody knows that somebody listening to a joke is not really listening; he is impatiently awaiting his turn to tell a joke of his own. Everybody knows that husbands give half an ear to the discourse of their wives—and vice versa. Why do these highly disciplined attempts at human dialogue fail? The reason, says Abraham Kaplan, a professor of philosophy at the University of Michigan, is that they are not really dialogues at all. Before a conference on human and animal communication at Minnesota's Gustavus Adolphus College this month, Kaplan introduced his own word for all those human occasions when everybody talks and nobody listens. He calls them "duologues."

Kaplan applies his coinage widely. "Duologue," he says, "takes place in schools, churches, cocktail parties, the U.S. Congress and almost everywhere we don't feel free to be wholly human." In his view, a duologue is little more than a monologue mounted before a glazed and exquisitely indifferent audience, as in the classroom: "First the professor talks and the students don't listen; then the students talk or write and the professor doesn't listen or read."

The duologue has its unforgiving rules: "You have to give the other his turn, and you give signals during his turn, like saying 'uh huh' or laughing at what he says, to show that he is having his turn. You must also refrain from saying anything that really matters to you as a human being, as it would be regarded as an embarrassing intimacy." A near-perfect example of duologue is the televiewer, transfixed by that mesmeric eye. A truly perfect duologue would be two TV sets tuned in and facing each other.

Open to you The prevalence of the duologue saddens Philosopher Kaplan, a devoted student of the late Jewish philosopher Martin Buber, whose I-thou philosophy was based on the conviction that each man defines himself by genuinely engaging others; humanity is a meeting. Kaplan applied this notion to the laryngeal noise that fills humanity's crowded corners and rooms. And honest dialogue, says Kaplan, is never rehearsed. "I don't know beforehand who I will be, because I am open to you just as you are open to me." Dialogue involves serious listening—listening not just to the other, but listening to oneself. This rare and wondrous event Kaplan calls "communion" instead of communication.

"It seems to me impossible," he says, "to teach unless you are learning. You cannot really talk unless you are listening." The student is also the professor; the joke teller should also be part of the audience. To Kaplan, there is nothing lonelier than two humans involved in a duologue—and nothing more marvelous than two genuinely engaged listeners. "If we didn't search so hard for our own identities but occupied ourselves with the other, we might find precisely what we were not seeking. If we listen, it may be that we will find it at last possible to respond: "Here I am."

Time Magazine

Listening More Effectively

Now that we've come this far you probably realize that you don't listen as much as you think you do. As we've said, it's almost impossible to listen carefully to everything you hear, and so the key is to at least realize when you're just pretending to pay attention. But there are times when you do want very much to understand others. At times like these you may try hard to get the other person's meaning and yet *still* seem to wind up with misunderstandings.

What can you do in such cases? It takes more than good intentions to listen well—there are skills that you can learn to use. As a way of beginning to understand these skills, try the following exercise.

One- and Two-Way Communication

1 Copy the following chart onto a blackboard so that everyone in your group can see it:

One-Way			Two-Way		
Time _____			Time _____		
Number Correct			Number Correct		
Estimate	**Actual**		**Estimate**	**Actual**	
		5			
		4			
		3			
		2			
		1			
		0			

2 Select one member of your group to act as a sender. The sender's job will be to describe two simple drawings to the rest of the group.

3 Select two observers, one to observe and make notes of the sender's behavior in the exercise, and the other to watch and note the behavior of the group members.

4 Supply the group members with a sheet of unlined 8½ × 11-inch paper.

5 Make sure everyone hears and understands the following directions:

"In a minute the sender will describe a simple set of figures that the group members should draw as accurately as possible. The group members should ask no questions or respond in any way to the sender's directions. The idea is to create a one-way communication situation."

6   The sender now stands or seats himself so he can't see or be seen by the group. The instructor then gives him a copy of the drawing contained in the Instructor's Manual for this book. (Actually, any simple drawing will work in this exercise. A variation is to have the sender create his own drawing and describe it to the group. Remember, however, that the drawing should be quite uncomplicated; the exercise is hard enough this way!)

7   The sender should describe this drawing to the group as quickly and accurately as possible. The instructor should make sure that the group members don't communicate with each other during this step. All should understand that a glance at another's drawing furnishes an additional source of information, thus destroying a one-way communication situation.

8   After the sender has finished, note the time that his description took, and place it on the chart. Next, find out how many group members think they've drawn all five figures exactly, how many think they got four, three, and so on. Place the numbers in the appropriate spaces on the chart.

9   Now the sender should move so that he can see and be seen by the group. The instructor will give him a second drawing, which he's to describe. This time, however, the group members should ask necessary questions to make sure they understand the drawing being described. This should be two-way communication. The only limitation on communication here is that the sender must use words only; he can't use gestures to describe his picture to the group.

10   Remember, the goal is to have all group members reproduce the drawing perfectly, so everyone should feel free to ask plenty of questions.

11   Repeat step 8.

12   Now show the drawings one at a time to the group members so they can see how accurate their reactions were. The instructor should then record the accuracy of the group's drawings. For a figure to be correct, its size should be correct proportionately, and it should be positioned in the correct relationship to the preceding and following ones.

13   Now note the data the exercise has produced on your chart. After looking it over, what assumptions might you make about one- and two-way communication? Which takes longer? Which is more accurate?

14   Which is more frustrating for the sender? for the receiver?

15   What parallels does this exercise have in your everyday life? Does the exercise tell you anything about the way *you* listen?

So the first simple feeling I want to share with you is my enjoyment when I can really *hear* someone. I think perhaps this has been a long-standing characteristic of mine. I can remember this in my early grammar school days. A child would ask the teacher a question and the teacher would give a perfectly good answer to a completely different question. A feeling of pain and distress would always strike me. My reaction was, "But you didn't *hear* him!" I felt a sort of childish despair at the lack of communication which was (and is) so common.

Carl R. Rogers

After completing the previous exercise, it's clear that two-way communication is more effective than one-way. To understand why, recall the communication model we described in Chapter 1. At that time we talked about the importance of feedback as a device for increasing understanding. Feedback occurs whenever a receiver informs the sender of his idea of the message. If there was some misunderstanding, the sender can then recognize it and in so doing retransmit the message so that the receiver can understand it more clearly.

There are at least two types of feedback you can use as a listener to check your understanding. The first is *questioning*, which involves asking for additional information to clarify your idea of the sender's message. In the previous exercise some questions might have been "Is the second figure below or above the first one?" or "Did you say a square or a circle is the next figure?" In asking directions to a friend's house, typical questions might be "Is your place an apartment?" or "How long would it take to get there from here?" Note that one key element of questioning is that it requests the speaker to elaborate on information already given.

Questioning is often a valuable tool for increasing understanding. Sometimes, however, it won't help you receive a speaker's ideas any more clearly, and it can even lead to further communication breakdown. To see how this can be so, consider again our example of asking directions to a friend's home. Suppose the instructions you've received are to "Drive about a mile and then turn left at the traffic signal." Now imagine that a few common problems exist in this simple message. First, suppose that your friend's idea of a mile is different from yours: Your mental picture of the distance is actually closer to two miles, while hers is closer to 300 yards. Next, consider the very likely occurrence that while your friend said "traffic signal" she meant "stop sign"; after all, it's common for us to think one thing and say another. Keeping these problems in mind, suppose you tried to verify your understanding of the directions by asking, "After I turn at the light, how far should I go?" to which your friend replied that her house is the third from the corner. Clearly, if you parted after this exchange, you would encounter a lot of frustration before finding the elusive residence.

What was the problem here? It's easy to see that questioning wouldn't have helped you, for your original idea of how far to drive and where to turn were mistaken. And contained in such mistakes is the biggest problem with questioning, for such inquiries don't tell you whether you have accurately received the information that has *already* been sent.

Now consider another kind of feedback—one that would tell you whether you understand what had already been said before you asked additional questions. This sort of feedback involves restating in your own words the message you thought the speaker has just sent, without adding anything new. In the example of seeking directions we've been using, such rephrasing might sound like this: "So you're telling me to drive down to the traffic light by the high school and turn toward the mountains, is that it?" Immediately

"I have a pet at home"

"Oh, what kind of a pet?"

"It is a dog."

"What kind of a dog?"

"It is a St. Bernard."

"Grown up or a puppy?"

"It is full grown."

"What color is it?"

"It is brown and white."

"Why didn't you say you had a full-grown, brown and white St. Bernard as a pet in the first place?"

sensing the problem, your friend could then reply, "Oh no, that's way too far. I meant that you should drive to the four-way stop by the park and turn there. Did I say stop light? I always do that when I mean stop sign!"

This simple step of restating what you thought the speaker has said before going on is commonly termed *active listening*, and it is a very important tool for effective listening. The thing to remember in active listening is to *paraphrase* the sender's words, not to parrot them. In other words, restate what you think the speaker has said in your own terms as a way of cross-checking the information. If you simply repeat the speaker's comments *verbatim*, you'll sound like you're foolish or hard of hearing, and just as importantly, you still might be misunderstanding what's been said.

To see how useful active listening can be, try the following exercise.

Active Listening

1 Find a partner, then move to a place where you can talk comfortably. Designate one person as *A* and the other *B*.

2 Find a subject on which you and your partner apparently disagree—a current events topic, a philosophical or moral issue, or perhaps simply a matter of personal taste.

3 *A* begins by making a statement on the subject. *B*'s job is then to paraphrase the idea back, beginning by saying something like "What I hear you saying is . . ." It is very important that in this step *B* feeds back only what she heard *A* say without adding any judgment or interpretation. *B*'s job is simply to *understand* here, and doing so in no way should signify agreement or disagreement with *A*'s remarks.

4 *A* then responds by telling *B* whether or not her response was accurate. If there was some misunderstanding, *A* should make the correction and *B* should feed back her new understanding of the statement. Continue this process until you're both sure that *B* understands *A*'s statement.

5 Now it's *B*'s turn to respond to *A*'s statement, and for *A* to help the process of understanding by correcting *B*.

6 Continue this process until each partner is satisfied that she has explained herself fully and has been understood by the other person.

7 Now discuss the following questions:

a. As a listener, how accurate was your first understanding of the speaker's statements?

b. How did your understanding of the speaker's position change after you used active listening?

c. Did you find that the gap between your position and that of your partner narrowed as a result of your both using active listening?

d. How did you feel at the end of your conversation? How does this feeling compare to your usual emotional state after discussing controversial issues with others?

e. How might your life change if you used active listening at home? at work? with friends?

Listening to Help

So far we've talked about how becoming a better listener can help you to understand other people more often and more clearly. If you use the skills presented so far, you should be rewarded by communicating far more accurately with others every day. But there's another way in which listening can improve your relationships. Strange as it may sound, often you can help other people solve their own problems simply by learning to listen—actively and with concern.

To understand how listening to others can be so helpful, you need to realize that you can't solve people's problems for them. You can, however, help them work things out for themselves. This is a difficult lesson to learn. When someone you care for is in trouble and feeling bad, your first tendency is to try and make things better—to answer his questions, soothe his hurts, fix whatever is bothering him. But even in cases when you're sure you know what's right for a person, most of the time it's necessary to let that person discover the solution for himself.

This need to let people find their own answers doesn't mean that you have to stand by and do nothing when a friend is in trouble. Fortunately there's a way of responding that you can use to help others find solutions to their problems—even when you don't know these solutions yourself. But before we introduce this technique, here's a chance for you to discover your present style of responding to someone's problem.

What Would You Say?

1 In a moment you'll read a list of situations in which someone shares a problem with you. In each case write out the words you'd use in responding to this person.

2 Here are the statements:

a. I just don't know what to do about my parents. It seems like they just don't understand me. Everything I like seems to go against their values, and they just won't accept my feelings as being right for me. It's not that they don't love me—they do. But they don't accept me.

b. I've been pretty discouraged lately. I just can't get a good relationship going with any guys. . . . I mean a romantic relationship . . . you know. I have plenty of boys whom I'm good friends with, but that's always as far as it goes. I'm tired of being just a pal. . . . I want to be more than that.

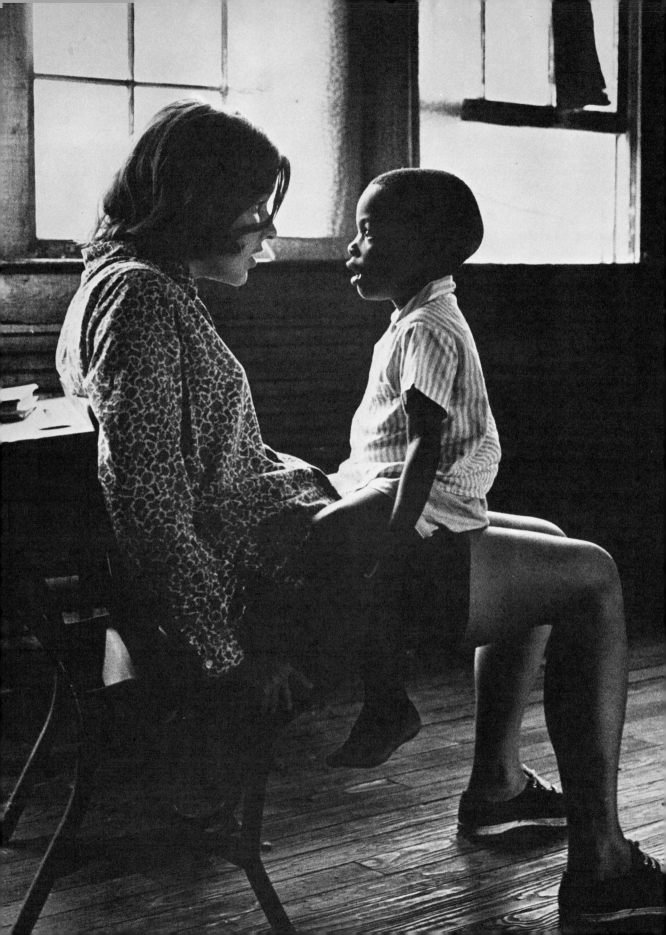

c. (child to parent) I hate you guys! You always go out and leave me with some stupid sitter. Why don't you like me?

d. I'm really bummed out. I don't know what I want to do with my life. I'm pretty tired of school, but there aren't any good jobs around, and I sure don't want to join the service. I could just drop out for a while, but that doesn't really sound very good either.

e. Things really seem to be kind of lousy in my marriage lately. It's not that we fight too much or anything, but all the excitement seems to be gone. It's like we're in a rut, and it keeps getting worse. . . .

f. I keep getting the feeling that my boss is angry at me. It seems like lately he hasn't been joking around very much, and he hasn't said anything at all about my work for about three weeks now. I wonder what I should do?

3 When you've finished writing down your responses, move into triads.

4 Now, as a group share the responses you made to each statement. See if you can decide which ones would be most helpful. As a way of testing the consequences of different responses, you might have two group members role-play each statement and your initial responses. Continue improvising responses to see the way a conversation might really go.

5 After deciding which (if any) responses might be helpful, put your paper aside. You'll be looking back over your answers in a few minutes.

6 Read the next section of the text.

7 After you've read this next section, classify your responses. Were they advising, judging, analyzing, supporting, questioning, or something else? Work with your triad in this classifying process.

Some Typical Ways of Responding to Problems

Most of the responses your group made probably fell into one of four categories. None of these ways of responding is good or bad in itself, but it often happens that we use these ways in situations when they aren't best suited to helping someone we care about solve her problem. There's a proper time and place for each kind of response. The problem, however, usually occurs when we use them in the wrong situations or depend upon one of two styles of responses for all situations.

As you read the following descriptions of these ways of responding, see which ones you most frequently used in the previous exercise and notice the results that probably would have occurred from your response.

Advising When approached with another's problem, the most common tendency is to try to help by offering a solution. While such a response is sometimes valuable, often it isn't as helpful as you might think.

Often your suggestion may not offer the best course to follow, in which case it can even be harmful. There's often a temptation to tell others how *we* would behave in their place, but it's important to realize that what's right for one person may not be right for another. A related consequence of advising is that it often allows others to avoid responsibility for their decisions. If a partner follows your suggestion and things don't work out, he can always pin the blame on you. Finally, often people simply don't want advice: They may not be ready to accept it, instead needing simply to talk out their thoughts and feelings.

Judging A judging response evaluates the sender's thoughts or behaviors in some way. The judgment may be favorable—"That's a good idea" or "You're on the right track now"—or unfavorable—"An attitude like that won't get you anywhere." But in either case it implies that the person doing the judging is in some way qualified to pass judgment on the speaker's thoughts or actions.

As you'll remember from Chapter 3, judging or evaluative language is very likely to make someone defensive. Thus, responding in this way might tend to put the speaker on guard and in so doing end the conversation and the possibility of helping him.

Analyzing The analyzer's response suggests that she understands the sender better than the sender does himself: "What's bothering you is. . . ." or "What you really think is. . . ." In a sense, the analyzer tries to read the speaker's mind or give him a lesson in psychology.

There are two problems with analyzing. First, your interpretation may not be correct, in which case the sender may become even more confused by accepting it. Second, even if your analysis is accurate, sharing it with the sender might not be useful to him. There's a chance that it'll make him defensive (since analyzing implies superiority and evaluativeness), and even if this doesn't occur, he may not be able to understand your view of the problem until he's worked it through for himself.

There are times when analyzing can be a way of helping a person see the "blind parts" of himself, but this style of responding is one many of us use too often.

Questioning   Although questioning is often a helpful way for you to understand the unclear parts of a person's statements, it can also be used as a tool to direct her thoughts. We've all been questioned by a parent, teacher, or other authority figure who seemed to be trying to trap us. In this way questioning is a strategy and often implies that the person doing the asking already has some idea of what direction the discussion should take.

Supporting   Sometimes a person needs encouragement, and in these cases a supporting response might be the best thing. But in many cases this kind of help isn't helpful at all. Telling a person who's obviously upset that "everything's all right" or joking about his problem can communicate a message that you don't accept his feelings or that there isn't justification in the problem for feeling the way he does.

All these responses may be helpful at times, but they often confuse the person asking for help, making him feel worse than before he shared his problem or making him defensive. To understand how these responses can be harmful, look at this example:

Tom: Boy, there must be something wrong with me. Last night I blew it on my first date with Linda. That's the way it always goes—I never seem to do anything right. I'm really a clod.
Bill: Oh, well, cheer up; you'll probably forget about it in a few days. **(Supporting)**
Tom: No I won't. This dating thing really has me depressed. I feel like a social outcast or something.
Bill: Well, I think you're worrying about it too much. It's probably your worrying that messes things up in the first place. **(Judging, analyzing)**
Tom: But I can't help worrying about it. How would you feel if you hadn't had a girl really like you in about three years?
Bill: Well, what do you think the problem is? Have you been polite to them? Do you get drunk or something? There must be some reason why you blow it. **(Questioning)**
Tom: I don't know. I've tried all kinds of approaches and none of them works.

Bill: Well, there's your problem. You're just not being yourself. You have to be natural, and then girls will like you for what you are. There's really nothing to it—just be yourself and everything will be cool. (Judging, analyzing, supporting)

We've used this example to illustrate how good intentions aren't always helpful. Bill may have been right about what caused Tom's dating problem and how he could solve it, but because Tom didn't discover the answer himself, it most likely wasn't useful to him. As you know, people can often ignore the truth, even when it's so obvious that you'd think they would trip over it.

If you were working on the exercise "What Would You Say," now's the time to go back and complete step 7.

To get a clearer idea of how often you use these styles of responding, try the following exercise.

Responding Exercise

1 Read the following examples, and on a separate sheet of paper write down the words you'd use in making each style of response.

a. What can I do? My old man has booted me out of the house. He said I'm not going to live off him if I can't do what he tells me. He's so far out of it he doesn't know what's going on with young people these days. I haven't got any place to stay and I can't get to my savings account at least 'til Monday.

Advising _____
Judging _____
Analyzing _____
Supporting _____
Questioning _____

b. My girl says she doesn't want to go steady this summer while I'm working on road construction. I've told her I'll be out in the boondocks and won't get home more than once or twice all summer. She says she wants to get around a little bit, and she knows if she doesn't go out with other guys she'll just sit home. she claims it won't make any difference with us, but I think she wants to break it off permanently. I don't know, I just can't seem to talk about it with her.

Advising _____
Judging _____
Analyzing _____
Supporting _____
Questioning _____

c. My roommate and I can't seem to get along. She's always having her boyfriend over and he doesn't know when to go home. You've seen our apartment, and you know I can't go to bed until he's gone. I don't know, maybe I'm just a prude. Anyway, I don't want to break up our arrangement. It's good for both of us. Neither of us can afford to live by ourselves or the expense of moving. But I can't put up with this much longer.

Advising _____
Judging _____
Analyzing _____
Supporting _____
Questioning _____

2 After you've made your responses, join two others to make a triad and compare them.

3 For each statement select one or more responses you'd be likely to make. Role-play this response to find the consequences.

4 How helpful were these styles of responding in the exercises?. How helpful are they in your life?

Another Way of Responding

Fortunately there's another way of responding that can often be much more helpful in letting a person work out his problems. This style of responding is simply to *listen actively,* using the techniques of giving feedback we introduced earlier in this chapter. Actively listening tells the speaker that you're interested in understanding what he has to say, that you care about him. And amazingly enough, simply feeding back a person's ideas often helps him sort out and solve the problems for himself. If you're lucky, you probably know people who can help you understand things better simply by sitting and listening. These people are probably active listeners, even though they don't know it.

Take a look at how the previous conversation might have gone if Bill had used active listening:

Tom: Boy, there must be something wrong with me. Last night I blew it on my first date with Linda. That's the way it always goes—I never seem to do anything right. I'm really a clod.
Bill: You're pretty upset because things never seem to work out on your dates, huh?
Tom: Yeah. And I don't know what my problem is. I'm not stupid or anything. I always take them to nice places, and I don't get loaded and act like a fool or anything. But I always blow it.
Bill: So you always try to do everything just right—be a gentleman and all that, but it never works out.
Tom: Yeah. I really want to make it work, and so I wind up maybe being too much of a gentleman. I don't act natural. And then when that doesn't work I get even more nervous the next time, which makes the girl uptight, and on it goes. It's a vicious circle.
Bill: So it's your nervousness that you think hangs you up? You're afraid of not being a good date, and so you try too hard, which the girls don't like.
Tom: Yeah. I guess what I have to do is just be myself—not try to force things or act like I'm right out of some suave movie or something. Maybe I'll try that. . . .

Notice that in the above example Bill's answers reflected Tom's *feelings* as well as his *thoughts*. This sort of two-barreled response is important in helping others sort out their problems. A moment's reflection will show you the importance of focusing on emotions in problem-solving. Often the emotion a person experiences is more important than the idea that triggered it. Is the problem one of sadness or anger? Is your partner worried or resigned? By reflecting back your perception of the other's feeling you'll help her identify it. Don't be afraid to guess the wrong emotion: If you do so, your partner will correct you, and in so doing clarify the situation for herself.

Here's an exercise designed to sharpen your skill at detecting the feeling behind the words spoken.

Listening for Feelings

1 Below are fifteen statements that people might make. Read each one separately, trying to listen carefully for the possible feeling behind the words.

2 On a piece of paper write down the number of the example and any and all feelings you think you hear in the statement. Write in only feelings, not content. Try to identify the feeling with a single word, but if you need to use a phrase, feel free.

3 After you've finished, join two other group members and compare your list of feelings with the others.

4 Find the areas in which you generally agree. When only one person lists a feeling, refer back to the example. Could it be a legitimate feeling for a person saying those words? How would you find out whose interpretation is correct?

5 Did you find you weren't hearing all the feelings others heard?

The Person Says	The Person Might Be Feeling
(Example) It seems to me that you aren't paying much attention to me. Is there something I should know?	Puzzled, hurt

a. I wonder if I ought to start looking for another job. They're reorganizing the company, and what with drop in business and all, maybe this is one of the jobs they'll cut back on. But if my boss finds out I'm looking around, maybe he'll think I don't like it here and let me go anyway.

b. That's really a beautiful dress! Where'd you get it?

c. I said I'd do the collecting for him, but I sure don't feel like it. But I owe him a favor so I guess I'll have to do it.

d. I've got a report due tomorrow, an exam the next day, rehearsals every night this week, and now a meeting this afternoon. I don't think I can even fit in eating, and this has been going on all month.

DEAR ABBY: I am a recently retired woman who once enjoyed a successful and fulfilling business career. I've remained single by choice.

I live alone, but I'm far from lonely. I have all the friends I want. I like my privacy and have never encouraged visitors to drop in.

The high-rise in which I live has excellent security, and no one gets into this building without being screened.

One evening about 7:30, there was a knock on my door. I wasn't expecting anyone so I asked who was there. It was a widow who lives on my floor and with whom I had had only a nodding acquaintance. She said she was "lonely," and didn't know what to do with herself, and asked if she could come in and visit for a while.

I told her politely but bluntly that I was busy, and didn't approve of visitors dropping in without phoning first. (I have an unlisted phone number, which I did not give her.) She apologized for bothering me and left.

Abby, I've always felt that people who intrude on others should be treated with the same lack of consideration they give those upon whom they intrude. I felt quite proud of myself for not getting trapped by a bore who would probably be difficult to get rid of.

The next evening a friend telephoned to ask if I knew the woman in my building who had committed suicide the night before.

If you have already guessed that she was the woman who knocked on my door, you are right.—HARD LESSON LEARNED

e. Sure she gets better grades than I do. She's a housewife, takes only two classes, and all she has to do is study. I have to work a job and go to school too. And I don't have anyone to support me.

f. I can't understand why they haven't written. They've never been gone this long without at least a card, and I don't even know how to get in touch with them.

g. Thanks for a great evening. The dinner was fantastic, so was the party. Let's do it again.

h. My daughter got straight A's this year, and the high school has a reputation for being very hard. She's a natural student. But sometimes I wonder if she isn't all books. I wish I could help her get interested in something besides studying.

i. Boy, the teacher tells us he'll mark off on our grade every time we're late, but it doesn't seem to bother him when he comes in late. He must figure it's his privilege.

j. I worked up that whole study—did all the surveying, the compiling, the writing. It was my idea in the first place. But he turned it into the head office with his name on it, and he got the credit.

k. I don't know whether I'm doing a good job or not. She never tells me if I'm doing well or need to work harder. I sure hope she likes my work.

l. She believed everything he said about me. She wouldn't even listen to my side, just started yelling at me.

m. Look, we've gone over and over this. The meeting could have been over an hour ago if we hadn't gotten hung up on this one point. If we can't make a decision, let's table it and move on.

n. Look, I know I acted like a rat. I apologized, and I'm trying to make up for it. I can't do anymore, can I? So drop it!

o. How can I tell him how I really feel? He might get mad and then we'd start arguing. He'll think I don't love him if I tell him my real feelings.

Most conversations seem to be carried out on two levels, the verbal level and the emotional level. The verbal level contains those things which are socially acceptable to say, but it is used as a means of satisfying emotional needs. Yesterday a friend related something that someone had done to her. I told her why I thought the person had acted the way he had and she became very upset and started arguing with me. Now, the reason is clear. I had been listening to her words and had paid no attention to her feelings. Her words had described how terribly this other person had treated her, but her emotions had been saying, "Please understand how I felt. Please accept my feeling the way I did." The last thing she wanted to hear from me was an explanation of the other person's behavior.

Hugh Prather

SO PENSEROSO

Come, megrims, mollygrubs and collywobbles!
Come, gloom that limps, and misery that hobbles!
Come also, most exquisite melancholiage,
As dank and decadent as November foliage!
I crave to shudder in your moist embrace,
To feel your oystery fingers on my face.
This is my hour of sadness and of soulfulness,
And cursed be he who dissipates my dolefulness.
I do not desire to be cheered,
I desire to retire, I am thinking of growing a beard,
A sorrowful beard, with a mournful, a dolorous hue in it,
With ashes and glue in it.
I want to be drunk with despair,
I want to caress my care,
I do not wish to be blithe,
I wish to recoil and writhe,
I will revel in cosmic woe,
And I want my woe to show.
This is the morbid moment,
This is the ebony hour.
Aroint thee, sweetness and light!
I want to be dark and sour!
Away with the bird that twitters!
All that glitters is jitters!
Roses, roses are gray,
Violets cry Boo! and frighten me.
Sugar is stimulating,
And people conspire to brighten me.
Go hence, people, go hence!
Go sit on a picket fence!
Go gargle with mineral oil,
Go out and develop a boil!
Melancholy is what I brag and boast of,
Melancholy I mean to make the most of,
You beaming optimists shall not destroy it.
But while I am it, I intend to enjoy it.
Go, people, stuff your mouths with soap,
And remember, please, that when I mope, I mope!

OGDEN NASH

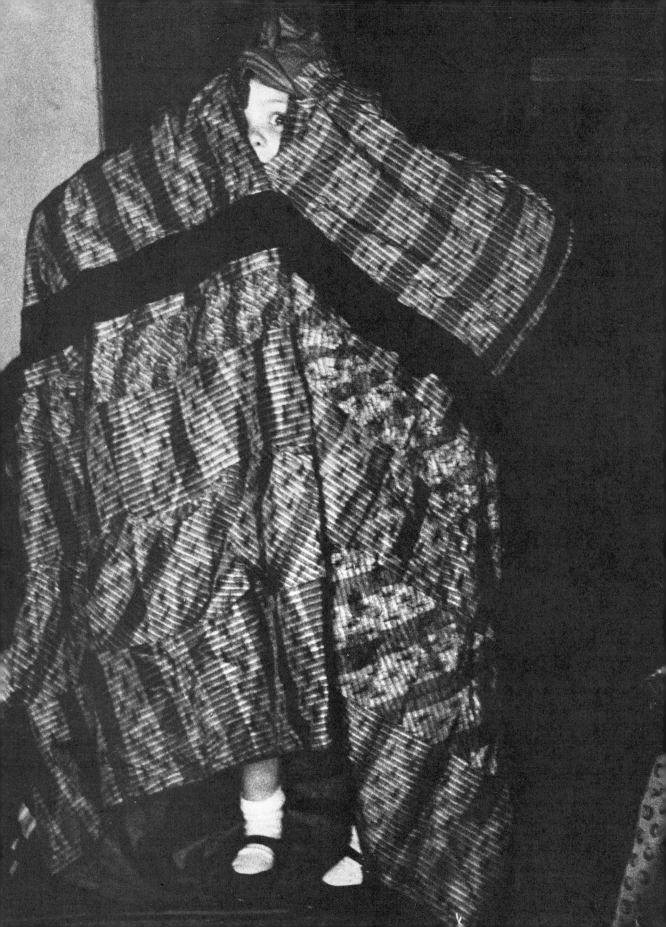

Danny

(Active listening really works, even with young kids. Here's an actual example of how one mother used her skills to solve a typical family problem.)

Mother: It's late. Turn out the light and go to sleep.

Danny: I'm not going to sleep.

Mother: You have to, it's late. You'll be tired tomorrow.

Danny: I'm not going to sleep.

Mother (harshly): Turn that light off immediately!

Danny (flatly): I'm *never* going to sleep.

Mother (I feel like strangling him. I'm so tired, I can't stand this tonight . . . I go into the kitchen, smoke a cigarette, decide that I'm going in there and try active listening even if it kills me! Entering Danny's room): ''C'mon, it's late but I'll sit on your bed for a while and rest my feet before I do the dishes. [She takes the book from him, turns off the light, closes the door, and sits on the bed beside him, leaning back against the wall.]

Danny: Gimme that book! Don't turn off the light. Get out of here. I don't want you in here. I'm not going to sleep. I hate you!

Mother: You're feeling angry.

Danny: Yeah, I hate school, and I'll never go back, never!

Mother (He loves school.): You're fed up with school.

Danny: It's horrible. I'm not good in school. Don't know anything. I ought to be in second grade. [He's in third.] Math, I don't know it. [He is very good at it.] The teacher must think we're in a high school or something.

Mother: Math's pretty hard for you.

Danny: No! It's easy. Just don't feel like doing it.

Mother: Oh.

Danny (sudden shift): I sure like baseball. Much rather play baseball than go to school.

Mother: You really like baseball.

Danny: Do you *have* to go to college? [Oldest brother will soon enter college and there is much family talk about it.]

Mother: No.

Danny: How long do you have to go to school?

Mother: You have to finish high school.

Danny: Well, I'm not going to college. Don't have to, right?

Mother: Right.

Danny: Good, I'll play baseball.

Mother: Baseball's really fun.

Danny: Sure is. [Completely calmed down, talking comfortably, no anger.] Well, good night.

Mother: Good night.

Danny: Will you sit up with me some more?

Mother: Uh huh.

Danny (pulls up covers which had been kicked off; carefully covers up Mother's knees and pats them): Comfortable?

Mother: Yes, thank you.

Danny: You're welcome. [Period of quiet, then Danny starts snorting and sniffing with much exaggerated clearing of throat and nose.] Snort, snort, snort. [Danny does have slight allergy with stuffy nose, but the symptoms are never acute. Mother has never heard Danny snort like this before.]

Mother: Nose bugging you?

Danny: Yeah, sure is. Think I need the stuffy nose medicine?

Mother: Do you think it would help?

Danny: No. (Snort, snort.)

Mother: Nose really bugs you.

Danny: Yeah [snort]. [Sigh of anguish.] Oh, I wish you didn't have to breathe through your nose when you sleep.

Mother (very surprised at this, tempted to ask where that idea came from): You think you have to breathe through your nose when you sleep?

Danny: I *know* I have to.

Mother: You feel sure about it.

Danny: I know it. Tommy told me, a long time ago. [Much admired friend, two years older.] He said you have to. You can't breathe through your mouth when you sleep.

Mother: You mean you aren't supposed to?

Danny: You just *can't* [snort]. Mommy, that's so, isn't it? I mean, you *gotta* breathe through your nose when you sleep, don't you? [Long explanation—many questions from Danny about admired friend. "He wouldn't lie to me."]

Mother (explains that friend is probably trying to help but kids get false information sometimes. Much emphasis from Mother that everyone breathes through the mouth when sleeping.)

Danny (very relieved): Well, good night.

Mother: Good night. [Danny breathing easily through mouth.]

Danny (suddenly): Snort.

Mother: Still scary.

Danny: Uh huh. Mommy, what if I go to sleep breathing through my mouth—and my nose is stuffy—and what if in the middle of the night when I'm sound asleep—what if I closed my mouth?

Mother (realizes that he has been afraid to go to sleep for years because he is afraid he would choke to death; thinks, "Oh, my poor baby"): You're afraid you might choke maybe?

Danny: Uh huh. You *gotta* breathe. [He couldn't say, "I might die."]

Mother (more explaining): It simply couldn't happen. Your mouth would open—just like your heart pumps blood or your eyes blink.

Danny: Are you *sure*?

Mother: Yes, I'm sure.

Danny: Well, good night.

Mother: Good night, dear. [Kiss. Danny is asleep in minutes.]

Thomas Gordon, *Parent Effectiveness Training*

Advantages of Active Listening

There are several reasons why active listening works so well. First, it takes the burden off you as a friend. Simply being there to understand what's on a person's mind often makes it possible for her to clarify her own problems. This means you don't have to know all the answers to help. Also, helping by active listening means you don't need to guess at reasons or solutions that might not be correct. Thus, both you and your friend are saved from going on a wild goose chase after incorrect solutions.

A second advantage of active listening is that it's a great way to get through layers of hidden meanings. Often people express their ideas, problems, or feelings in strangely coded ways. Active listening can sometimes help cut through to the real meaning. Not too long ago a student came to an instructor and asked, "How many people get D's and F's in this class?" The instructor could have taken the question at face value and answered it, but instead he tried active listening. He replied by saying, "Sounds like you've got some fears of doing poorly in here." After a few minutes of listening he learned that this girl had a very poor self-concept and was afraid that getting a low grade in a communication class would be equal to failing as a person. He assured her that if she were as honest and open throughout the class as she'd been in their talk, she'd have little to worry about as far as grades were concerned.

The third advantage of active listening is that it's usually the best way to encourage someone to share more of himself with you. Knowing that you're interested in him will encourage less feeling of threat, and he'll be willing to let down some of his defenses. In this sense active listening is simply a good way to learn more about someone and a good foundation on which to build a relationship.

Now What Would You Say

1 Refer back to the "What Would You Say" exercise in this chapter.

2 Using the six situations there, role-play the speaker and listener. This time the listener is to practice active listening in a way that tells the speaker he's interested in understanding what he has to say.

3 Small groups allow more participation, so work in groups of three to five persons.

4 Remember you're not judging, analyzing, supporting, or questioning—you're listening actively and giving feedback that tells the speaker you're with him and understanding what he's saying.

5 When the conversation lags, go to another situation and a different group member's role-playing. Work through all six situations.

When to Use Active Listening

Active listening isn't appropriate in all situations when someone wants help. Sometimes people are simply looking for information and not trying to work out their feelings. At times like this active listening would be out of place. If someone asks you for the time of day, you'd do better to simply give her the information than to respond by saying "You want to know what time it is." If you're fixing dinner and someone wants to know when it will be ready, it would be exasperating to reply, "You're interested in knowing when we'll be eating."

However, people do often hide an important feeling behind an innocent-sounding statement or question, and in such cases active listening on your part can usually bring their real concern into the open. But don't go overboard with the technique. Usually, if there's a feeling hidden behind a question, you'll recognize some accompanying nonverbal clue—a change in your friend's facial expression, tone of voice, posture, and so on. But it takes attention, concentration, and "caring" on your part.

Claude Brown in his book *Manchild in the Promised Land* describes how he wants to say he cares for his mother, but even in his imagination he can't be that open. Thus the words he decides he would have used only hint at his feelings.

Isn't this often the case?

... Those tears shining on Mama's face were falling for me. When the bus started down the street, I wanted to run back and say something to Mama. I didn't know what. I thought, maybe, I woulda said, "Mama, I didn't mean what I said, 'cause I really do care." No, I wouldn'a said that. I woulda said, "Mama, button up your coat. It's cold out here." Yeah, that's what I forgot to say to Mama.

Claude Brown,
*Manchild in the
Promised Land*

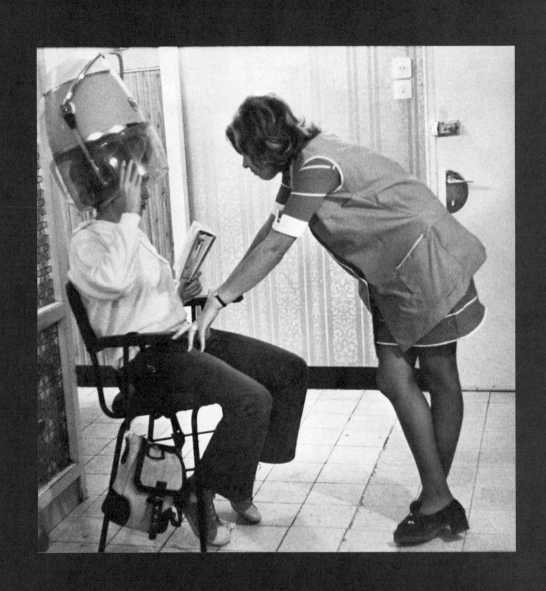

They Learn To Aid Customers By Becoming Good Listeners

Do you need someone to listen to your troubles? Have your hair done.

Beauty salon chairs may be to today's women what conversation-centered backyard fences were to their grandmothers and psychiatrists' couches are to their wealthier contemporaries.

"We are not as family-oriented as our ancestors were," says counselor-trainer Andy Thompson. "They listened to and helped each other. Now that we have become a society of individuals isolated from one another by cars, telephones, jobs and the like, we have had to find other listeners."

Community training program director for Crisis House, Thompson has designed and is conducting human relations training sessions for workers to whom customers tend to unburden their woes most frequently—cosmetologists, bartenders and cab-drivers.

□ □ □

"People can definitely help others just by letting them talk," he said. "Relatives, friends or spouses who listen do a lot to keep the mental health of this country at a reasonable rate. Workers in situations that encourage communications can make the same meaningful contribution."

Thompson explained that his training is not meant to replace, or be confused with, professional treatment or counseling. His students fill a gap between family and professionals.

"There are not enough psychiatrists or psychologists to go around," he said. "And, some professionals become so technical that their help doesn't mean much to persons who just need a someone who will let them get problems and questions out in the open where they can look at them."

Thompson's first course of training, completed recently, was for cosmetologists.

□ □ □

The human relations training program attempts to make the most of these built-in assets by using a method Thompson calls "reflective listening."

"The purpose is to let the customer talk enough to clarify her own thinking," he said. "We are not interested in having cosmetologists tell women what to do, but to give them a chance to choose their own course of action.

"There is a tendency among listeners to try to rescue a person with problems and pull them out of negative situations. People don't really want that. They just want to discuss what is on their minds and reach their own conclusions."

Cosmetologists are taught to use phrases that aid customers in analyzing their thoughts. Some of the phrases are, "You seem to think . . ." "You sound like . . ." "You appear to be . . ." "As I get it, you . . ." and "It must seem to you that . . ."

There also are barriers to conversation that the cosmetologists are taught to avoid.

"A constant bombardment of questions can disrupt communications," Thompson said. "Commands will have the same effect. Many of them are impossible to follow anyway.

"How many can respond to orders to 'Stop feeling depressed,' 'Don't be so upset,' or 'Don't think about it.'"

"The same applies to negative criticism, 'That's dumb,' for instance; and evaluations, such as 'Oh, you're just confused.'

"Comments that seem threatening—'You had better stop feeling sad,' as an example—will end a conversation as quickly as changing the subject or not paying attention."

Classes for bartenders, to be held Nov. 16–18, and cabdrivers, set for Dec. 7–9, at National University, will be similar to those given the cosmetologists.

"The environments and roles of the three are different, but I have a feeling that we will only have to redesign the fringes and keep the core of the training," Thompson said. "Giving people a chance to talk about themselves is a very fundamental thing."

The current series, for 100 cosmetologists, bartenders and cabdrivers in the East County areas, is being financed by a grant from the state Department of Health.

"I feel that we have taken the cap off something people have been waiting for," Thompson said. "There is a need for training that will help us work more effectively with one another. We will continue the classes, but those attending will have to pay for future courses."   *San Diego Union*

A Matter of Attitude

Now you're almost ready to begin active listening for yourself. But before you do, you should realize that your success in using this skill will depend on the attitude you bring to a situation. Too often people will think of active listening as a kind of gimmick they can use when some unpleasant situation arises. If you think about the technique this way, it is almost sure to fail. In fact, unless you truly mean what you say, you'll come across as being manipulative, phony, and uncaring. So as you practice your listening skill, try to keep these points in mind:

First, don't actively listen unless you truly want to help the person. There's nothing wrong with being too preoccupied to help. But you'll be doing both yourself and the other person a disservice if you pretend to care when you really don't.

Second, don't try to listen actively if you're not willing to take the necessary time. As the exercise on one-way–two-way communication showed, listening with feedback takes time. If you're willing to make the effort, you'll be rewarded, but you'll only lose the speaker's trust if you commit yourself and then don't follow through.

Third, don't try to impose your ideas on the other person. Active listening means accepting the speaker's feelings and trusting that p/he ¢ can find his own solutions. If you try to moralize, suggest, or otherwise change the speaker, you won't really be actively listening, and it's less likely that you'll be of much help.

Fourth, keep your attention focused on the sender. Sometimes, as you listen to another person share his feelings, it's easy to become defensive, to relate his thoughts to your own life, or to busy yourself thinking of an answer. Remember that active listening is a form of helping someone else. Try to keep your energy focused on this goal.

Active Listening Practice

Here's a chance to try out your active listening skills.

1   Divide into pairs.

2   One member should tell the other about some problem that has been bothering her lately. The problem may be big or small.

3 The receiver is to practice active listening. Remember that the goal here is not judging, analyzing, supporting, or questioning, but rather understanding and clarifying.

4 Your understanding responses should be appropriate in language and depth to the problem. If the problem is a serious one and you took it lightly (or vice versa), you would be failing at active listening.

5 Let this conversation develop and see what happens.

6 When each person in the pair has shared a problem, compare notes on how you felt throughout the exercise. Was the sender helped in any way? Was the receiver comfortable? How can you use active listening in your life?

On Your Own

1 In the next five days try to listen actively whenever an appropriate situation arises. See if you can recall and use all the skills introduced in this chapter. Remember, the most important thing you can bring to a conversation is your *care* for the other person.

2 Write a brief account of how your conversation went. Try to explain as much of the encounter as you can without violating any confidences. How successful was your active listening style?

Check Your Listening

Nobody's a perfect listener. Here's a chance for you to see just how often you truly listen and how much of the time you just pretend.

1 For the next five days pay attention to your listening behavior. Don't try to change the way you act; just observe the times when you're really trying to understand someone and the times when you're behaving in one of the nonlistening ways described previously.

2 Keep track of your findings in a briefly written journal. Here's a form you might find useful for your journal. For each entry include

    a. The day and time

    b. The person or people involved

    c. The situation: What was the background for this conversation? What subject were you discussing? What emotions were you and your partner experiencing?

    d. The style of listening you used: one-way, questioning, active, pseudo-listening, stage hog, ambushing, insensitive listening, selective listening, defensive listening, insulated listening, advising, judging, analyzing, or supporting.

    e. The outcome of your listening style. Did it help bring the conversation to a conclusion that satisfied everyone involved?

f. Your level of satisfaction with your listening. If you had it to do over, would you listen in the same way?

3 At the end of the five-day period answer these questions:

a. About what percentage of the time do you use each of the listening styles described in this chapter? With whom and in what situations do you most commonly use each?

b. How satisfied are you with your listening behavior? In what situations and with what people would you like to change the way you listen? What must you do to start making this change?

If things have gone well, you have a new appreciation of the importance of listening in interpersonal communication. Our hope is that you'll put the skills introduced here into use in your own interpersonal relationships. All the theory in the world can do little good if you can't integrate it into your actions. We suggest you try to develop a listening style that's both effective and suits you personally. Good luck!

Roads Not Taken

1 Observe the listening behavior of those around you—at home, on the job, at school, in social situations. Do the styles of listening various people use differ from one situation to another? What are the consequences of each style?

2 Work on improving your listening behavior. Begin by defining which styles you would like to use with various people in different situations. Next, keep a journal in which you record the kind of listening you actually do use. See if you can move closer to your goal over the time you keep your journal.

3 Investigate some of the studies that have been conducted on human listening. What does the information contained in these studies have to do with your listening behavior?

4 Our educational system provides many opportunities for learning how to speak, write and read, but the skill of listening is relatively neglected. Try to find information about courses on listening that exist in various educational settings. Where do such courses exist? What is taught in them?

More Readings on Listening

Axline, Virginia M. *Dibs: In Search of Self*. New York: Ballantine Books, 1967.

This is a fascinating account of a child's transition from isolation to happy normality. Beautifully illustrates how active listening can be a therapeutic tool.

Axline, Virginia M. *Play Therapy.* New York: Ballantine Books, 1969.
A description of the author's technique for working with troubled children. An important part of her work involves the skillful use of active listening.

Barker, Larry L. *Listening Behavior.* Englewood Cliffs, N.J.: Prentice-Hall, 1971.
This book is helpful because it's concerned with just listening: the variables, identifying problems, listening to biased communication, and feedback. A good collection of recent thinking on the subject.

Beier, Ernst G., and Evans G. Valens. *People-Reading: How We Control Others, How They Control Us.* New York: Stein and Day, 1975.
Chapter 2: How to Listen, Chapter 3: How Not to Listen, and Chapter 4: Listening to Feelings expand on the information that we have been able to include in our one chapter. The many examples are extremely helpful in adding to your understanding of the art of listening.

Nichols, R., and L. A. Stevens. *Are You Listening?* New York: McGraw-Hill, 1957.
This is the pioneer book about the subject. It deals mostly with listening accurately for information.

Rogers, Carl R. *On Becoming a Person.* Boston: Houghton Mifflin, 1961.
Rogers' technique of helping others centers around actively listening. This is a readable, helpful book.

Films on Listening

Listen, Please. Color. 10 min. 1959. Central Arizona Film Cooperative.
Depicts a day in the life of an average plant supervisor, emphasizing the high proportion of his time and attention that must go to listening. From the Modern Management Series.

Listening Skills, An Introduction. Color. 11 min. 1965. Iowa University.
Provides pointers for improving listening habits: paying close attention, thinking about and mentally reviewing what is being said, and responding to the communicator. Studies distractions and how to cope with them. Beginning or remedial level.

Speech: Effective Listening. B/W. 15 min. 1959. Central Arizona Film Cooperative.
Demonstrates the importance of skilled listening in the communicative process. Discusses ways to develop good listening habits.

Task of the Listener. B/W. 30 min. NET. 1959. Iowa University.
This selection from Hayakawa's Language in Action series may seem dated, but the emphasis on the nature of self and the importance of self-concept and self-disclosure to communication is relevant.

6

Nonverbal Communication: Messages Without Words

Nonverbal Communication Means:

smiling, frowning
laughing, crying, sighing
standing close to others
being stand-offish

the way you look:
your hair, your clothing
your face, your body

your handshake (sweaty palms?)
your postures
your gestures
your mannerisms

your voice:
soft-loud
fast-slow
smooth-jerky

the environment you create:
your home, your room
your office, your desk
your kitchen
your car

The Adventures of Sherlock Holmes

One night—it was on the twentieth of March, 1888—I was returning from a journey to a patient (for I had now returned to civil practice), when my way led me through Baker Street. As I passed the well-remembered door, which must always be associated in my mind with my wooing, and with the dark incidents of the *Study in Scarlet,* I was seized with a keen desire to see Holmes again, and to know how he was employing his extraordinary powers. His rooms were brilliantly lit, and, even as I looked up, I saw his tall, spare figure pass twice in a dark silhouette against the blind. He was pacing the room swiftly, eagerly, with his head sunk upon his chest and his hands clasped behind him. To me, who knew his every mood and habit, his attitude and manner told their own story. He was at work again. He had risen out of his drug-created dreams and was hot upon the scent of some new problem. I rang the bell and was shown up to the chamber which had formerly been in part my own.

His manner was not effusive. It seldom was; but he was glad, I think, to see me. With hardly a word spoken, but with a kindly eye, he waved me to an armchair, threw across his case of cigars, and indicated a spirit case and a gasogene in the corner. Then he stood before the fire and looked me over in his singular introspective fashion.

"Wedlock suits you," he remarked. "I think, Watson, that you have put on seven and a half pounds since I saw you."

"Seven!" I answered.

"Indeed, I should have thought a little more. Just a trifle more, I fancy, Watson. And in practice again, I observe. You did not tell me that you intended to go into harness."

"Then, how do you know?"

"I see it, I deduce it. How do I know that you have been getting yourself very wet lately, and that you have a most clumsy and careless servant girl?"

"My dear Holmes," said I, "this is too much. You would certainly have been burned, had you lived a few centuries ago. It is true that I had a country walk on Thursday and came home in a dreadful mess, but as I have changed my clothes I can't imagine how you deduce it. As to Mary Jane, she is incorrigible, and my wife has given her notice; but there, again, I fail to see how you work it out."

He chuckled to himself and rubbed his long, nervous hands together.

"It is simplicity itself," said he; "my eyes tell me that on the inside of your left shoe, just where the firelight strikes it, the leather is scored by six almost parallel cuts. Obviously they have been caused by someone who has very carelessly scraped round the edges of the sole in order to remove crusted mud from it. Hence, you see, my double deduction that you had been out in vile weather, and that you had a particularly malignant boot-slitting specimen of the London slavey. As to your practice, if a gentleman walks into my rooms smelling of iodoform, with a black mark of nitrate of silver upon his right forefinger, and a bulge on the right side of his top-hat to show where he has secreted his stethoscope, I must be dull, indeed, if I do not pronounce him to be an active member of the medical profession."

I could not help laughing at the ease with which he explained his process of deduction. "When I hear you give your reasons," I remarked, "the thing always appears to me to be so ridiculously simple that I could easily do it myself, though at each successive instance of your reasoning I am baffled until you explain your process. And yet I believe that my eyes are as good as yours."

"Quite so," he answered, lighting a cigarette, and throwing himself down into an armchair. "You see, but you do not observe."

Sir Arthur Conan Doyle, *A Scandal in Bohemia*

Sometimes it's difficult to know how other people really feel. Often they don't know for sure themselves, and other times they have some reason for not wanting to tell us, but in either case there are times when we can't find out what is going on inside another's mind simply by asking.

What should we do in these cases? They happen every day, and often in the most important situations. Sherlock Holmes said the way to understand people was to watch them—not only to see, but to observe.

Observing yourself and others is what this chapter is about. In the following pages you'll become acquainted with the field of nonverbal communication—the way we express ourselves, not by what we say, but by what we *do*. Psychologist Albert Mehrabian claims that less than ten percent of what we communicate comes from our words; the rest is sent by nonverbal messages. Whether this figure is precise or not, the point is important: To communicate better you need to be sensitive to body language.

So let's begin.

□ □ □

Verbal and Nonverbal Communication

Here's an experiment you can try either at home or in class. It will help you begin learning how nonverbal communication works.

1   Pick a partner, and find a place where you have some space to yourselves.

2   Now sit back-to-back with your partner, making sure that no parts of your bodies are touching. You should be seated so that you can talk easily without seeing each other.

3   Once you're seated, take two minutes to carry on a conversation about whatever subject you like. The only requirement is that you not look at or touch each other. Communicate using words only.

4   Next, turn around so that you're facing your partner, seated at a comfortable distance. Now that you can both see and hear each other, carry on your conversation for another two minutes.

5   Continue to face each other, but for the next two minutes don't speak. Instead, join hands with your partner and communicate whatever messages you want to through sight and touch. Try to keep aware of how you feel as you go through this step. There isn't any right or wrong way to behave here—there's nothing wrong with feeling embarrassed, silly, or any other way. The only requirement is to *remain silent.*

After you've finished the experiment, take some time to talk it over with your partner. Start by sharing how you felt in each part of the experience. Were you comfortable, nervous, playful, affectionate? Did your feelings change from one step to another? Could your partner tell these feelings without our expressing them? If so, how? Did he communicate his feelings too?

well that's it
i have nothing
more to say
i said
and went on to play
many variations
on this theme

i said it upstairs
down stairs
in the kitchen
in the bedroom
nothing more to say

it's finished
i'm going to bed
where i will set
the electric blanket
at body temperature
take the fetal
position
and wait it out

i put the dust cover
on my silent
typewriter
and laid it to rest
beside
my silent grandmother

i mean
what can you say
when it's all been said

and like a pat
on the head
you smile

perhaps
we could try
silence
for awhile

Ric Masten

Characteristics of Nonverbal Communication

If this experiment seemed strange to you, we hope you still went through with it, because it points out several things about nonverbal communication.

Nonverbal communication exists   Even when you were in the nontalking stage, you probably could pick up some of your partner's feelings by the touch of her hands, her posture, and expressions—maybe more than you could during your conversation. We hope that this exercise showed you that there are other languages besides words that carry messages about your relationships.

The point isn't so much *how* you or your partner behaved during the exercises—whether you were tense or relaxed, friendly or distant. We wanted to show you that even without any formal experience you can recognize and to some degree interpret messages that other people send nonverbally. In this chapter we want to sharpen the skills you already have, to give you a better grasp of the vocabulary of nonverbal language, and to show you how this understanding can help you understand yourself and others better.

You can't not communicate   The fact that communication without words took place between you and your partner brings us to this second important feature of nonverbal communication. To understand what we mean here, think back to the experience you just finshed. Suppose we'd asked you not to communicate any messages at all while with your partner. What would you have done? Closed your eyes? Withdrawn into a ball? Left the room? You can probably see that even these behaviors communicate messages that mean you're avoiding contact.

HE THAT HAS EYES TO SEE AND
EARS TO HEAR MAY CONVINCE
HIMSELF THAT NO MORTAL CAN
KEEP A SECRET. IF HIS LIPS ARE
SILENT, HE CHATTERS WITH HIS
FINGER TIPS; BETRAYAL OOZES
OUT OF HIM AT EVERY PORE.

FREUD

Take a minute now to try *not* communicating. Make a dyad with the person sitting next to you, and spend some time trying not to communicate anything to one another. What happened?

This impossibility of not communicating is extremely important because it means that each of us is a kind of transmitter that cannot be shut off. No matter what we do, we send out messages that say something about ourselves.

Stop for a moment and examine yourself as you read this. If someone were observing you now, what nonverbal clues would they get about how you're feeling? Are you sitting forward or reclining back? Is your posture tense or relaxed? Are your eyes wide open or do they keep closing? What does your facial expression communicate now? Can you make your face expressionless? Don't people with expressionless faces communicate something to you?

The fact that you and everyone around you are constantly sending off nonverbal clues is important because it means that you have a constant source of information available about yourself and others. If you can tune into these signals, you'll be more aware of how those around you are feeling and thinking, and you'll be better able to respond to their behavior.

Nonverbal communication transmits feelings As you study this subject, you'll find that even though feelings are communicated quite well nonverbally, thoughts don't lend themselves to nonverbal channels.

Think back to the exercise at the beginning of the chapter. Do you recall the different kinds of messages that you sent and received in the talking and nontalking parts of it? Most people find that in the first parts (where they communicate verbally) they talk about what they *think*: "Does the exercise seem like a good or bad one?"; "What have you been doing lately?"; "Did you do your reading?"; and so on. Quite different kinds of messages usually come across in the last step, however. Without being able to use words, peoples' bodies generally express how they *feel*—nervous, embarrassed, playful, friendly, et cetera.

You can test this another way. Here's a list that contains both thoughts and feelings. Try to express each item nonverbally, and see which ones come most easily:

You're tired.

You're in favor of capital punishment.

You're attracted to another person in the group.

You think marijuana should be legalized.

You're angry at someone in the group.

Beware of the man
whose belly does not
move when he laughs.

Chinese Proverb

Double messages   Knowing that people express their feelings by their actions is important when you keep in mind this fourth characteristic of nonverbal communication. People often simultaneously express different and even contradictory messages in their verbal and nonverbal behaviors. A common example of this sort of "double message" is the experience we've all had of hearing someone with a red face and bulging veins yelling, "Angry? No, *I'm not angry!*"

Usually, however, the contradiction between words and nonverbal clues isn't this obvious. At times we all try to seem different than we are. There are many reasons for this contradictory behavior: to cover nervousness when giving a speech or in a job interview, to keep someone from worrying about us, or to appear more attractive than we believe we really are.

As we discuss the different kinds of nonverbal communication throughout this chapter, we'll point out a number of ways in which people contradict themselves by either conscious or unconscious behaviors. Thus, by the end of this chapter you should have a better idea of how others feel, even when they can't or won't tell you with their words.

Nonverbal communication is ambiguous   Before you get the idea that merely reading this chapter will turn you into some sort of mind reader, we want to caution you and in so doing introduce a fifth feature of nonverbal communication: A great deal of ambiguity surrounds nonverbal behavior. To understand what we mean, how would you interpret silence from your spouse, date, or companion after an evening in which you both laughed and joked a lot? Can you think of at least two possible meanings for this nonverbal behavior? Or suppose that a much admired person with whom you've worked suddenly begins paying more attention to you than ever before. What could the possible meanings of this be?

The point is that although nonverbal behavior can be very revealing, it can have so many possible meanings that it's foolish to think that your interpretations will always be correct. Our suggestion is that when you become aware of nonverbal messages in your everyday life, you should think of them not as facts but as *clues* that need to be checked out.

Reading Body Language

Before we begin discussing the many channels of communication besides words that exist, here's an exercise that will both increase your skill in observing nonverbal behavior and show you the dangers of being too sure that you're a perfect reader of body language. You can try the exercise either in or out of class, and the period of time over which you do it is flexible, from a single class period to several days. In any case begin by choosing a partner, and then follow these directions:

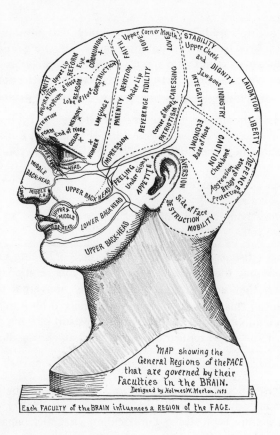

MAP showing the
General Regions of the FACE
that are governed by their
Faculties in the BRAIN.
Designed by Holmes W. Merton. 1899

Each FACULTY of the BRAIN influences a REGION of the FACE.

1 For the first period of time (however long you decide to make it), observe the way your partner behaves. Notice how she moves, her mannerisms, postures, the way she speaks, how she dresses, et cetera. To remember your observations, jot them down. If you're doing this exercise out of class over an extended period of time, there's no need to let your observations interfere with whatever you'd normally be doing: Your only job here is to compile a list of your partner's behaviors. In this step you should be careful *not* to *interpret* your partner's actions; just record what you *see*.

2 At the end of the time period share what you've seen with your partner. She'll do the same with you.

3 For the next period of time your job is to not only observe your partner's behavior but also to *interpret* it. This time in your conference you should tell your partner what you thought her actions said about her. For example, if she dressed carelessly, did you think this meant she overslept, that she's losing interest in her appearance, or that she was trying to be more com-

fortable? If you noticed her yawning frequently, did you think this meant she was bored, tired from a late night, or sleepy after a big meal? Don't feel bad if your guesses weren't all correct. Remember, nonverbal clues tend to be ambiguous. You may be surprised how checking out the nonverbal clues you observe can help build a relationship with another person.

4   At the end of the third and final time period again tell your partner what behaviors you observed and what you think they meant. But this time you should also share how they made *you* feel. For example, your partner may have looked at you with an expression that you interpreted as anger or disgust. In such a case explain

    a. what you saw
    b. what you thought it meant
    c. how you felt

Don't get into a discussion about the correctness of having such a feeling: You did have it, and that makes it important to your relationship. You may find, however, that your interpretation of the nonverbal behavior was mistaken, and in this case your feeling was caused by a mistake. If this happened, you might ask yourself how often this sort of thing occurs in your life. What can you do to reduce this kind of misunderstanding?

This exercise should have showed you the difference between merely observing somebody's behavior and interpreting it. Noticing someone's shaky hands or smile is one thing, but deciding what such behaviors mean is quite another. If you're like most people, you probably found that a lot of your guesses were incorrect. Now, if that was true here, it may also be true in your daily life. Being a sharp nonverbal observer can give you some good hunches about how people are feeling, but the only way you can find out if these hunches are correct is to *check them out* verbally.

You may also have found that sharing your feelings with your partner expanded your relationship with that person. As we said in the defensiveness chapter, simply describing your feelings using "I" language is a good way of gaining understanding.

Keeping the five characteristics of nonverbal communication in mind, let's take a look at some of the ways we communicate in addition to words.

Proxemics—Distance as Nonverbal Communication

Proxemics is the study of the way people and animals use space. As you'll see by the end of this chapter, you can sometimes tell how people are feeling toward each other simply by noting the distance between them. To begin to understand how this is so, try this exercise.

I suppose it was something you said
That caused me to tighten
And pull away.
And when you asked,
"What is it?"
I, of course, said,
"Nothing."

Whenever I say, "Nothing,"
You may be very certain there is something.
The something is a cold, hard lump of
Nothing.

Lois Wyse

Distance Makes a Difference

1   Choose a partner, and go to opposite sides of the room and face each other.

2   Very slowly begin walking toward each other while carrying on a conversation. You might simply talk about how you feel as you experience the activity. As you move closer, try to be aware of any change in your feelings. Continue moving slowly toward each other until you are only an inch or so apart. Remember how you feel at this point.

3   Now, while still facing each other, back up until you're at a comfortable distance for carrying on your conversation.

4   Share your feelings with each other and/or the whole group.

During this experiment your feelings most likely changed at least three times. During the first phase, when you were across the room from your partner, you probably felt unnaturally far away. Then, as you neared a point about three feet from him, you probably felt like stopping; this is the distance at which two people in our culture normally stand while conversing socially. If your partner wasn't someone you're emotionally close to, you probably began to feel quite uncomfortable as you moved through this normal range and came closer; it's possible that you had to force yourself not to move back. Some people find this phase so uncomfortable that they can't get closer than twenty inches or so to their partner.

The reason for your discomfort has to do with your territorial needs. Each of us carries around a sort of invisible bubble of personal space

an example of a person

You

wherever we go. We think of the area inside this bubble as our private territory—almost as much a part of us as our own bodies. As you moved closer to your partner, the distance between your bubbles narrowed and at a certain point disappeared altogether: Your territory had been invaded, and this is the point at which you probably felt uncomfortable. As you moved away again, your partner retreated out of your bubble, and you felt more relaxed.

Of course, if you were to try this experiment with someone very close to you—your husband, wife, girl- or boyfriend, you might not have felt any discomfort at all, even while touching. On the other hand, if you'd been approaching someone who made you uncomfortable—a total stranger or someone you dislike—you probably would have stopped farther away from them. The reason for this is that our personal bubbles vary in size according to the person we're with and the situation we're in. And it's precisely this variable size of our personal space—the distance that we put between ourselves and others—which gives a nonverbal clue about our feelings.

Anthropologist Edward T. Hall has defined four distances that we use in our everyday lives. He says that we choose a particular one depending upon how we feel toward the other person at a given time and that by "reading" which distance a person takes, we can get some insight into his feelings.

Intimate distance The first of Hall's zones begins with skin contact and ranges out to about eighteen inches. We usually use intimate distance with people who are emotionally very close to us, and then mostly in private situations—making love, caressing, comforting, protecting. By allowing someone to move into our intimate distance we're letting them enter our territory. When we do this voluntarily, it's usually a sign of trust: We've willingly lowered our defenses. On the other hand, when someone invades this most personal area without our consent, we usually feel threatened. This explains the feeling you may have had during the last exercise when your partner intruded into your space without any real invitation from you. It also explains the discomfort we sometimes feel when forced into crowded places like buses or elevators with strangers. At times like these the standard behavior in our society is to draw away or tense our muscles and avoid eye contact. This is a nonverbal way of signaling, "I'm sorry for invading your territory, but the situation forced it."

In courtship situations a critical moment usually occurs when one member of a couple first moves into the other's intimate zone. If the partner being approached does not retreat, this usually signals that the relationship is moving into a new stage. On the other hand, if the reaction to the advance is withdrawal to a greater distance, the initiator should get the message that it isn't yet time to get more intimate. We remember from our dating experiences the significance of where on the car seat our companions chose to sit. If they moved close to us, it meant one thing; if they stayed jammed against the passenger's door, we got quite a different message.

Nonverbal Communication: Messages Without Words

Some thirty inches from my nose
The frontier of my Person goes,
And all the untilled air between
Is private *pagus* or demense.
Stranger, unless with bedroom eyes
I beckon you to fraternize,
Beware of rudely crossing it:
I have no gun, but I can spit.

W. H. Auden

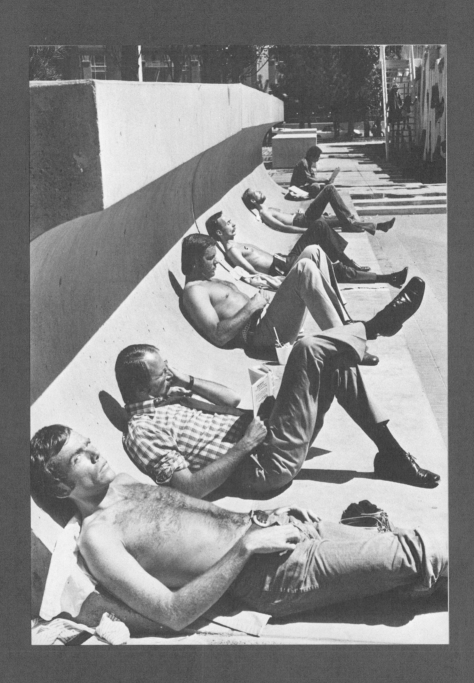

Personal distance This second spatial zone ranges from eighteen inches at its closest point to four feet at its farthest. Its closer phase is the distance at which most couples stand in public. But if someone of the opposite sex stands this near one partner at a party, the other partner is likely to feel uncomfortable. This "moving in" often is taken to mean that something more than casual conversation is taking place. The far range of personal distance runs from about two and a half to four feet. It's the zone just beyond the other person's reach. As Hall puts it, at this distance we can keep someone "at arm's length." This choice of words suggests the type of communication that goes on at this range: The contacts are still reasonably close, but they're much less personal than the ones that occur a foot or so closer.

Test this for yourself. Start a conversation with someone at a distance of about three feet, and slowly move a foot or so closer. Do you notice a difference? Does the distance affect your conversation?

Social distance This third zone ranges from four to about twelve feet out. Within it are the kinds of communication that usually occur in business situations. Its closer phase, from four to seven feet, is the distance at which conversations usually occur between salespeople and customers and between people who work together. Most people feel uncomfortable when a salesclerk comes as close as three feet, whereas four or five feet nonverbally signals "I'm here to help you, but I don't mean to be too personal or pushy."

Take a minute now to role play a customer-salesperson scene. Try it first at five feet and then at three. Which one seems most natural?

We use the far range of social distance—seven to twelve feet—for more formal and impersonal situations. This is the range at which we sit from our boss (or other authority figure) as he stares across his desk at us. Sitting at this distance signals a far different and less relaxed type of conversation than if we were to pull a chair around to the boss's side of the desk and sit only three or so feet away.

The interrogator should sit fairly close to the subject, and between the two there should be no table, desk, or other piece of furniture. Distance or the presence of an obstruction of any sort constitutes a serious psychological barrier and also affords the subject a certain degree of relief and confidence not otherwise attainable. . . .

As to the psychological validity of the above suggested seating arrangement, reference may be made to the commonplace but yet meaningful expressions such as "getting next" to a person, or the "buttonholing" of a customer by a salesman. These expressions signify that when a person is close to another one physically, he is closer to him psychologically. Anything such as a desk or a table between the interrogator and the subject defeats the purpose and should be avoided.

INBAU AND REID, *Criminal Interrogation and Confessions*

Public distance This is Hall's term for the farthest zone, running outward from twelve feet. The closer range of public distance is the one that most teachers use in the classroom. In the farther reaches of public space—25 feet and beyond—two-way communication is almost impossible. In some cases it's necessary for speakers to use public distance due to the size of their audience, but we can assume that anyone who voluntarily chooses to use it when he could be closer is not interested in having a dialog.

Physical invasion isn't the only way people penetrate our spatial bubble; we're just as uncomfortable when someone intrudes on our visual territory. If you've had the unpleasant experience of being stared at, you know this can be just as threatening as having someone get too close. In most situations, however, people respect each others' visual privacy. You can test this the next time you're walking in public. As you approach another person notice how he'll shift his glance away from you at a distance of a few paces, almost like a visual dimming of headlights. Generally, strangers maintain eye contact at a close distance only when they want something—information, assistance, signatures on a petition, recognition, a handout, et cetera.

The way people use space can communicate a good deal about power and status relationships. Generally we grant people with higher status more personal territory and greater privacy. We knock before entering our boss's office, whereas she can usually walk into our work area without hesitating. In traditional schools professors have offices, dining rooms, and even toilets

. . . *Leipold . . . studied the distance at which introverted and extroverted college students placed themselves in relation to an interviewer in either a stress or a nonstress situation. When the student entered, he was given either the stress, praise, or neutral instructions. The stress instructions were, "We feel that your course grade is quite poor and that you have not tried your best. Please take a seat in the next room and Mr. Leipold will be in shortly to discuss this with you." The neutral control instructions read, "Mr. Leipold is interested in your feelings about the introductory course. Would you please take a seat in the next room." [The praise instructions were, "You are doing very well in this course and Mr. Leipold wants to talk to you further. Please take a seat in the next room."] After the student had entered and seated himself, Mr. Leipold came in, recorded the student's seating position, and conducted the interview. The results showed that students given praise sat closest to Leipold's chair, followed by those in the neutral condition, with students given the stress instructions maintaining the most distance from Leipold's chair behind the desk. It was also found that introverted and anxious individuals sat further away from him than did extroverted students with a lower anxiety level.*

ROBERT SOMMER, *Personal Space*

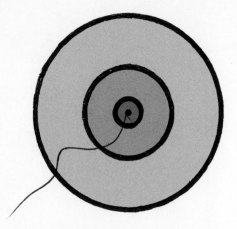

that are private, while the students, who are presumably less important, have no such sanctuaries. In the military greater space and privacy usually come with rank: Privates sleep forty to a barracks, sergeants have their own private rooms, and generals have government-provided houses.

For a period of several days keep track of the role space plays in your life. Notice the distance between you and others. Does it change according to the situation? What does the distance between you and someone else say about your relationship? How would the relationship change if you moved closer or farther away? How would it change if the other person moved?

The next area of nonverbal communication we want to talk about is the broad field of *kinesics,* or body motion. In this section we'll explore the role that posture, gestures, body orientation, facial expressions, and eye behaviors play in our relationships with each other.

Body Orientation

We'll start with body orientation—the degree to which we face toward or away from someone with our body, feet, and head. To understand how this kind of physical positioning communicates nonverbal messages you might try an experiment.

You'll need two friends to help you. Imagine that two of you are in the middle of a personal conversation when a third person approaches and wants to join you. You're not especially glad to see this person, but you don't want to sound rude by asking her to leave. Your task is to signal to the intruder that you'd rather be alone, using only the position of your bodies. You can talk to the third person if you wish, but you can't verbally tell her that you want privacy.

she dresses in flags
comes on
like a mack truck
she paints
her eyelids green
and her mouth
is a loud speaker
rasping out
profanity

at cocktail parties
she is everywhere
like a sheep dog
working a flock
nipping at your sleeve
spilling your drink
bestowing
wet sloppy kisses

but i
have received
secret messages
carefully written
from the shy
quiet woman
who hides
in this
bizarre
gaudy castle

Ric Masten

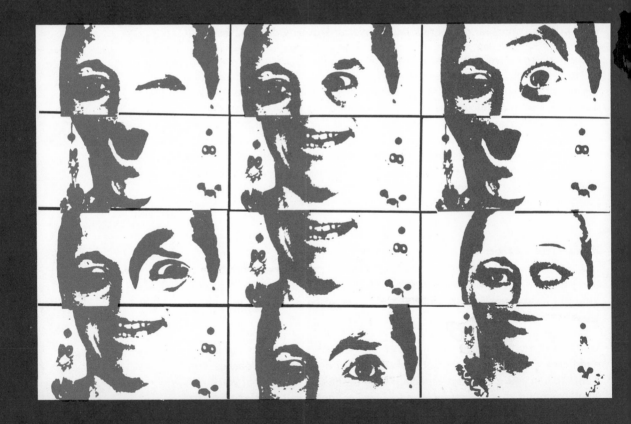

When you've tried this experiment, or if you've ever been in a real-life situation similar to it, you know that by turning your body slightly away from an intruder you can make your feelings very clear. An intruder finds herself in the difficult position of trying to talk over your shoulder, and it isn't long before she gets the message and goes her way. The nonverbal message here is "Look, we're interested in each other right now and don't want to include you in our conversation." The general rule this situation describes is that facing someone directly signals your interest, and facing away signals a desire to avoid involvement. This explains how we can pack ourselves into intimate distance with total strangers in places like a crowded elevator without offending others. Because there's a very indirect orientation here (everyone is usually standing shoulder to shoulder, facing in the same direction), we understand that despite the close quarters everyone wants to avoid personal contact.

By observing the way people position themselves you can learn a good deal about how they feel. Next time you're in a crowded place where people can choose whom to face directly, try observing who seems to be included in the action and who is being subtly shut out. And in the same way, pay attention to your own body orientation. You may be surprised to discover that you're avoiding a certain person without being conscious of it or that at times you're "turning your back" on people altogether. If this is the case, it may be helpful to figure out why. Are you avoiding an unpleasant situation that needs clearing up, communicating your annoyance or dislike for the other, or sending some other message?

Posture

Another way we communicate nonverbally is through our posture.

To see if this is true, stop reading for a moment and notice how you're sitting. What does your position say nonverbally about how you feel? Are there any other people near you now? What messages do you get from their present posture? By paying attention to the postures of those around you, as well as your own, you'll find another channel of nonverbal communication that can furnish information about how people feel about themselves and each other.

An indication of how much posture communicates is shown by our language. It's full of expressions that link emotional states with body postures:

I won't take this lying down!
He can stand on his own two feet.

She has to carry a heavy burden.

Take a load off your back.

'He's all wrapped up in himself.

Don't be so uptight!

Such phrases show that an awareness of posture exists for us, even if it's often unconscious. The main reason we miss most posture messages is that they aren't very obvious. It's seldom that a person who feels weighted down by a problem hunches over so much that he stands out in a crowd, and when we're bored we usually don't lean back and slump enough to embarrass the other person. In reading posture, then, the key is to look for small changes that might be shadows of the way people feel inside.

For example, a teacher who has a reputation for interesting classes told us how he uses his understanding of micropostures to do a better job. "Because of my large classes I have to lecture a lot," he said, "And that's an easy way to turn students off. I work hard to make my talks entertaining, but you know that nobody's perfect, and I do have my off days. I can tell when I'm not doing a good job of communicating by picking out three or four students before I start my talk and watching how they sit throughout the class period. As long as they're leaning forward in their seats, I know I'm

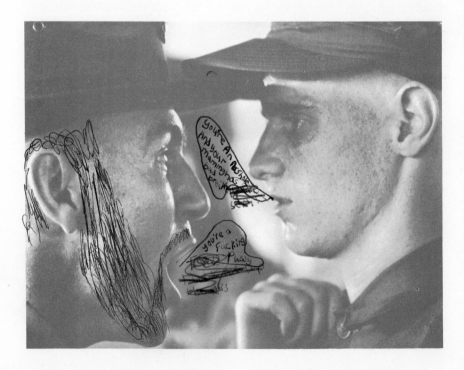

Nonverbal Communication: Messages Without Words

doing okay, but if I look up and see them starting to slump back, I know I'd better change my approach."

Psychologist Albert Mehrabian has found that other postural keys to feelings are tension and relaxation. He says that we take relaxed postures in nonthreatening situations and tighten up when threatened. Based on this observation he says we can tell a good deal about how others feel simply by watching how tense or loose they seem to be. For example, he suggests that watching tenseness is a way of detecting status differences: The lower-status person is generally the more rigid, tense-appearing one, whereas the one with higher status is more relaxed. This is the kind of situation that often happens when we picture a "chat" with the boss (or professor, judge, et cetera) where we sit ramrod straight while she leans back in her chair. The same principle applies to social situations, where it's often possible to tell who's uncomfortable by looking at pictures. Often you'll see someone laughing and talking as if he were perfectly at home, but his posture almost shouts nervousness. Some people never relax, and their posture shows it.

Try spending an hour or so observing the posture of those around you. See if you can get some idea of how they're feeling by the way they carry themselves. Also, pay attention to your own posture. In what situations do you tense up? Is this a sign of anger, aggressiveness, excitement, fear? Do you ever find yourself signaling boredom, interest, attraction, or other emotions by your posture? Do the feelings you find yourself expressing posturally ever surprise you?

Gestures

Gestures are another good source of nonverbal communication. In an article titled "Nonverbal Leakage and Clues to Deception" Paul Eckman and Wallace Friesen observed how gestures transmit emotions. They explained that because most of us, at least unconsciously, know that the face is the most obvious channel of expressing emotions, we're especially careful to control our facial expressions when trying to hide our feelings. But most of us are less aware of the ways we move our hands, legs, and feet, and because of this these movements are better indicators of how we truly feel.

Probably the clearest example of someone whose feelings show through her gestures is the fidgeter. She's the kind of person who assures us that "everything is fine" while almost ceaselessly biting her fingernails, flicking her cigarette, bending paperclips, and so on. Even when the fidgeter is aware of these gestures and tries to control them, her nervousness usually finds another way of leaking out, such as toe tapping, leg crossing and uncrossing, or other restless movements.

Besides nervousness, you can often detect other emotions from a person's gestures. It's possible to observe her anger by looking beyond her smile and noticing her whitened knuckles and clenched fists. When she'd like to express her friendship or attraction toward us, but for some reason feels she can't, we can sometimes notice her slightly reaching out or maybe even opening her hands. We've even seen those who proclaim to all how open and honest they want to be while their gestures suggest something different: talking from behind a hand, folding their arms across their chests, or turning away from us. In one article, Paul Scheflen, a psychiatrist, tells how a person's sexual feelings can be signaled through gestures. He describes "preening behaviors" that draw attention to the sender's body and advertise a "come-on" message. Movements such as stroking or combing the hair, glancing in a mirror, and rearranging the clothing are often signals of sexual interest in another person.

Eckman and Friesen describe another kind of double message—the "lie of omission." The deceiver nonverbally shows his true feelings by failing to accompany his words with the appropriate gestures. This is the kind of behavior we see from a person who says he's excited or happy while sitting almost motionless with hands, arms, legs, and posture signaling boredom, discomfort, or fatigue.

Nonverbal Feedback

1 Choose a partner, and form a group of about five pairs.

2 Sit in two concentric circles, with one partner in each circle. People on the outside should sit so they can easily see their partner.

3 Now, for fifteen minutes or so the inside group should carry on a discussion about some subject that will generate lots of personal feelings. (Some possible topics are: would you want your teenage child to smoke marijuana, and should capital punishment be abolished?)

4 During this time people in the outside circle should observe their partner, noticing as many characteristic gestures, postures, facial expressions, and other nonverbal clues as possible.

5 After fifteen minutes the partners should meet. The observer can now feed back his partner's nonverbal behavior, being careful only to describe and not to interpret it. After this description the partner who was observed may want to discuss what nonverbal messages she might have been sending.

6 Now switch places and repeat steps 2 to 5, discussing a new topic.

I don't want to disgrace you—

    I've shined up my bones and
    smoothed my skin in quiet
    folds around me, arranged
    my limbs tastefully
    in elegant lines that none may see
    elbow or knee, i've instructed
    my jaw not to grin nor jape,
    my lips to stay firmly in place:

    I shall not blink nor stare
    nor will a hair upon my head
    move, and I can hold my feet
    still, that not a toe will tumble:

I don't want to disgrace you—

    but my hands have their own
    history and instinctively
    at your entrance

    rise to your face

                    Gerald Huckaby

CLOSE TO THE VEST

. . . the expert [poker player] is a psychologist.

He is continually studying the other players to see, first, if they have any telltale habits, and second, if there are any situations in which they act automatically.

In connection with general habits, I divide poker players into three classes

    (a) the ingenuous player,

    (b) the tricky, or coffee-housing player,

    (c) the unreadable player.

The ingenuous player When the ingenuous player looks worried, he probably is worried.

When he takes a long time to bet, he probably doesn't think much of his hand.

When he bets quickly, he fancies his hand.

When he bluffs, he looks a little guilty, and when he really has a good hand, you can see him mentally wishing to be called.

This ingenuousness, incidently, is seldom found in veteran players. A player of this type usually quits poker at an early stage on account of his "bad luck."

The tricky or coffee-housing player At least ninety percent of all poker players fall into this category.

The tricky player has a great tendency to act just opposite of the way he really feels. Thus with a very good hand, he trembles a little as he bets, while with a poor hand, he fairly exudes confidence. Of course, he may be triple-crossing, but year-in and year-out I have played in a great many games, and have found that at least two times out of three when another player makes a special effort to look confident, he has nothing, while when he tries to look nervous, he is loaded.

There is one mild little coffee-housing habit that practically never fails to act as a giveaway.

That is showing too much nonchalance. For instance, it is my turn to bet, and as I am about to put my chips in the pot, one of the other players casually lights a cigarette. Experience tells me that this casual player is at least going to call me, and is very likely to raise me if I bet.

Accordingly, if I do see that sign, unless my hand is really very good, I refuse to bet for him and simply check.

The unreadable player This particular individual is, of course, the hardest opponent of all.

Invariably, he knows all the rules of correct play, but departs from all of them on occasion. Unlike the ingenuous player, who acts the way he feels, or the coffee-house, who acts the way he doesn't feel, this player has no consistency.

Accordingly, the fact that he exudes confidence or looks nervous gives no clue to the nature of his hand.

The preceding discussion has been of a very general nature. Here are a few specific giveaway habits I have noticed.

(It should be borne in mind that poker has no ethics, except in a few obvious and specific instances and that short of actually cheating, which, by the way, includes attempting to peek at another player's hand, you have the right to any advantage you can gain.)

Glancing to the left In the early stages of betting, a player with a normal calling hand usually comes into the pot with no fuss whatsoever. However, a player with a good hand is going to consider raising, and before betting, is likely to cast a covert glance toward the players in back of him (on his left) to see if he can get any idea of what they are going to do.

If it looks to him as if two or three of them are

going to call, he sandbags. If it looks as if they are all going to drop, he raises.

Accordingly, when I see this glance, even though the player merely calls, I am fairly sure that his hand is fully strong enough for a raise.

Looking at the hole card the second time The very best stud players, of course, look at their hole card once, and then know it for the rest of the hand, but the average player, particularly with a low card in the hole, is likely to be careless and not remember it.

Accordingly, there are many instances where a second glance at the hole card gives a lot of information.

For instance:

The first bettor shows an ace. On the next card, he receives a six, and promptly looks at his hole card. At this point, there is a very strong presumption that his hole card is a six or very close to it.

Piling chips on your hole card This is probably the most telltale giveaway habit of all.

Before the second card is dealt, a player looks at his hole card. If it is a low card, he pays no attention to it, but if it is a high card he is quite likely to put it down and pile some chips on top of it immediately, to prevent any possibility of it blowing over.

I know I must have seen chips piled on top of the hole card in that situation hundreds of times, and I do not recall more than two or three instances where the card was lower than a jack, and very few when it was not an ace or a king.

Looking at your draw In Draw Poker, it is the exceptional player who will simply pick up the cards and look at them. The average player has various methods of mixing his draw with his hand, squeezing the cards, looking at them one at a time, etc.

While little can be learned about the nature of a player's hand from the manner in which he looks at his draw, there is one pretty general giveaway in connection with a one-card draw.

A player drawing to a flush or two pair is likely to put the card he draws in the middle of his hand. A player drawing to an open straight invariably puts the card either on top or bottom.

Oswald Jacoby, *Oswald Jacoby on Poker*

The Face and Eyes

The face and eyes are probably the most noticed parts of the body, but this doesn't mean that their nonverbal messages are the easiest to read. The face is a tremendously complicated channel of expression for several reasons.

First, it's hard even to describe the number and kind of expressions we commonly produce with our face and eyes. For example, researchers have found that there are at least eight distinguishable positions of the eyebrows and forehead, eight more of the eyes and lids, and ten for the lower face. When you multiply this complexity by the number of emotions we experience, you can see why it would be almost impossible to compile a dictionary of facial expressions and their corresponding emotions.

Another reason for the difficulty in understanding facial expressions is the speed with which they can change. For example, slow-motion films have been taken that show expressions fleeting across a subject's face in as short a time as a fifth of a second. Also, it seems that different emotions show most clearly in different parts of the face: happiness and surprise in the eyes and lower face, anger in the lower face and brows and forehead, fear and sadness in the eyes, and disgust in the lower face.

In spite of the complex way in which the face shows emotions, you can still pick up messages by watching it. One of the easiest ways is to look for expressions that seem to be overdone. Often when someone is trying to fool himself or another he'll emphasize his mask to a point where it seems too exaggerated to be true. Another way to detect a person's feelings is by watching his expression at moments when he isn't likely to be thinking about his appearance. We've all had the experience of glancing into another car while stopped in a traffic jam or looking around at a sporting event and seeing expressions that the wearer would probably never show in more guarded moments. At other times it's possible to watch a microexpression as it flashes across a person's face. For just a moment we see a flash of emotion quite different from the one a speaker is trying to convey. Finally, you may be able to spot contradictory expressions on different parts of someone's face: His eyes say one thing, but the expression of his mouth or eyebrows might be sending quite a different message.

The eyes themselves can send several kinds of messages. Meeting someone's glance with your eyes is usually a sign of involvement, while looking away signals a desire to avoid contact. As we mentioned earlier, this is why solicitors on the street—panhandlers, salesmen, petitioners—try to catch our eye. Once they've managed to establish contact with a glance, it becomes harder for the approached person to draw away. A friend explained how to apply this principle to hitchhiking. "When I'm hitching a ride, I'm always careful to look each driver in the eye as he comes toward me. Most of them will try to look somewhere else as they pass, but if I can catch somebody's eye, he'll almost always stop." Most of us remember trying to avoid a question we didn't understand by glancing away from the teacher. At times like these we usually became very interested in our textbooks, fingernails, the clock—anything but the teacher's stare. Of course, the teacher always seemed to know the meaning of this nonverbal behavior and ended up picking on those of us who signaled our uncertainty.

Another kind of message the eyes communicate is a positive or negative attitude. When someone glances toward us with the proper facial expression, we get a clear message that the looker is interested in us, thus the expression "making eyes." At the same time, when our long glances toward someone else are avoided by him, we can be pretty sure that the other person isn't as interested in us as we are in him. (Of course, there are all sorts of courtship games in which the receiver of a glance pretends not to notice any message by glancing away, yet signals his interest with some other part of the body.)

The eyes communicate both dominance and submisson. We've all played the game of trying to stare down somebody, and in real life there are also times when downcast eyes are a sign of giving in. In some religious orders, for example, subordinate members are expected to keep their eyes downcast when addressing a superior.

Even the pupils of our eyes communicate. E. H. Hess and J. M. Polt of the University of Chicago measured the amount of pupil dilation while showing men and women various types of pictures. The results of the experiment were very interesting: A person's eyes grow larger in proportion to the degree of interest they have in an object. For example, men's pupils grew about eighteen percent larger when looking at pictures of a naked woman, and the rate of dilation for women looking at a naked man's picture was twenty percent. Interestingly enough, the greatest increase in pupil size occurred when women looked at a picture of a mother and infant. A good salesman can increase his profits by being aware of pupil dilation, as Edward Hall describes. He was once in a Middle East bazaar, where an Arab merchant insisted that a customer looking at his jewelry buy a certain piece that the shopper hadn't been paying much attention to. But the vendor had been watching the pupils of the buyer's eyes and had known what the buyer really wanted.

Voice

The voice itself is another channel of nonverbal communication. We don't mean the words we say, which after all make up verbal communication, but rather *how* we say them. If you think about it for a moment, you'll realize that a certain way of speaking can give the same word or words many meanings. For example, look at the possible meanings from a single sentence just by changing the word emphasis:

This is a fantastic communication book.
   (Not just any book, but *this* one in particular.)

This is a *fantastic* communication book.
   (This book is superior, exciting.)

This is a fantastic *communication* book.
   (The book is good as far as communication goes; it may not be so great as literature, drama, et cetera.)

This is a fantastic communication *book.*
   (It's not a play or record, it's a book.)

It's possible to get an idea across without ever expressing it outright by emphasizing a certain word in a sentence. In his book *Nonverbal Communication in Human Interaction,* Mark Knapp quotes an example from *Newsweek* on how this is done. It describes how Robert J. McCloskey, a State Department official in the Nixon administration, was able to express the government's position in an off-the-record way:

McCloskey has three distinct ways of saying, "I would not speculate": spoken without accent, it means the department doesn't know for sure; emphasis on the "I" means "I wouldn't, but you may—and with some assurance"; accent on "speculate" indicates that the questioner's premise is probably wrong.

There are many other ways our voice communicates—through its tone, speed, pitch, and number and length of pauses, volume, find disfluencies (such as stammering, use of "uh," "um," "er," and so on). All these factors together can be called "paralanguage," and they can do a great deal to reinforce or contradict the message our words convey.

Sarcasm is one instance in which we use both emphasis and tone of voice to change a statement's meaning to the opposite of its verbal message. Experience this yourself with the following three statements. First time through mean them literally, and then say them sarcastically.

Darling, what a beautiful little gown!

I really had a wonderful time on my blind date.

There's nothing I like better than calves' brains on toast.

Albert Mehrabian and others have conducted experiments which indicate that when the vocal factors (tone of voice, disfluencies, emphasis, et cetera) contradict the verbal message (words), the vocal factors carry more meaning. They had subjects evaluate the degree of liking communicated by a message in which vocal clues conflicted with the words and found that the words had very little effect on the interpretation of the message.

Communication through paralanguage isn't always intentional. Often our voices give us away when we're trying to create an impression different from our actual feelings. For example, you've probably had experiences of trying to sound calm and serene when you were really exploding with inner nervousness. Maybe your deception went along perfectly for a while—just the right smile, no telltale fidgeting of the hands, posture appearing relaxed—and then, without being able to do a thing about it, right in the middle of your relaxed comments your voice squeaked! The charade was over.

Nonverbal Communication: Messages Without Words   257

When a husband comes home from the office, takes off his hat, hangs up his coat, and says "Hi" to his wife, the way in which he says "Hi", reinforced by the manner in which he sheds his overcoat, summarizes his feelings about the way things went at the office. If his wife wants the details she may have to listen for a while, yet she grasps in an instant the significant message for her; namely, what kind of evening they are going to spend and how she is going to have to cope with it.

Edward Hall, *The Silent Language*

Voice Messages

Here's an experiment that can give you an idea of some messages your voice communicates.

1 Choose a partner, and find a space for yourselves.

2 Now close your eyes. You'll be focusing on the voice as a means of communication; this will help screen out other kinds of nonverbal messages.

3 For five minutes carry on a conversation about whatever you want. As you talk, listen to your partner's voice. Try not to concentrate as much on the *words* as the way your partner *sounds*. Imagine what messages you'd receive if you were listening to a foreign language.

4 Now with your eyes still shut tell your partner what messages you received from the sound of her voice. Did it sound tired, relaxed, happy, tense? Share your perceptions.

5 Still keeping your eyes closed, take turns performing the following step. The first person begins a sentence with the words "I am my voice . . . ," completing the statement by describing whatever he hears his voice communicating. For example: "I am my voice and I'm very excited. I'm high-pitched and fast, and I can go on and on without stopping"; or "I am my voice, and I'm tired. I hardly ever say anything, and when I do, it's very quietly. It hardly takes anything to make me stop."

6 After both partners have completed the previous step, take turns sharing your perceptions of your partner's description of her voice. Do you agree with the interpretation, or did you pick up different messages?

7 As you talk with others both in and outside of class, try to listen to the messages your voice sends. Can you tell when you're sincere and when you're being untruthful? Do you have a different voice for certain occasions with: parents, employers, teachers, certain friends? Do you have a happy, bored, angry voice? What do these different voices say about the relationships in which you use them?

An interesting variation of this exercise is to spend five minutes or so holding a conversation with your partner in gibberish. Say whatever nonsense syllables come to your mind, and see what happens. If you can get over the fear of sounding foolish for a few minutes (is this so horrible?), you'll probably find that you can communicate a great deal with your voice, even without words.

THE GIRL WITH THE BRACES

Sometimes a commercial—yes, a commercial!—portrays a real-life situation with such accuracy and perception that you find yourself deeply affected by it. Colgate's recent spot is a notable example.

On TV, you wait for the moments of truth. Sometimes it's a long wait between moments, and of course it's a chancy thing because you can't watch everything on the tube, so a choice moment may crop up while you're busily watching something else. But fortunately, since moments of truth are more likely to be found on TV commercials than on regular programming, the constant repetition of commercials—usually a viewer's bane—practically guarantees that you will confront the moment sooner or later.

The reason such moments happen in commercials rather than in TV dramatic or sitcom shows is that the latter, for the most part, have given up any effort at truthconveying—that is, dealing with real people in real situations, instead of stereotypes in cartoon-strip situations—while commercials, quite frequently, do attempt to deal with reality, not out of any particular devotion to truth, but out of the conviction that viewers will be more apt to buy a product if the people shown using that product are presented believably. The trouble is, the real-life portrayed in TV commercials is not so real as to conceivably disturb viewers. It's a smoothed-over, less serious real-life, most of the angst removed. The people depicted, although they are fairly recognizable as real people, are—in the immortal words of the old-time Hollywood mogul—happy people with happy problems.

But once in a while, in these commercials that venture to the edge of reality, something happens to push them right over the edge. Occasionally a mo-

ment occurs that strikes the viewer as so truly, sharply observed that it almost has the force of a revelation. It doesn't need to be anything more than a gesture, an inflection, a turn of phrase, a glance—but it hits you so hard, and it moves you so much, that you find yourself looking forward to seeing the same commercial again and again, in order to relive the experience, the moment of truth.

Let's add The Girl With The Braces to this select group of TV epiphanies. By now, most TV viewers west of Zambia are happily familiar with the charming, appealing, anxious pre-teener from the Colgate dental cream commercial ordering a cheeseburger on the lunch line at school while trying unsuccessfully to hide her newly installed braces. Those braces! So ugly, so prominent, such an obvious handicap to a sensitive adolescent struggling uncertainly toward self-esteem.

For most viewers, the great moment in the commercial comes at the end when the girl, her lips closed tight over the braces as the boy is introduced to her, breaks into a delighted, relieved smile as the young man reveals his own extensive orthodontic works. This is a nice moment, all right, but for me it's not *the* moment. *The* moment, in my opinion, comes earlier, when the girl is still in that lunch line and her friend observes, with an excess of enthusiasm, "Oh, you got your braces"—to which our mortified heroine responds: "Wonderful."

That "wonderful" is wonderful. Think about it. The girl might have responded with a tight-lipped, inaudible, inexpressive "YesIgotmybraces," or with an offhand, jocular "Yes, aren't they perfectly awful." Or she simply could have blushed and not replied at all. But instead—and for this a round of applause is due the perceptive creators of the commercial—she says "Wonderful," in a tone of voice and with a look on her face that convey a wealth of feeling and meaning. Discomfort is there in that response, and miserableness, and shy embarrassment. Also, a sort of wry resignation, which betrays an attractively ironic approach to life that, one feels, will serve the kid well in years to come. That expressive "wonderful" acknowledges, too, that she is aware that her friend's innocent observation—OH, YOU GOT YOUR BRACES—just might have a touch of malice to it (the friend seems to have very straight teeth).

Martin Fox

Big Brother Is Listening

It could change forever the relationships between husbands and wives, witnesses and juries, political leaders and voters, businessmen and customers. It could sharply reduce the output of talk all over by making everyone think twice before speaking. It could also bring closer the Orwellian society of *1984*. The remarkable but ominous device that might cause these changes is the P.S.E. (for Psychological Stress Evaluator) which, its inventors believe, can use voice recordings to detect lies without the cooperation or even the presence of the speaker.

The new lie detector is a creation of Dektor Counterintelligence and Security, Inc. of Springfield, Va. It uses an ordinary tape recording of a voice on radio or TV or in any of the numerous settings where lies may be told: in a police station, perhaps, at a press conference, on the speaker's platform at a political meeting, or in the bedroom of a married—or unmarried—couple. The tape is fed into a machine that measures muscular microtremors in the voice, faint quivers that come from the muscles in the voice box and cause slight changes in pitch. Changes are not detectable by ear, but they can be traced on a chart by a pen linked to the machine. It is the capacity to detect and reproduce these tremors—apparently produced by the freely undulating throat muscles of a relaxed speaker—that gives the P.S.E. its awesome powers. For the throat muscles of a person under stress are so tense that they produce practically no microtremors.

Government intelligence agencies have already bought four of the machines (at $3,200 each), allegedly for testing purposes only. Also, by agreement of prosecution and defense, the P.S.E. has been used in four Maryland court cases. In three, negative findings by the device led to dropping one murder and two bad-check charges; in the fourth case, a positive report ensured conviction in a shoplifting incident. In addition, Dektor reports that it has monitored the TV program *To Tell the Truth* and been 94.7% successful in finding out who the truth tellers really were.

P.S.E.'s reliability still has not been proved. No independent agency has double checked the company's TV experiment. Moreover, some lie detector experts caution that the weakness of the stress evaluator may lie in its dependence on a single measure of bodily function (the polygraph, or conventional lie detector, records several: pulse rate, blood pressure, respiration and sweat-gland activity). Besides, experts agree that although both the old and new devices can spot stress, neither can prove absolutely that the stress results from lying. The most serious objection to the P.S.E. is ethical. As the company itself suggests, the machine can be used covertly, thus invading the privacy to which, presumably, even liars are entitled.

Time Magazine

The unconscious parental feelings communicated through touch or lack of touch can lead to feelings of confusion and conflict in a child. Sometimes a "modern" parent will say all the right things but not want to touch his child very much. The child's confusion comes from the inconsistency of levels: if they really approve of me so much like they say they do, why won't they touch me?

William Schutz, *Here Comes Everybody*

Touching

Besides being the earliest means we have of making contact with others, touching is essential to our healthy development. During the nineteenth and early twentieth centuries a large percentage of children born every year died from a disease then called *marasmus,* which translated from Greek means "wasting away." In some orphanages the mortality rate was nearly 100 percent, but even children in the most "progressive" homes, hospitals, and other institutions died regularly from the ailment. When researchers finally tracked down the causes of this disease, they found that the infants suffered from lack of physical contact with parents or nurses, rather than nutrition, medical care, or other factors. They hadn't been touched enough, and as a result they died. From this knowledge came the practice of "mothering" children in institutions—picking the baby up, carrying it around, and handling it several times each day. At one hospital that began this practice, the death rate for infants fell from between 30 and 35 percent to below 10 percent.

As a child develops, his need for being touched continues. In his excellent book *Touching: The Human Significance of the Skin*, Ashley Montagu describes research which suggests that allergies, eczema, and other health problems are in part caused by a person's lack of contact as an infant with his mother. Although Montagu says that these problems develop early in life, he also cites cases where adults suffering from conditions as diverse as asthma and schizophrenia have been successfully treated by psychiatric therapy that uses extensive physical contact.

Touch seems to increase a child's mental functioning as well as his physical health. Dr. L. J. Yarrow has conducted surveys which show that babies who have been given plenty of physical stimulation by their mothers have significantly higher IQs than those receiving less contact.

The society we live in places less importance on touch than on other, less immediate senses such as sight or hearing. Our language is full of visual and aural figures of speech such as "Seeing is believing," "I'll be hearing from you," "Here's looking at you," and "Sounding something out." As Bernard Gunther points out, when leaving someone we say, "See you later," never "touch," "smell," or "taste" you later.

What are the consequences of not touching? The studies we mentioned here, as well as many others, suggest that physical contact is essential for healthy development. Little research has been done yet on the effects of touch in our adult lives, but the recent popularity of sensory-awareness groups indicates a feeling among many people that an element of warmth is missing from their lives which they want to recapture. The belief is growing that as adults we sometimes suffer from a kind of emotional marasmus—a wasting away of the intense feelings of love, anger, friendship, and fear.

If you're interested in exploring the role of touching in your life, you might try the following exercise. It's designed to let you reexperience this little-used medium of communication and see how it can help you get more in touch with yourself and others.

Blind Milling

1   Begin by forming a circle so that there are a few feet between you and the people to each side of you. Members should either blindfold themselves or close their eyes.

2   Now, for a period of fifteen or twenty minutes the members of your group can do whatever they wish—move around the room, or stay still, encounter others, or keep to yourself. The only requirements are that everyone remains "blind" and that nobody speaks during the experience.

3   There's no "correct" behavior. If you want to meet others, go ahead. If you'd rather be alone, that's all right too. You may need to communicate your wants to people who approach you, but remember to do it nonverbally.

4 At the end of fifteen or twenty minutes (perhaps on some signal from your instructor) say good-bye to anyone you may be with and find a space of your own.

5 Now take a few minutes to reflect on the experience you just had. You might ask yourself whether the way you related to other people here is similar to the kind of relationships you have in your everyday life. Did you aggressively seek out others, or did you wait for them to approach you? Did you find it easy to express your feelings? If you encountered two or more other people already together, did you feel comfortable joining in, or did you assume that you wouldn't be welcome? Did you make your wants known to the people you encountered, or did you assume that they knew what kind of communication you wanted to have?

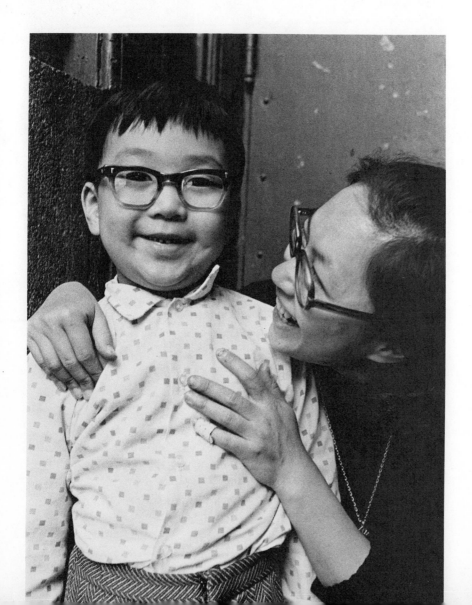

Touch Sparks Love

Our little girl was retreating into a walled-off world until we found the key to unlock her love.

"Debbie, please brush that hair out of your face. It's even getting into the food on your fork!"

It was suppertime; I had been late getting home from work, and I was edgy. My irritation was apparent in my voice. Slowly, mechanically, Debbie reached up and pushed her hair back. Then The Look began to come over her face.

I had seen it before. She had been perhaps four years old when it began. Her eyes became flat and expressionless, her face lost all animation. Even her coloring seemed to fade, and with her pale lashes and brows, she looked like an unpainted wooden doll. I knew that I could pass my hand in front of her face and she wouldn't even see it. Nor would she respond to anything that was said to her.

"There she goes again, feeling sorry for herself," commented Don, her big brother.

And so it appeared. The middle child in a family of seven children, it was understandable that she might feel sorry for herself. The older children bossed her around, nagged her, and seemed to pick on everything she said. The younger children demanded their own way, and often got it through the privilege of their ages. Pushed from above, threatened from below, Debbie didn't feel that she mattered to anyone.

The rest of the family continued with supper, ignoring Debbie. From past experience, we knew that it was useless to try to bring her back into the group. As the others were excused I led Debbie away from her half-eaten dinner to the living room, where I sat her down in front of the television set. Here she would gradually forget her grievances and join in again.

I couldn't help but have mixed feelings, though. Poor little thing! Six years old, and so unhappy! I wished desperately that I had more time to spend with her as an individual. I knew I had nagged her again. But why must she resort to that "Sorrowful Sal" act at every offense, either real or imagined? It was positively exasperating for her to tune us all out when it was quite clear that she could see and hear everything around her.

When Debbie had first begun to get The Look, we thought she was funny. "Isn't she cute when she's angry? See how she refuses to pay any attention to you! She's got a mind of her own!" But as time passed, it was no longer funny. It was angering to be intentionally ignored. We coaxed. We reasoned. We scolded. We even spanked her for her stubbornness, all to no avail.

But as long as it didn't happen often, we didn't pay much attention to such behavior. In a large family, it's easy to put a problem aside when a minor crisis has passed. Our older children were starting school; we had one in the "terrible twos" and an infant, as well as a chronic invalid who required extensive home nursing care. Our hands were full. The more-urgent-appearing problems received our attention, and Debbie's increasing needs went unrecognized.

Debbie was in the first grade when one of the older children said to me one afternoon, "Mom, Debbie's teacher wants to talk to you." The normal pangs of worry hit me that night. What trouble had Debbie gotten herself into? I made an appointment for the next afternoon with her teacher.

"I'm worried about Debbie," Mrs. Voorhees told me. "She's so . . . alone. She craves attention and she desperately needs more of it from you." She was telling me as gently as she could that I was failing my daughter.

I turned the problem over and over in my mind. How could I give Debbie more attention without incurring the resentment of the other children? Knowing that siblings in a large family are intensely competitive, I decided it would be best to enlist their help. I called the older children together and repeated what Mrs. Voorhees had told me. "So I'm going to try to give Debbie what she needs. It means that she has a greater need for attention at this time, and I'm trying to help her. I'd do the same for any of you."

For a while this seemed to help. But as weeks went by, I found that even the knowledge of reasons for my actions could not compensate for the unequal distribution of my attention. Don began to take pokes and pinches at his little sister, or to kick her as she went by, for no apparent reason.

Denise would keep track of every favor that I might give Debbie, and accused me, "You've read to her four times in the past month, and only once to me."

It was true. I was now working full time and trying to divide the remaining time between the children. With the small amount of time that there was to be divided, the inequality was obvious. The resentment of the other children over the extra time given to Debbie alone only made them more quarrelsome and belittling toward her. It was defeating my original purpose.

Still, I wondered, what could I do? What should I do? Debbie was getting good grades in school, so it didn't seem that she was too badly in need of attention. I began to spend more time in group activities with the family and less time with Debbie as an individual.

The Look returned more frequently, and Debbie ran away that summer—several times. "Where will you live?" I asked her. "Under a bush," she would reply poignantly. My heart ached for her.

Her comments began to reveal her feelings. "I wish I'd never been born."; "I wish I was dead."; Or "Some day I'm going to kill myself."

One afternoon she climbed up on the family car, and walked around on it in her gritty shoes, scratching the paint. Her exasperated father spanked her vigorously. Afterward I sat down beside her at the foot of the stairway, where she sat sobbing. "Why ever did you do that, Debbie? You knew Daddy would get angry and spank you," I asked her.

"Because I don't like myself."

"Why don't you like yourself?"

"Because nobody likes me."

Because nobody likes me. Oh, Debbie!

"I like you Debbie. I love you. You're my little girl." Words. Just words. Again, The Look. She tuned me out. She didn't see or hear me.

What a desperate cry for help! A little girl, six years old, invoking the wrath of her parents because she didn't think she was a person worth liking!

It took me a long time to acknowledge that Debbie—that WE—needed help. "How could a six-year-old have any serious problems?" I would ask myself. "How could so young a child be too much for you to manage? Don't bring outsiders into it. We can handle our own problems if we work on them."

But we weren't handling them. By the time Debbie was seven years old, The Look became a routine part of our daily life.

After a long inner struggle I finally decided to go to the county mental-health center. "What if someone sees me there and thinks I'm a kook?" I wondered. But I swallowed my pride and went. It was the turning point in Debbie's life.

After I discussed the problem with the psychiatric social worker, he set up an appointment for the entire family. "I want to see how they interact," he told me. After several such appointments, he began to see Debbie alone. A few weeks later he was able to give some help.

"She's a very unhappy little girl," he told me. "You must give her the love and attention she needs. If you don't, her problems will probably come to a head when she is a teenager. Then there is a strong chance that she will either commit suicide, or turn for affection to the first fellow who will give her a little attention. And you know what that means. These girls often become unwed mothers in their teens."

"But how?" I asked. "I'm working full time; I must

work. I've so little time to give any of the children and when I try to give Debbie a little extra attention, the other children become jealous and are cruel to her. And how do I cope with her when she tunes me out?"

"She's tuning you out to protect herself. Think about it," the social worker said, "When does she do it? When you scold her or criticize her? When the other children argue with her or deride her? These things hurt her so much that she can't cope with them. But if she can't see you or hear you, then you can't hurt her like that any more. So she withdraws. It's a defense mechanism she uses to keep from being hurt by other people."

He paused, then continued gently, "But you can reach her. There is one means you haven't tried yet. And that is—touch."

Touch? A strange thought. Communication without words. She could close her eyes and her ears, but she could still feel love.

"Touch her every chance you get. Ruffle her hair when you go by her. Pat her bottom. Touch her arm when you talk to her. Caress her. Put your hand on her shoulder, your arm around her. Pat her back. Hold her. Every chance you get. Every time you talk to her."

"Even when she refuses to see or hear you, she will feel you. And, incidently, this is something you can use to communicate with all your children. But pour it on Debbie."

Pour it on I did. And in a short time the results began to show noticeably. Debbie gradually became alive again. She smiled. She laughed. She had fun. She began to talk with me again. The Look became less and less frequent. And the other children never seemed to notice a thing, nor did they show any resentment of Debbie, possibly because I was touching them too.

Debbie is nine now, and she is like a different child. In addition to her new cheerful outlook on life, she has begun to discover some self-esteem. She stood in front of the mirror recently and told me, "I like my hair. It's pretty." What she was really telling me was that she has learned to like herself again. How far she has come! How far we all have come since I finally admitted that we needed professional help for a problem we hadn't been able to solve by ourselves.

The social worker's suggestion that I begin to communicate my love to my children by touching them was not guaranteed to be a miracle cure for Debbie's problems—or anyone else's. It did work for us, but not without a serious re-evaluation of ourselves as individuals and as a family unit. We have had to learn a lot about ourselves, and we had to try hard to understand one another better, to accept one another as distinctly different human beings, each with intense feelings and needs.

I know the road ahead of us will have many rough spots and that the struggle to work out family difficulties is not an easy one. Debbie's problems are not over yet by any means. Strong rivalry remains among the children and she is still right in the middle of it. She has many crucial years in front of her, and we'll have to continue to boost her ego. We'll have to pay attention to her; give her the opportunity to express her feelings and listen to her when she does.

But no matter what the future holds, I have learned at least one invaluable lesson: to let my children feel my love. Love can be shown in many ways—in facial expressions, in attitudes, in actions. Love can be heard. But—and perhaps this is most important of all—love can be felt, in one of the simplest means of communication there is: touch.

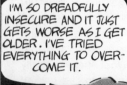

Clothing

The way we dress tells others something about us. The armed forces have developed uniforms partly as a way of showing who has a particular job and who's in charge of whom. Thus, uniforms are a sort of nonverbal badge that describes the wearer's place in the military social system. Although many of us have a tendency to criticize what looks like a rigid system that puts people into classes, in many ways we use clothing to categorize people too.

Think about the people you know. See if you can tell anything about their political or social philosophies by the way they dress. A good place to begin your survey is with the faculty at your school. Is there any relationship between the way an instructor dresses and his teaching style? Take a look at your friends. Do you find that the people who spend time together share the same ideas about clothing? Is there a "uniform" for political radicals and one for conservatives? Is there a high fashion "uniform" that tells the public who's in style and who's out of it?

A student proved to himself how clothing labels a person's social position by trying an experiment. He spent a week hitchhiking back and forth from Santa Barbara to Los Angeles, a distance of about 100 miles. Every other day he would alternate his clothing style. On Monday, Wednesday, and Friday he wore old Levi's, sandals, and a tie-dyed sweatshirt; and on Tuesday, Thursday, and Saturday he put on stay-pressed bell-bottomed pants, well-shined leather shoes, and a freshly ironed shirt. Other than his clothing, he kept all factors constant: He began at the same time each day, stood in the same spot, and signaled with his thumb in exactly the same way. The results seemed to prove how much clothes can say to others. As he described:

> It was incredible! On my three grubby days I got rides from people who looked just like I did. Two of them drove old V.W. buses, and the third had a '55 Ford pickup truck. They all wore Levi's, boots, et cetera, and all had pretty much the same life style. On the days when I dressed up, I got rides in shiny new Oldsmobiles and Cadillacs from people who were completely opposite from the ones I'd driven with the day before. The very first thing one guy said after picking me up was how nice it was to see a young person who wasn't one of those "hippie types!"

As well as illustrating the influence clothing has in our culture, this story points out a real danger inherent in reading many nonverbal messages. That danger is that we find ourselves stereotyping others on skimpy evidence, and often our interpretations are mistaken. By jumping to conclusions about another human from these surface appearances, we may very well be stereotyping ourselves out of some important relationships. There's an old generalization that you can't judge a book by its cover. In light of what we know about nonverbal communication we could change it to "You can tell only a little about a book from its cover; you need to have more information before you'll be able to speak with any authority about it."

The Groomer

John T. Molloy believes in the old saw that clothes make the man. He believes it so much that two years ago he became America's first wardrobe engineer, a veritable B. F. Skinner of haberdashery who believes that a man's clothing can be chosen to evoke conditioned responses from anyone he meets. Operating out of a cluttered office in Manhattan, Molloy teaches dress habits that, he says, enable salesmen to sell more insurance, trial lawyers to win more cases and executives to exert more authority. Wardrobe engineering, Molloy says, "is just putting together the elements of psychology, fashion, sociology and art."

Molloy began to develop his theory in the late 1950s, when as an instructor at a prep school in Connecticut, he discovered that a teacher's dress could subtly affect student performance. In one case, two teachers taught the same class in separate half-day sessions: one consistently wore penny loafers while the other wore traditional lace-up shoes. The students, it turned out, worked longer and harder for the teacher in lace-ups, and Molloy concluded that the shoes were responsible. "I felt we were on to something big," he recalls, "but nobody noticed."

Chintzy ties Nobody, that is, but Molloy. Over the next decade, he refined his techniques and conducted other experiments that convinced him he was right. During his early research, for example, he discovered that the Boston Strangler invariably wore beige or gray repairman-like outfits; the light colors tended to reassure housewives and helped him get into their homes. Last year Molloy planted an actor posing as a trainee in a New York City corporate office, and instructed him to ask 100 secretaries to retrieve some information from their files. First the actor dressed in "lower-middle-class" style: black shoes with large buckles, a greenish-blue suit, a white shirt and a chintzy blue polyester tie, thick glasses and a gold expansion watch band. In that garb, he was able to get only twelve secretaries out of 50 to go to the files for him. Later, in an "upper-middle-class" outfit—styled hair, expensive blue suit, beige shirt, silk polka-dot tie and brown cordovan shoes—he visited 50 more secretaries. This time, 42 of the 50 did as they were bade.

Based on such findings, Molloy has put together a number of courses designed to teach clients how to dress more effectively. For $300, he will teach an "upper-middle-class set of color and pattern values" that will help boost the wearer in the corporate world. For those with three years and $1,000 to invest, he will conduct a full-fledged, complex "credibility study" designed to find the "clothing trend" that will best project a desired image.

Molloy has already had plenty of takers. At his suggestion, the owner of an insurance agency in a Boston suburb replaced his flashily attired sales force with men in gray suits, simple ties and button-down collars—and sales boomed. A trial lawyer with a folksy courtroom manner and a losing record was persuaded to abandon his pin-stripe suits and wire-rimmed spectacles (which were more suitable for a remote "authority figure") in favor of solid blue suits and glasses with thicker frames that gave him a friendlier image. He is now winning more cases.

One of Molloy's most satisfying experiences occurred a few years ago, when a conservatively dressed corporate recruiter at Columbia University insisted to him that clothes did not matter. It was a time when militant students were throwing recruiters off campus, and Molloy guaranteed that he could dress him so that a student would punch him in the nose. Dressed in dark blue clothing "just like a cop," the recruiter ventured back onto campus—and caught a fast one in the chops. Molloy collected his fee and won a convert.

Time Magazine

Clothes and Communication*

In this exercise you can get some idea of whether your clothes communicate the messages you want them to.

1 Copy the following chart on a piece of paper:

Item of clothing	What I want my clothes to say about me	What others think my clothing says about me

2 In the first column list item by item the clothes you're wearing right now—for example: tennis shoes, T-shirt, corduroy pants, sunglasses.

3 In the middle column list what message you'd like the clothes you've chosen to say—for example, "I want to look casual," "I want people to notice me," or "I want to look sexy."

4 Now join two other people. Have them fill in the third column by describing what your clothes *do* say about you. Continue this process until everyone has received feedback.

5 Now discuss in your group how the feedback you've received makes you feel. Are you happy with the way your clothes communicate?

Environment and Nonverbal Communication

To conclude our look at nonverbal communication we want to emphasize the ways in which physical settings, architecture, and interior design affect our communication. Begin your thinking by recalling for a moment the different homes you've visited lately. Were some of these homes more comfortable to be in than others? Certainly a lot of these kinds of feelings are shaped by the people you were with, but there are some houses where it seems impossible to relax, no matter how friendly the hosts are. We've spent what seemed like endless evenings in what Mark Knapp calls "unliving

*Based on an exercise developed by Sidney B. Simon, Leland W. Howe, and Howard Kirschenbaum in *Values Clarification: A Handbook of Practical Strategies for Teachers and Students* (New York: Hart, 1972).

rooms," where the spotless ashtrays, furniture coverings, and plastic lamp covers seemed to send nonverbal messages telling us not to touch anything, not to put our feet up, and not to be comfortable. People who live in houses like this probably wonder why nobody ever seems to relax and enjoy themselves at their parties. One thing is quite certain: They don't understand that this environment they have created can communicate discomfort to their guests.

There's a large amount of research that shows how the design of an environment can shape the kind of communication that takes place in it. In one experiment at Brandeis University Maslow and Mintz found that the attractiveness of a room influenced the happiness and energy of people working in it. The experimenters set up three rooms: an "ugly" one, which resembled a janitor's closet in the basement of a campus building; an "average" room, which was a professor's office; and a "beautiful" room, which was furnished with carpeting, drapes, and comfortable furniture. The subjects in the experiment were asked to rate a series of pictures as a way of measuring their energy and feelings of well-being while at work. Results of the experiment showed that while in the ugly room, the subjects became tired and bored more quickly and took longer to complete their task. When they moved to the beautiful room, however, they rated the faces they were judging higher, showed a greater desire to work, and expressed feelings of importance, comfort, and enjoyment. The results teach a lesson that isn't surprising: Workers generally feel better and do a better job when they're in an attractive environment.

Many business people show an understanding of how environment can influence communication. Robert Sommer, a leading environmental psychologist, described several such cases. In his book *Personal Space: the Behavioral Basis for Design,* he points out that dim lighting, subdued noise levels, and comfortable seats encourage people to spend more time in a restaurant or bar. Knowing this, the management can control the amount of customer turnover. If the goal is to run a high-volume business that tries to move people in and out quickly, it's necessary to keep the lights shining brightly and not worry too much about soundproofing. On the other hand, if the goal is to keep customers in the bar or restaurant for a long time, the proper technique is to lower the lighting and use absorbent building materials that will keep down the noise level.

Furniture design can control the amount of time a person spends in an environment too. From this knowledge came the Larsen chair, which was designed for Copenhagen restaurant owners who felt their customers were occupying their seats too long without spending enough money. The chair is constructed to put an uncomfortable pressure on the sitter's back if occupied for more than a few minutes. (We suspect that many people who are careless in buying furniture for their homes get much the same result without trying. One environmental psychologist we know refuses to buy a chair or couch without sitting in it for at least half an hour to test its comfort.)

Sommer also describes how airports are designed to discourage people from spending too much time in waiting areas. The uncomfortable chairs, bolted shoulder to shoulder in rows facing outward, make conversation and relaxation next to impossible. Faced with this situation, travelers are forced to move to restaurants and bars in the terminal, where they're not only more comfortable but where they're also likely to spend money.

Casino owners in places such as Las Vegas also know how to use the environment to control behavior. To keep gamblers from noticing how long they've been shooting craps, playing roulette and blackjack, and feeding slot machines, they build their casinos without windows or clocks. Unless he has his own watch, the customer has no way of knowing how long he has been gambling, or, for that matter, whether it's day or night.

In a more therapeutic and less commercial way physicians have also shaped environments to improve communications. One study showed that simply removing a doctor's desk made patients feel almost five times more at ease during office visits. Sommer found that redesigning a convalescent ward of a hospital greatly increased the interaction between patients. In the old design seats were placed shoulder to shoulder around the edges of the ward. By grouping the chairs around small tables so that patients faced each other at a comfortable distance, the amount of conversations doubled.

Explore Your Classroom

1 Who are the people with whom you interact most in your classroom? Where do they sit in relation to you?

2 Is there any relationship between the way people behave in class and the place they usually sit? Do talkers sit together or apart? How about friends? People who argue? What kind of people sit near the instructor?

3 How would your communication change if you sat in a different place in the room? Why not find out?

4 How would the communication differ if you changed the seating arrangement
  a. into rows
  b. into a circle
  c. removed all chairs

5 How could you change the room into a place where
  a. it's hard to stay awake
  b. it's easiest to stay awake
  c. the teacher dominates the class
  d. it's easy for all members to discuss a subject
  e. only a few people can comfortably join a discussion
  f. it's easy to make friends
  g. it's hard to make friends

Nonverbal Communication: Messages Without Words

Bill Bernbach, when he was building the most exciting advertising agency of his time, had a round conference table in his office. He tried the customary rectangular one, but, as he said, "The junior men always sat at the foot and I sat at the head, and I learned that the light of conviction is often in the eyes of junior men. With a round table, I was closer to them and less likely to miss it."

Robert Townsend, *Up the Organization*

On the Grand Avenue corner is the Hearing Room, a sloping auditorium big enough for 706 people, and it was there, at one of the regular weekly meetings of the board, that we began our tour—and began to see the cause of the problem.

Citizens who want to address the board stand at two microphones in front of the first row of spectator seats. Beyond them, behind a solid oak fence running the width of the room and raised three steps, sit the supervisors' top aides: the clerk, the county counsel and the chief administrative officer. Beyond them, still another step up, sit the supervisors themselves, arrayed behind a curving bench like justices of some high court, each one rocking in his own reclining chair.

Bob Abernathy and Art White,
West Magazine—Los Angeles Times

The hospital building disregards physical factors that might promote recovery. Colors are bland, but instead of being restful, are more often depressing; space is badly distributed, so that a patient may be stranded in a large room, or crowded in a small one; private and semi-private patients often feel isolated in their rooms. . . . Windows are badly placed, and the view most often shows an adjacent large hospital building or a parking lot. . . .

One may immediately object that despite all this, the majority of patients adjust well to the hospital, recover, and go home. That is true, but as an argument it is a little like saying that the world got on perfectly well without electricity, which is also true.

Michael Crichton, M.D., *Five Patients*

Even the design of an entire building can shape communication among its users. Architects have learned that the way housing projects are designed will control to a great extent the contact neighbors will have with each other. People who live in apartments near stairways and mailboxes have many more neighbor contacts than do those living in less heavily traveled parts of the building, and tenants generally have more contacts with immediate neighbors than with people even a few doors away. Architects now use this information to design buildings that either encourage communication or increase privacy, and house hunters can use the same knowledge to choose a home that gives them the neighborhood relationships they want.

Sometimes the matter of designing an environment can become absurd. During 1968 the United States, South Vietnam, and North Vietnam spent eight months arguing over the shape of the table at which they would hold their peace talks. The argument centered on the nonverbal statement that the design of the conference room would make. The North Vietnamese wanted a square table, which would have given the National Liberation Front (NLF) guerillas a separate side all to themselves. As the Communists saw it, this arrangement would have given the guerillas equal status as an independent government. The United States and South Vietnamese were not about to give in to the demand. They wanted two rectangular tables, one seating themselves and the other for the North Vietnamese and NLF. This design would have kept the guerillas from having a whole table side to themselves, and symbolically denied them clear-cut status as an equal power. Several thousand lives later both sides finally compromised on a round table, which, having no sides at all, allowed each side to claim victory.

Nonverbal Communication: Messages Without Words

Those Maddening Modalities

Two hundred years ago, Jean Jacques Rousseau described peace parleys as ''a species of general diets where one deliberates in common as to whether the table will be round or square, whether the chamber will have more or fewer doors, whether such and such a plenipotentiary will have his face or his back turned toward the window, whether such and such another will take two steps more or less while making a visit, and upon a thousand other questions of equal importance, uselessly debated for the past three centuries.'' Things have scarcely changed since.

To dignify their often absurd arguments over such ceremonial questions, diplomats talk about ''modalities.'' The word is derived from ''modal,'' which pertains to form as opposed to substance—and history is studded with episodes where wrangles over form all but prevented negotiators from ever getting down to substance.

Most maddening of all the modalities has been the problem of precedence. It took nearly six months to sign the Peace of Ryswick in 1697, for example, because the representatives of France and the Holy Roman Empire never could agree about who should walk into the conference room first; they finally agreed to enter together, and so ended what was known as the War of the Grand Alliance. In 1801, Thomas Jefferson adopted the rule of ''pell-mell'' for diplomatic meetings—whoever arrived first, entered first. That solution has long since been dropped by protocol-conscious officials. Numerous efforts have been made to regulate matters of precedence. The Congress of Vienna in 1815 established four classes of diplomatic representatives (ambassadors and Papal legates; ministers plenipotentiary; ministers resident; *chargés d'affaires*). Heads of state remained a problem; at Vienna, the conference hall had no fewer than five doors to cope with the attending monarchs.

The problems persisted. Thus the 1945 Potsdam Conference ground to a halt while whole phalanxes of foreign officers fretted over who should enter first. They finally found a room with three doors so that Churchill, Stalin and Truman could come in simultaneously. Another near impasse was averted at the conference's end when Stalin insisted that he be the first to sign, since the British Prime Minister and the U.S. President had each been first in two previous conferences. Harry Truman refused to make a fuss about it. ''You can sign any time you want to,'' he snorted. ''I don't care.''

The size and shape of negotiating tables is another problem that has confounded many a diplomat. At the 1959 Geneva Conference of the Big Four, a protracted dispute was finally ended when the U.S., Russia, Britain and France agreed to sit at a round table while the East and West Germans sat at small, square, separate tables precisely six pencil widths from the main table. To solve the present impasse in Paris, some officials have suggested that no formal tables be used—but then the negotiators would argue over the size and shape of the coffee tables that would be needed to accommodate their ashtrays, water pitchers and doodling pads.

The Korean armistice talks, which have dragged on through 275 sessions, have provided some classic examples of the use of punctilio to shatter a rival's composure. At one of the first meetings, North Korea's General Nam II provided himself with a particularly high chair and seated U.S. Admiral C. Turner Joy on a low one. Joy saw to it that the chairs were of equal height from then on. When the allies set out a small United Nations table flag, the North Koreans followed suit—only theirs was six inches taller. In this case, however, Joy ''hastened to veto any tendency toward such competition,'' as he wrote in his book, *How Communists Negotiate,* "thereby perhaps averting construction of the two tallest flagpoles on earth."

Probably the nastiest problems of all are posed when heads of state get together. In 1475, England's Edward IV and France's Louis XI met in the middle of a bridge spanning the Somme near Amiens, with a thick oaken lattice separating them, to settle a war in Picardy. The three feuding princes of Laos—Souphanouvong, Souvanna Phouma and Boun Oum, similarly met in the middle of a bridge over the Nam Lik River in 1961 to launch the talks that eventually led to the country's tenuous neutralization. When Napoleon and Alexander I of Russia met in 1807 to carve up Europe in the Treaty of Tilsit, the site for preliminary talks was an elaborate barge anchored in the River Memel in Prussia. The precedence problem was solved by having the two monarchs set out simultaneously for the barge from the river banks; Napoleon, naturally, provided himself with the faster boat and arrived first.

Time Magazine

So far we've talked about how designing an environment can shape communication, but there's another side to consider. Watching how people use an already existing environment can be a way of telling what kind of relationships they want. For example, Sommer watched students in a college library and found that there's a definite pattern for people who want to study alone. While the library was uncrowded, students almost always chose corner seats at one of the empty rectangular tables. Finally each table was occupied by one reader. New readers would then choose a seat on the opposite side and far end of an occupied table, thus keeping the maximum distance between themselves and the other readers. One of Sommer's associates tried violating these "rules" by sitting next to and across from other female readers when more distant seats were available. She found that the approached women reacted defensively, either by signalling their discomfort through shifts in posture, gesturing, or by eventually moving away.

A person's position in a room can also communicate his status. Research shows that during conferences people who take leadership roles usually seat themselves at the ends of a meeting table. This pattern carries over to many households, where the father as head of the family sits at the end of the dinner table.

House Tour*

1 Draw a map of your house or apartment. Include all the working and living areas, both indoors and out.

2 Choose one color of ink, and with it put a plus sign (+) in each area you enjoy and feel comfortable in.

3 Now with your same color put a circle (○) in each area you don't like or where you feel uncomfortable.

*Based on a design by Mayer Spivack, Harvard Laboratory of Community Psychiatry.

Nonverbal Communication: Messages Without Words

4 Outline with your color ink the areas of the house that are your territory.

5 Give the map to the other people who live with you, and have them complete steps 2 to 4. Use a different color of ink for each person.

6 After looking at the map together, answer the following questions:
   a. What are the characteristics of each person's enjoyable spaces?
   b. What are the characteristics of each person's unpleasant spaces?
   c. How many enjoyable spaces are shared by more than one person? How many aren't?
   d. What does the completed map say about your relationship—the time you share, the activities you enjoy, your need for privacy?
   e. How can you redesign your home to make it a place that fits everyone's wants and needs?

As we draw this discussion of nonverbal communication to a close, there are some points we'd like to reemphasize. First, in a normal two-person conversation the words or verbal components of the message carry far less of the social meaning of the situation than do the nonverbal components. This statistic may have been difficult for you to believe when we cited it at the beginning of the chapter, but by this time you know how many channels nonverbal communication includes: spatial distance, touch, body posture and tension, facial expression, hand and body movement, dress, physique, tone of voice, speed of speech, as well as disfluencies of speech and even the

A good house is planned from the inside out. First, you decide what it has to do for its occupants. Then, you let the functions determine the form. The more numerous and various those functions, the more responsive and interesting the house should be. And it may not look at all like you expect.

Dan MacMasters, *Los Angeles Times*

environment we create. Our hope is that the information and experiences of the chapter have placed some importance on nonverbal communication in your life.

We also want to reemphasize that when we compare nonverbal behavior with verbal language it's very limited. Our nonverbal communication is concerned mostly with the expression of feelings, likings, or preferences, and these usually *reinforce* or *contradict* the message we're expressing verbally.

Third, we need to realize that although nonverbal behaviors are more powerful in expressing feelings than are words, they're ambiguous and difficult to "read" accurately. They'll always stand checking out.

Our fourth point is to remind you that the gestures, glances, postures, and other behavior we've discussed here are culturally learned and don't necessarily apply to other cultures or even to subcultures within our society. At this point most nonverbal research has been done on middle- and upper-middle-class college students and shouldn't be automatically generalized to other groups.

Finally, we hope you now understand the importance of *congruency*—the matching of your verbal and nonverbal expressions. Contradicting messages from two channels are a pretty good indication of deliberate or unconscious deception, and matching signals reinforce your messages.

We haven't tried to teach you *how* to communicate nonverbally in this chapter—you've always known this. What we do hope you've gained here is a greater *awareness* of the messages you and others send, and we further hope that you can use this new awareness to understand and improve your relationships.

Roads Not Taken

1   Research such as that cited in the readings section of this chapter shows that the design of an environment can have a great effect on what takes place within it. Investigate some of the studies that have been done in this area and report your findings.

2   Touching plays a necessary role in human relationships and adjustment. Familiarize yourself with some research in this area and report your findings.

3   Apply the statement, "It's easier to lie verbally than nonverbally," to various communication settings—business, school, social, family, and romantic relationships, and the legal system.

4   Gestures are a large part of nonverbal language. Make an investigation into the universality of the meaning of gestures. Do the same movements have the same meanings around the world?

5   Report on the different nonverbal customs and rules in various cultures and subcultures that interest you. What is the importance of knowing these rules for travelers from one culture to another?

Nonverbal Communication: Messages Without Words

More Readings in Nonverbal Communication

Bakker, Cornelis B., and Marianne Bakker-Rabdau. *No Trespassing! Explorations in Human Territoriality.* San Francisco: Chandler & Sharp, 1973.
   This book explores the various aspects of human territoriality. The authors are convinced that human territoriality deserves a central position in the understanding of human behavior and interpersonal communication.

Deasy, C. M. "When Architects Consult People." *Psychology Today* 3:10 (March, 1970).
   A readable article that discusses how architects can design buildings to encourage certain types of relationships. It shows how social science applies to the "real world."

Eckman, Paul, and Wallace V. Friesen, "Nonverbal Leakage and Clues to Deception." *Psychiatry* 32 (1969):88–106.
   The title of this article is self-explanatory. Eckman and Friesen discuss the various types of nonverbal emotional clues that people unintentionally send as well as indicators of deliberate deception.

Hall, Edward T. *The Hidden Dimension.* Garden City, N.Y.: Anchor Books, Doubleday, 1969.
   Hall has probably done more work on proxemics than anyone else, and this book gives you a good survey of the field, including the research with animals that led to our knowledge about how humans use space. It also contains chapters on how different cultures handle space.

_____. *The Silent Language,* Greenwich, Conn.: Fawcett Books, 1959.
   A good blend of theory and anecdotes, this book introduces several kinds of nonverbal communication and their cultural implications. As a quote on the cover says, "Diplomats could study this book with profit."

Knapp, Mark L. *Nonverbal Communication in Human Interaction.* New York: Holt, Rinehart and Winston, 1972.
   If you're interested in finding out how much and what kinds of work have been done in nonverbal communication, this is the book to read. As we go to press this is the most complete survey of the field and a book you should have if you're seriously interested in the subject.

Mehrabian, Albert. *Nonverbal Communication.* Chicago: Aldine-Atherton, 1972.
   This book falls into the same category as Knapp's, although it's organized differently. Mehrabian has probably written more articles and books about nonverbal communication than anyone else, and this work reviews his and most everyone else's work in this area.

Molloy, John T. *Dress for Success.* New York: Wyden, 1975.
   An elaboration of Molloy's ideas on dressing as described in this chapter.

Montagu, Ashley, *Touching: The Human Significance of the Skin.* New York: Harper & Row, 1971.

Montagu has written 335 mostly fascinating pages about our skins and the importance they have in our development. It's a book you'll probably want to read before you plan to have children.

Rosenfeld, Lawrence B., and Jean M. Civikly. *With Words Unspoken: The Nonverbal Experience.* New York: Holt, Rinehart and Winston, 1976.

This is a new text for a study of the importance of the nonverbal in our lives. The treatment of the material is contemporary and inviting to the college student. Materials are drawn from all parts of our society. Subjects covered range from biorhythm cycles to weight. The book is hard to put down once you pick it up.

Scheflen, Albert E. *How Behavior Means.* Garden City, N.Y.: Anchor Books, 1974.

This book explores kinesics, posture, interaction, setting, and culture as to their importance in human communication.

Sommer, Robert. *Personal Space: The Behavioral Basis of Design.* Englewood Cliffs, N.J.: Prentice-Hall, 1969.

Sommer is a leading authority on environmental psychology, and this book is a good introduction to the field. It shows how manipulating space controls communication.

Thompson, James J. *Beyond Words: Nonverbal Communication in the Classroom.* New York: Citation Press, 1973.

This is a highly readable, nontechnical explanation of the many ways nonverbal communication affects the performances of both students and teachers.

Films on Nonverbal Communication

Communication By Voice And Action. Color. 13 min. 1969. Central Arizona Film Cooperative.

Shows how communication is a two-way proposition between the speaker and listener and that posture, voice, facial expression, and body movement contribute to correct interpretation.

Communication: The Non-Verbal Agenda. Color. 30 min. 1975. Iowa University.

Alerts viewers to the constant, inevitable flow of interpersonal nonverbal communication, which occurs universally.

Face. Color. 11 min. 1968. Central Arizona Film Cooperative.

Shows experimentalism in cinema but also the potential of facial expression in communication through animation of an engraving of a woman's face, with expressions ranging from elegant beauty to absurdity.

Invisible Walls. B/W. 12 min. 1955. University of California.

This film investigates human territoriality. Hidden cameras catch people reacting to actors who violate their intimate distance barriers.

Orpheon. Color. 8 min. 1966. Iowa University.

An amusing portrayal of the potential of nonverbal communication, done with humorous and imaginative animation.

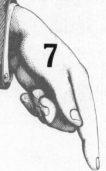

7

Semantics:
Where Words
Go Astray

*A*ND THE WHOLE EARTH WAS OF ONE LANGUAGE AND ONE SPEECH. AND IT CAME TO PASS, AS THEY JOURNEYED FROM THE EAST, THAT THEY FOUND A PLAIN IN THE LAND OF SHINAR; AND THEY DWELT THERE.

2 AND THEY SAID TO ONE ANOTHER, GO TO, LET US MAKE BRICK, AND BURN THEM THOROUGHLY. AND THEY HAD BRICK FOR STONE, AND SLIME HAD THEY FOR MORTAR.

3 AND THEY SAID, GO TO, LET US BUILD US A CITY AND A TOWER, WHOSE TOP MAY REACH UNTO HEAVEN; AND LET US MAKE US A NAME, LEST WE BE SCAT-TERED ABROAD UPON THE FACE OF THE WHOLE EARTH.

4 AND THE LORD CAME DOWN TO SEE THE CITY AND THE TOWER, WHICH THE CHILDREN OF MEN BUILDED.

5 AND THE LORD SAID, BEHOLD, THE PEOPLE IS ONE, AND THEY HAVE ALL ONE LANGUAGE; AND THIS THEY BEGIN TO DO: AND NOW NOTHING WILL BE RE-STRAINED FROM THEM, WHICH THEY HAVE IMAGINED TO DO.

6 GO TO, LET US GO DOWN, AND THERE CONFOUND THEIR LANGUAGE, THAT THEY MAY NOT UNDERSTAND ONE ANOTHER'S SPEECH.

7 SO THE LORD SCATTERED THEM ABROAD FROM THENCE UPON THE FACE OF ALL THE EARTH; AND THEY LEFT OFF TO BUILD THE CITY.

8 THEREFORE IS THE NAME OF IT CALLED BABEL; BECAUSE THE LORD DID THERE CONFOUND THE LANGUAGE OF ALL THE EARTH; AND FROM THENCE DID THE LORD SCATTER THEM ABROAD UPON THE FACE OF ALL THE EARTH.

Genesis 11:1–9

Sometimes it seems as if *none* of us speak the same language. How often have you felt that nobody understood what you were saying? *You* knew what you meant, but people just didn't seem to understand you. How often have the tables been turned—you couldn't understand somebody else's ideas? And how many times have you had the feeling that someone was deliberately playing tricks with words—using language to fool you or hide what was on his mind?

In this chapter we'll examine these problems by taking a quick look at the subject of semantics—the relationship between words and things. We'll try to show you some of the ways language can trip us up and some of the things you can do to make it work better. We'll also talk about how language not only describes how we see the world but shapes our view of it.

Semantics: Where Words Go Astray

Attitude Survey

You can begin this chapter by filling out the following questionnaire. It's a series of statements someone might make while discussing politics; you've probably heard comments like these many times. Signify your response by putting a number next to each statement according to the following scale:

5 strongly agree

4 agree

3 undecided

2 disagree

1 strongly disagree

1 ____ In many cases revolutions are justifiable ways of getting rid of repressive governments.

2 ____ All groups can live in harmony in this country without changing the system very much.

3 ____ It's not really undemocratic to recognize that the world is divided into superior and inferior people.

4 ____ If you start trying to change things very much, you usually make them worse.

5 ____ You can usually depend more on a man who owns property than one who doesn't.

6 ____ Police brutality is never justified.

7 ____ I prefer the practical man anytime to the intellectual.

8 ____ Private ownership of property is necessary if we're to have a strong nation.

9 ____ No matter how much ordinary people like to talk about it, political power doesn't come from them but from some higher powers.

10 ____ It's better to stick with what you have than to be trying new things you don't really know.

11 ____ Increasing government control in our lives is taking away our freedom.

12 ____ A man has the right to protect himself from physical threats, no matter what the law says.

13 ____ It's never wise to introduce changes rapidly, in government or in the economic system.

"Well, at any rate it's a great comfort," she said as she stepped under the trees, "after being so hot, to get into the—into the—into what?" she went on, rather surprised at not being able to think of the word. "I mean to get under the—under the—under this, you know!" putting her hand on the trunk of the tree. "What does it call itself, I wonder? I do believe it's got no name—why to be sure it hasn't!"

Lewis Carroll,
Through the Looking Glass

14 ____ Our society is so complicated that if you try to reform parts of it, you're likely to upset the whole system.

15 ____ A man doesn't really get much wisdom until he's well along in years.

16 ____ If something grows up over a long time, there's bound to be much wisdom in it.

17 ____ I'd want to be sure that something would really work before I'd be willing to take chances on it.

18 ____ You can't change human nature.

19 ____ The heart is as good a guide as the head.

After writing down your response to the questions, compare them with the answers of other people who have taken the survey. Where do you agree? disagree? Talk over your responses and see if anyone's mind is changed. Do you ever get the feeling in such conversations that all you're doing is talking in circles? Why do you think this is so?

What happened when you discussed the survey? It's likely that you found yourself in one of those unsatisfying arguments where you not only disagreed with other respondants about the answers you gave, but you couldn't even be sure you were talking about the same questions.

If this did happen, you can probably see why. The statements you responded to were so vague that they meant different things to every person who read them. Take question 1, for example. What kind of revolution were you thinking about—violent or nonviolent? Are all revolutions alike? If so, to defend one means you have to defend them all. If you don't believe all revolutions are justified, did you explain in your discussion which ones you do support? And what about "repressive governments"? Do you think everybody you argued with shared the same idea of what constitutes one? Probably not, but did you take much time trying to find a common definition for this term? In discussions like the ones you probably had here it almost seems sometimes that the people involved are speaking different languages which only look alike.

Now you might say that this vague kind of language in the survey was obvious, that in your everyday communications you'd never be this careless in your use of language. But would this really be true? How often do you recall arguing with someone about one or more of these topics, and how many times have such discussions turned into frustrating arguments?

We think you'll find as you read on that a great many communication problems you encounter each day are caused by semantic difficulties. If this is true, how can you use language better?

COON!!

HONKIE!!

Words don't mean—**people** mean!

Words and Meanings

The first thing to realize is that meanings rest more in people than in words themselves. Words are *symbols,* which each of us interprets, often in very different ways. As we said in Chapter 6, the tone of voice somebody uses in calling you an old fool will determine whether you react with anger or laughter. Similarly, an Englishman might think nothing about telling you to "keep your pecker up" (which in his country means something like our expression "keep your chin up"), but you, being unfamiliar with this expression, would probably be very surprised (at the least) and maybe shocked or angry to hear it.

In each of these cases it wasn't the words themselves that had any meaning. Rather, the meaning came from the sender as he chose the words and from the listener as he heard and interpreted them. Now if everyone interpreted words in the same way, this fact that meanings are in people and not words wouldn't be important, but unfortunately this isn't the case. The 500 words most commonly used in everyday communications have over 14,000 definitions listed in the dictionary, and often people use words in ways you'd never be able to look up. Because most of us forget this simple fact—that everyone doesn't use words the way we do—we wind up in all sorts of misunderstandings. Sometimes they're only small ones, such as driving a few miles out of the way after misunderstanding some directions; but in other cases they can ruin friendships and careers and even influence the course of history, as the following article shows.

The Great *Mokusatsu* Mistake

Was This the Deadliest Error of Our Time?

For many months after the Japanese collapse in 1945, people wondered whether it was the atomic bomb or Russia's entry into the war that had brought to an end the fighting in the Pacific. But it gradually became clear that the importance of these two events in persuading Japan to surrender had been overrated; that Japan had been a defeated nation long before August 1945.

"The Japanese had, in fact, already sued for peace before the Atomic Age was announced to the world with the destruction of Hiroshima, and before the Russian entry into the war," Fleet Admiral Chester W. Nimitz told Congress; and other American military leaders confirmed this report.

Why, then, did not Japan accept the Potsdam Declaration, which called upon Japan to surrender, when it was issued in late July of 1945, instead of waiting until the second week in August, after Hiroshima and Nagasaki had been blasted into radioactive rubble and the Russians had begun their drive into Manchuria? That question has never been satisfactorily answered.

The true story of Japan's rejection of the Potsdam Declaration *may* be the story of an incredible mistake—a mistake which so altered the course of history in the Far East that we shall never be able to estimate its full effect on our nation—a mistake which, ironically, was made by a Japanese and involved just one Japanese word.

I say that it "may be" because part of the actual truth lies buried in human motivations which will probably always puzzle historians. But another part of it is clearly demonstrable. Let me tell the story; then you can judge for yourself what really happened.

By the spring of 1945 there was no question in the minds of Japan's leaders that their nation had been badly beaten.

The plight of the nation was so desperate that the actual figures were kept secret even from some of the cabinet ministers. Japan's industrial complex had crumbled under the aerial assault. Steel production was down 79 percent, aircraft production down 64 percent. By September a lack of aluminum would halt the building of planes entirely.

Allied air attacks were destroying railroads, highways, and bridges faster than they could be replaced. Hundreds of thousands of bodies were buried in the smoking ruins of cities and towns. Millions were homeless. In Tokyo alone, almost half of the homes had been leveled. People were fleeing the cities. A combination of American surface, air, and undersea attack had cut off shipments from the occupied regions on which Japan depended for her life. Food was running out.

American planes destroyed the last of Japan's fleet in a battle off Kyushu on the very day in April when Suzuki took office. The aged Premier was an admiral without a navy.

"We must stop the war at the earliest opportunity," he said when he learned the true condition of his nation's war potential. The *jushin,* the senior statesmen, had advised the Emperor in February of 1945 that surrender was necessary *no matter what the cost.*

The Potsdam Declaration was issued on July 26, 1945. It was signed by the United States, Great Britain, and (to the surprise of the Japanese) China. The reaction among Japanese leaders was one of exultation. The terms were far more lenient than had been expected. The Japanese were quick to note that instead of demanding unconditional surrender from the *government,* the last item of the proclamation called upon the government to proclaim the unconditional surrender of the *armed forces.*

The document also promised that Japan would

not be destroyed as a nation, that the Japanese would be free to choose their own form of government, that sovereignty over the home islands would be returned to them after occupation, that they would be allowed access to raw materials for industry, and that Japanese forces would be allowed to return home.

Most important of all, the phrasing of the proclamation hinted strongly that the Emperor would be left on the throne, the one point which had been of most concern to the cabinet in all its discussions of surrender. The Japanese were expected to read between the lines, which they very quickly did.

Upon receiving the text of the proclamation, the Emperor told Foreign Minister Togo without hesitation that he deemed it acceptable. The full cabinet then met to discuss the Allied ultimatum.

Despite the fact that the cabinet members were considering acceptance of the Potsdam terms, they could not at first decide whether the news of the Allied proclamation should be released to the Japanese public. Foreign Minister Togo, anxious to prepare the people for the surrender, argued for four hours for its prompt release to the press. At six in the evening he won his point over strong army objections and late that night the declaration was released to the newspapers.

But there was another factor which the cabinet also was forced to consider. As yet the Japanese had received news of the statement of Allied policy at Potsdam only through their radio listening posts. It was not addressed to their government and the ultimatum had not yet reached them through official channels. Could the cabinet act on the basis of such unofficial information?

"After mature deliberation the hastily convened cabinet decided to keep silence for a while about the Potsdam proclamation pending further developments," says Kase.

The delay in announcing acceptance of the Allied terms was not expected to be long, but Prime Minister Suzuki was to meet the very next day with the press. The Japanese newsmen undoubtedly would question him about the proclamation. What should he say?

Hiroshi Shimomura, president of the powerful Board of Information—counterpart of Germany's propaganda ministry—and a member of the cabinet, recalls in his account of this fateful session that it was decided that the prime minister, if asked, should treat the subject lightly.

"This was to be done in order not to upset the surrender negotiations then under way through Russia," says Shimomura.

Premier Suzuki was to say merely that the cabinet had reached no decision on the Allied demands and that the discussion was continuing. Although the policy was to be one of silence, the very fact that the cabinet did not reject the ultimatum at once would make it clear to the Japanese people what was in the wind.

When Premier Suzuki confronted the press on July 28, he said that the cabinet was holding to a policy of *mokusatsu*. The word *mokusatsu* not only has no exact counterpart in English but it is ambiguous even in Japanese. Suzuki, as we know, meant that the cabinet had decided to make no comment on the Potsdam proclamation, with the implication that something significant was impending. But the Japanese were tricked by their own language. For in addition to meaning "to withhold comment," *mokusatsu* may also be translated as "to ignore."

The word has two characters in Japanese. *Moku* means "silence" and *satsu* means "kill," thus implying in an absolutely literal sense "to kill with silence." This can mean—to a Japanese—either to ignore or to refrain from comment.

Unfortunately the translators at the Domei News Agency could not know what Suzuki had in mind. As they hastily translated the prime minister's statement into English, they chose the wrong meaning. From the towers of Radio Tokyo the news crackled to the Allied world that the Suzuki cabinet had decided to "ignore" the Potsdam ultimatum.

The cabinet was furious at Suzuki's choice of words and the subsequent error by Domei. The reaction of Kase, who had fought long and hard for peace, was one of dismay.

"This was a piece of foolhardiness," he says. "When I heard of this I strongly remonstrated with

Semantics: Where Words Go Astray

the cabinet chief secretary, but it was too late. . . . Tokyo radio flashed it—to America! The punishment came swiftly. An atomic bomb was dropped on Hiroshima on August 6 by the Allies, who were led by Suzuki's outrageous statement into the belief that our government had refused to accept the Potsdam proclamation."

But for this tragic mistake, Kase laments, Japan might have been spared the atomic attack and the Russian declaration of war.

William J. Coughlin

One word, one mistaken interpretation by a news reporter, and the cost may have been tens of thousands of lives. Add to this the literally hundreds of small misunderstandings that almost certainly come between you and other people every week and you can probably begin to see the need for taking a close look at how our language works.

Where Words Go Astray

What are some of the most common problems we have in understanding each other? We'll start our survey of semantics by listing the most important ones and after doing so try to show you how you can keep them from occurring in your life.

Equivocal words One kind of semantic misunderstanding is caused by equivocal words, that is, words that can be interpreted in more than one way. Equivocal misunderstandings happen almost every day, usually when we least expect them. Not long ago we were ordering dinner in a Mexican restaurant and noticed that the menu described each item as coming with rice or beans. We asked the waitress for "a tostada with beans," but when the order came we were surprised to find that instead of a beef tostada with beans on the side as we expected, the waitress had brought a tostada *filled* with beans. At first we were angry at her for botching a simple order, but then we realized that it was as much our fault for not making the order clear as it was hers for not checking.

"I don't know what you mean by 'glory,'" Alice said.

Humpty Dumpty smiled contemptuously. "Of course you don't—till I tell you. I meant 'there's a nice knock-down argument for you!'"

"But 'glory' doesn't mean 'a nice knock-down argument,'" Alice objected.

"When I use a word," Humpty Dumpty said, in a rather scornful tone, "it means just what I choose it to mean—neither more nor less."

"The question is," said Alice, "whether you can make words mean so many different things."

"The question is," said Humpty Dumpty, "which is to be master—that's all."

Lewis Carroll, *Through the Looking Glass*

The Semantics of "I Love You"

. . . "I love you" [is] a statement that can be expressed in so many varied ways. It may be a stage song, repeated daily without any meaning, or a barely audible murmur, full of surrender. Sometimes it means: I desire you or I want you sexually. It may mean: I hope you love me or I hope that I will be able to love you. Often it means: It may be that a love relationship can develop between us or even I hate you. Often it is a wish for emotional exchange: I want your admiration in exchange for mine or I give my love in exchange for some passion or I want to feel cozy and at home with you or I admire some of your qualities: A declaration of love is mostly a request: I desire you or I want you to gratify me, or I want your protection or I want to be intimate with you or I want to exploit your loveliness.

Sometimes it is the need for security and tenderness, for parental treatment. It may mean: My self-love goes out to you. But it may also express submissiveness: Please take me as I am, or I feel guilty about you, I want, through you, to correct the mistakes I have made in human relations. It may be self-sacrifice and a masochistic wish for dependency. However, it may also be a full affirmation of the other, taking the responsibility for mutual exchange of feelings. It may be a weak feeling of friendliness, it may be the scarcely even whispered expression of ecstasy. "I love you,"—wish, desire, submission, conquest; it is never the word itself that tells the real meaning here.

J. A. M. Meerloo, *Conversation and Communication*

Often equivocal misunderstandings are more serious. A nurse gave one of her patients a real scare when she told him that he "wouldn't be needing" his robe, books, and shaving materials any more. After that statement the patient became quiet and moody for no apparent reason. When the nurse finally asked why, she found out that her statement had led the poor man to think he was going to die immediately; she really meant that he'd be going home soon.

As we mentioned earlier, most of the words we use can be interpreted in a number of ways. A good rule to remember if you want to keep misunderstandings to a minimum is "If a word can be interpreted in more than one way, it probably will be."

Relative words Relative words are ones that gain their meaning by comparison. For example, is the school you attend a large or small one? This depends on what you compare it to: Alongside a campus like UCLA, with its almost 28,000 students, it probably looks pretty small; but compared with a smaller institution it might seem quite large. In the same way relative words like fast and slow, smart and stupid, short and long depend for their meaning upon what they're compared to. (The "large" size can of olives is the smallest you can buy; the larger ones are "giant," "colossal," and "super-colossal.")

Using relative terms without explaining them can lead to communication problems. Have you ever responded to someone's question about the weather by telling her it was warm, only to find out that she thought it was

Liddy Error Alleged: Thought He Must Kill

NEW YORK (UPI)—Convicted Watergate conspirator G. Gordan Liddy thought he had been ordered to assassinate columnist Jack Anderson during the 1972 campaign, Parade magazine reported Saturday.

The magazine said that during the course of a meeting with Jeb Stuart Magruder, deputy director of the Committee for the reelection of the President, Magruder mentioned Anderson and told Liddy: "We've got to get rid of this guy."

Liddy, according to Parade, left the meeting and ran into Robert Reisner, Magruder's assistant.

"I've just been ordered to kill Jack Anderson," the magazine quoted Liddy as telling him.

Alarmed, Reisner ran back into Magruder's office and confronted Magruder.

"Magruder and Reisner immediately got hold of Liddy," the magazine said. "Magruder explained that he had just been talking figuratively. He didn't want Anderson assassinated . . . all he meant was that Anderson's incisive reporting constituted a problem that he would prefer to be rid of."

According to Parade, Liddy answered: "Where I come from that means a rubout."

Semantics: Where Words Go Astray

cold? Or have you followed a friend's advice and gone to a "cheap" restaurant only to find that it was twice as expensive as you expected? Have you been disappointed to learn that classes you've heard were "easy" turned out to be hard, that journeys you were told would be "short" were long, that "unusual" ideas were really quite ordinary? The problem in each case came from failing to anchor the relative term used to a more precisely measurable one.

Emotive words Emotive words are ones that sound as if they're describing something but are really announcing the speaker's attitude toward it. Do you like that old picture frame? If you do, you'd probably call it an "antique," but if you think it's ugly you'd likely describe it as "a piece of junk." Now whether the picture frame belongs on the mantle or in the garbage can is a matter of opinion, not fact, but it's easy to forget this when you use emotive words. Emotive words may sound like statements of fact, but they're always opinions.

Here's a list of other emotive words:

If you approve, say	If you disapprove, say
Thrifty	Cheap
Traditional	Old-fashioned
Extrovert	Loudmouth
Cautious	Coward
Progressive	Radical
Information	Propaganda
Strategic withdrawal	Retreat
Military victory	Massacre

"Conjugating Irregular Verbs"

Here's a way to see how emotive words work. According to S. I. Hayakawa the idea of "conjugating irregular verbs" this way originated with Bertrand Russell.

1   The technique is simple: Just take an action or personality trait and show how it can be viewed either favorably or unfavorably, according to the label we give it. For example:

    I'm casual.
    You're a little careless.
    He's a slob.

Or try this one:

    I read love stories.
    You read erotic literature.
    She reads pornography.

Or:

> I'm thrifty.
> You're money conscious.
> He's a tightwad.

2 Now try a few conjugations yourself using the following statements:
  a. I'm tactful.
  b. I'm conservative.
  c. I'm quiet.
  d. I'm relaxed.
  e. My child is high spirited.
  f. I have a lot of self-pride.

3 Now recall at least two situations in which you used an emotive word as if it were a description of fact and not an opinion. A good way to remember these situations is to think of a recent argument you had and imagine how the other person involved might have described it. How would his words differ from yours?

Overly broad terms   Sometimes we use a word that says more to others than we intend it to. In such cases we've unintentionally chosen a word that covers a whole class of objects, but we only meant to describe some members of that class. For example, how many times has an instructor told you to study "everything we've covered so far" for an exam (causing you to loose sleep, neglect your other work, and generally ruin part of your life)? Then, when the day of the test came, you found he really meant you should study everything since the last midterm. In this case the words "everything we've covered so far" were too broad.

Fiction words   Semanticists use the label "fiction word" to describe terms such as freedom, truth, communism, democracy, justice, and so on. Fiction words make communication difficult because they have so many meanings that no two people use them the same way. The danger in using such words comes from assuming that their meaning is clear. For example, many voters will hear a candidate for office declare that he's in favor of "peace" and automatically vote for him, assuming his election will bring on a new era of international friendship. Later they may be disappointed to learn that their candidates' idea of peace involves bombing into submission any country whose governmental policies differ from his.

We'll have more to say about fiction words later in this chapter.

HOW TO TELL A
BUSINESSMAN
FROM A
BUSINESSWOMAN

A businessman is aggressive; a businesswoman is pushy.

He is careful about details; she's picky.

He loses his temper because he's so involved in his job; she's bitchy.

He's depressed (or hung over), so everyone tiptoes past his office; she's moody, so it must be her time of the month.

He follows through; she doesn't know when to quit.

He's firm; she's stubborn.

He makes wise judgments; she reveals her prejudices.

He is a man of the world; she's been around.

He isn't afraid to say what he thinks; she's opinionated.

He exercises authority; she's tyrannical.

He's discreet; she's secretive.

He's a stern taskmaster; she's difficult to work for.

Levels of Abstraction

After reading these last few pages you probably have a clearer idea of some ways that words can confuse as much as help our communication. You now understand better why it's a mistake to assume that words have fixed meanings that are the same for all of us, and you realize that meanings rest as much in people as in language.

Now that you've seen some of the most common ways that words get us into trouble, we can introduce the semantic problem they all share. Like many important ideas, this one seems clear enough at first, yet its implications are everywhere.

Stated most simply, the problem is that much of our language is too abstract. Often people use words that cover more territory than is necessary and in so doing not only make themselves harder to understand but also start us thinking in dangerous ways.

To see why this is so you have to realize that any idea can be described on a number of levels, some of which are more abstract than others. Take the thing you're reading now. What would you call it? Probably a book, right? But you could narrow your description by calling it a "communications book," or even more specifically, *Looking Out/Looking In.* You could be even more precise than this if you wanted: You could say that you're reading Chapter 7 of *Looking Out/Looking In* or even page 302 of Chapter 7 of

Looking Out/Looking In. In each case your description would be more precise, focusing more specifically on the object we asked you about while excluding other things that were members of the same categories but didn't apply in this case.

Instead of going down the abstraction ladder to more basic terms, you could go the other way. Rather than talking about this thing you're reading as a book, you could describe it as educational literature, nonfiction writing, or printed material, each description being less and less specific. The point is that the more precise your description, the less likely is your chance of being misunderstood by others.

To see how talking in abstract language can damage communication, imagine someone who has had a bad experience while traveling abroad and as a result blames an entire country. "Yeah, those damn Hottentots are a bunch of thieves. If you're not careful they'll steal you blind. I know, because one of 'em stole my camera last year." You can see here how lumping people into highly abstract categories ignores the fact that for every thieving Hottentot there are probably 100 honest ones. It's this kind of thinking that leads to mistaken assumptions that keep people apart: "None of those kids are any damn good!"; "You can't trust anybody in business."; "Those cops are all a bunch of goons." Each of these statements ignores the very important fact that sometimes our descriptions are too general, that they say more than we really mean.

When you think about examples like these, you begin to see how thinking in abstract terms can lead to ignoring individual differences, which can be as important as similarities. In this sense semantics isn't "just" a matter of words. People in the habit of using highly abstract language begin to *think* in generalities, ignoring uniqueness. And as we discussed in Chapters 2 and 3, expecting people to be a certain way can become a self-fulfilling prophecy. If I think all policemen are brutal, I'm more likely to react in a defensive, hostile way toward them, which in turn increases the chance that they'll react to me as a threat. If I think that no teachers care about their classes, then my defensive indifference is likely to make a potentially helpful instructor into someone who truly doesn't care.

Failing to recognize abstractions for what they are can lead to a great deal of unnecessary grief. We know a couple who were convinced that their child was abnormal because she hadn't learned to talk by the age of two. When we tried to tell them that some kids begin talking later than others and that there was nothing to worry about, the parents wouldn't accept our help. "But something must be wrong with Sally," they said, pointing to a book on child development. "It says right here that children should be talking by one year, and Sally only makes funny noises." What the parents had failed to do was read the first chapters of the book, in which the authors stressed that the term "child" is an abstraction—that there's no such thing as the "typical" child because each one is an individual.

"I know you believe you understand what you think I said, but I'm not sure you realize that what you heard is not what I meant."

Check Your Abstractions

To see how valid some of the abstractions you use in your language are, try the following exercise:

1 Form the class into groups of five or six.

2 Without thinking too much about it, each person should complete the following sentences. Don't be too analytical; write down the first thing that pops into your mind.

    a. Women are _____ .
    b. Men are _____ .
    c. When I think of the police I _____ .
    d. In my opinion, communism is _____ .
    e. My feelings about the military are _____ .
    f. I think that black people in this country want _____ .
    g. My opinion of the Republican party is _____ .
    h. I think movies about sex should _____ .

3 Now share your answers with those of the other group members. Were your reactions to these terms similar or different?

4 Now go back over the list. Reduce the subject of each sentence (women, men, police, et cetera) into as many individual, less abstract terms as you can. For example, instead of "Women" in sentence (a), you'd make a list of ten or twenty specific women you've known; for "movies about sex" in sentence (h), describe all the movies you can think of.

5 Now share your response to step 3 with your group. How similar or different are the individual responses this time?

6 Now that you've looked at the range of possible referents for each word on the original list, would you say that sometimes we're overly abstract in using such terms instead of more specific ones?

7 For the next two days keep track of the overly abstract terms that crop up in your life—in conversations, readings, TV and movies, lectures, et cetera. Can you see ways in which these abstractions endanger communication?

Just Look It Up . . .

Many times we use language that sounds clear enough to us but upon closer examination is very confusing. This especially happens when using highly abstract fiction words such as *peace, freedom,* and so on. At first you might say that the way to find out what these terms mean is simply to look them up in a dictionary. But this won't really help because the only thing a dictionary does is explain one word in terms of *other* words; this process often won't tell you any more about a term than you already know. In fact, it's possible to talk endlessly about a subject in a way that *sounds* very knowledgeable without ever having the slightest idea of what your words refer to. Jessica Davidson's quiz is an example of this. Read the paragraph and see if you can answer the questions:*

> Because public opinion is sometimes marsiflate, empetricious insoculences are frequently zophilimized. Nevertheless, it cannot be overemphasized that carpoflansibles are highly traculate.
>
> 1 In the authors' opinion, carpoflansibles are
>   a. Empetricious
>   b. Traculate
>   c. Zophilimized
> 2 Public opinion is sometimes
>   a. Insoculent
>   b. Variable
>   c. Marsiflate

*Jessica Davidson, "How to Translate English," in Joseph Fletcher Littell, ed. *The Language of Man,* vol. 4 (Evanston, Ill.: McDougal Littell, 1971).

On the basis of this article, explain in low-level terms Kleindienst's definition of "patriot."

3 According to the text insoculences are zophilimized
   a. Often
   b. Never
   c. Sometimes

You can see that the correct answers are 1(b), 2(c), and 3(a). But even if you scored perfectly on the quiz, do you know the meaning of the paragraph? Of course not, for the words are gibberish. But if you look closely, you'll find that many people use their own language in the same way, talking in terms which they can define only by other terms. For example, S. I. Hayakawa shows how "democracy" can be used without ever really being explained:

"What do you mean by *democracy?*"

"Democracy means the preservation of human rights."

"What do you mean by rights?"

"By rights I mean those privileges God grants to all of us—I mean man's inherent privileges."

"Such as?"

"Liberty, for example."

"What do you mean by *liberty?*"

"Religious and political freedom."

"And what does that mean?"

"Religious and political freedom is what we enjoy under a democracy."*

It's this kind of language usage that makes high-level abstractions so dangerous because they can lead you to honestly belive that someone is talking about a clear, definite idea when they really may as well be speaking gibberish.

Down to Specifics: Avoiding Abstract Thinking and Language

If abstract language is so widespread, what can we do to eliminate it from our lives? Probably the best thing is to pay attention to your own everyday conversation. Every so often—especially when you're in an emotional argument—ask yourself whether you can translate your language down the ladder of abstraction to less vague terms. Often you'll find you've been using words that are really hard to explain.

One effective way to reduce the use of unnecessarily high-level abstractions, or at least to be sure you know what they mean, is through the use of *operational definitions.* Instead of defining a word with more words, an operational definition *points,* as it were, to the behaviors, actions, or properties that a word signifies.

We use operational definitions all the time: "The student union is that building with all the bikes in front"; "What I'd like more than anything is 30 acres of land on the Columbia River"; "My idea of a good time is eating a triple-decker, three-flavor, chocolate-dipped ice cream cone." Each of these statements is relatively clear; rather than using vague, more abstract language they tell in observable terms just what the speaker is talking about. Hayakawa points out that the best examples of operational definitions in our everyday lives are found in cookbooks. They describe a dish by telling you what ingredients are combined in what amounts by what operations. ("To make a pizza, begin with the crust. Mix ¼ cup water with 2 cups flour. . . .")

But as we've already seen, some definitions aren't operational. They never point down the ladder of abstraction to more clearly understandable operations; instead, they only explain words with more words. A nonoperational, highly abstract cookbook might define a pizza as "a delectable, flavorful treat that is both hearty and subtle." You can see that it would be extremely difficult to learn very much about a pizza from such a description. In much the same way it's far clearer to define words such as *freedom* and *democracy* operationally rather than abstractly.

"In that case," said the Dodo solemnly, rising to its feet, "I move that the meeting adjourn, for the immediate adoption of more energetic remedies—"

"Speak English!" said the Eaglet. "I don't know the meaning of half those long words, and, what's more, I don't believe you do either!" And the Eaglet bent down its head to hide a smile: some of the other birds tittered audibly.

"What I was going to say," said the Dodo in an offended tone, "was that the best thing to get us dry would be a Caucus-race."

"What **is** a Caucus-race?" said Alice.

"Why," said the Dodo, "the best way to explain it is to do it."

Lewis Carroll,
*Alice's Adventures in
Wonderland*

*S. I. Hayakawa, *Language in Thought and Action* (New York: Harcourt Brace Jovanovich, Inc., 1964).

Operational Opinions

1 Divide the class into groups of three to five.

2 Each person should select one statement from the following list. More than one person can choose the same statement. Take five minutes to jot down your response to the statement you've chosen.

    a. What I want from this course

    b. What changes need to be made in our society

    c. The things that bother me most about my _____ (parents, spouse, children, boss, et cetera)

    d. My political philosophy in a nutshell

3 Now each person in turn should read his answer to the rest of the group. After doing this, the group should pick out all the highly abstract words in the statement and ask the writer to translate them into operational terms.

4 The author may need some help in this clarifying process, but be careful to let her define her own terms.

5 Now compare the newly written statement to the original one.

    a. Which sounds clearer?

    b. How does the revised statement differ from the ways you usually think and speak?

Instant Blap

Anyone who is familiar with the academic, business or government worlds knows that there often seems to be a rule which says "When choosing between a simple and a more abstract term, always pick the more confusing one."

In the past this has been a great setback for clear-headed writers and speakers. But now modern technology has found a solution: the Systematic Buzz Phrase Projector.

The projector is simple to use. Whenever you want to say nothing in an authoritative way, simply pick any three-digit number, and then find the matching word from each column. For example, 424 produces "functional monitored programing," which should impress anyone untrained in detecting high-level abstractions.

Column 1	Column 2	Column 3
0 integrated	0 management	0 options
1 total	1 organizational	1 flexibility
2 systematized	2 monitored	2 capability
3 parallel	3 reciprocal	3 mobility
4 functional	4 digital	4 programing
5 responsive	5 logistical	5 concept
6 optional	6 transitional	6 time-phase
7 synchronized	7 incremental	7 projection
8 compatible	8 third-generation	8 hardware
9 balanced	9 policy	9 contingency

. . . It is doubtful if a people learned in semantics would tolerate any sort of supreme political dictator. . . . A typical speech by an aspiring Hitler would be translated into its intrinsic meaning, if any. Abstract words and phrases without discoverable referents would register a semantic blank, noises without meaning. For instance:

> The Aryan Fatherland, which has nursed the souls of heroes, calls upon you for the supreme sacrifice which you, in whom flows heroic blood, will not fail, and which will echo forever down the corridors of history.

This would be translated:

> The blab, blab, which has nursed the blabs of blabs, calls upon you for the blab blab which you, in whom flows blab blood, will not fail, and which will echo down the blabs of blab.

The "blab" is not an attempt to be funny; it is a semantic blank. Nothing comes through. The hearer, versed in reducing high-order abstractions to either nil or a series of roughly similar events in the real world of experience, and protected from emotive associations with such words, simply hears nothing comprehensible. The demagogue might as well have used Sanskrit.

STUART CHASE, *The Tyranny of Words*

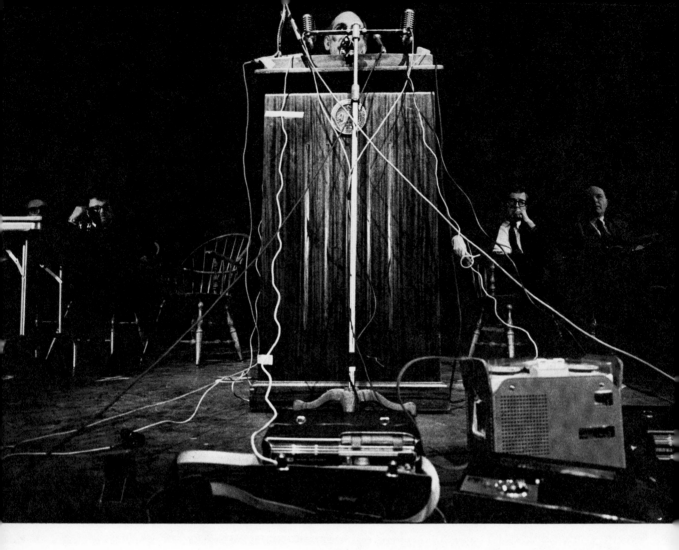

Euphemisms and Other Gobbledygook

So far we've been talking about cases where people use overly vague abstractions unintentionally. But there are other instances when abstractions can be used to deliberately obscure someone's intentions.

As we suggested earlier, probably the most widespread instance of this deliberate muddying of the waters is in the field of politics. People running for elective offices often use what we earlier termed fiction words to start the voters' glands working. Take Candidate X; he needs the support both of people who favor capital punishment and those who oppose it. How can he make a statement on the subject that won't cost him any votes? He can't say we should string up every felon in the state, yet he doesn't want to look "soft on crime" either. So after much deliberation, his office issues the following news release: "Candidate X declared today that under our great system of laws each man and woman must be guaranteed due process, with those found guilty receiving treatment which is both swift and fair. To do any less would be contrary to the principles of this nation."

Semantics: Where Words Go Astray

Now what do statements like this say? It's no accident that we don't know. In this age of widespread telecommunications every word a candidate speaks can be heard by anyone who cares to listen. In a statement like this candidates often are tempted to water down their words so that they sound good but say nothing . . . or everything.

Although more and more people are developing a healthy skepticism toward such statements, there's still a danger of a few high-level abstractions slipping through. Because of this it's necessary to keep on guard—to ask what those fine-sounding words refer to, what they mean in specific, operational terms to the person who spoke them.

Many times we use high-level abstractions to fool ourselves as well as others. When faced with a truth we'd rather ignore, often the easiest thing to do is rename it and in so doing remove some of its distastefulness. One way is through the use of euphemisms, words that soften the bluntness of unpleasant ideas. Often euphemisms are merely ways of avoiding shocking friends, as, for example, asking where the "rest rooms" are instead of asking "Where's the toilet?" In such cases there's nothing especially dangerous about using euphemisms instead of more straightforward language.

But there are many instances in which using vague, inoffensive terms instead of "telling it like it is" can block our thinking in important ways. Speaking of poor people as being "disadvantaged" somehow makes their plight less disturbing. Referring to "senior citizens' retirement communities" presents a happier picture than "old peoples' homes." And talking about someone's "passing on" instead of dying allows us to avoid facing and preparing for the eventual deaths of ourselves and our friends.

But it's in the field of international politics and war that euphemisms are probably most dangerous. As Aldous Huxley shows in the following reading, high-sounding phrases and noble generalities can lead to disastrous consequences.

A group of synonyms does not define an object. A careful description may help bring it into focus for the listener, but is not conclusive. Final identification is achieved only by pointing to the apple, touching it with the hand, seeing it with the eyes, tasting it with the mouth, and so recognizing it as nonverbal. Here is the base from which all our proud words rise—every last one of them—and to it they must constantly return and be refreshed. Failing this, they wander into regions where there are no apples, no objects, no acts, and so they become symbols for airy chunks of nothing at all. . . .

Stuart Chase, *The Tyranny of Words*

The Language of War

Words form the thread on which we string our experiences. Without them we should live spasmodically and intermittently. If, as so often happens, we choose to give continuity to our experience by means of words which falsify the facts, this is because the falsification is somehow to our advantage as egotists.

Consider, for example, the case of war. War is enormously discreditable to those who order it to be waged and even to those who merely tolerate its existence. Furthermore, to developed sensibilities the facts of war are revolting and horrifying. To falsify these facts, and by so doing to make war seem less evil than it really is, and our own responsibility in tolerating war less heavy, is doubly to our advantage. By suppressing and distorting the truth, we protect our sensibilities and preserve our self-esteem. Now, language is, among other things, a device which men use for suppressing and distorting the truth. Finding the reality of war too unpleasant to contemplate, we create a verbal alternative to that reality, parallel with it, but in quality quite different from it. That which we contemplate thenceforward is not that to which we react emotionally and upon which we pass our moral judgments, is not war as it is in fact, but the fiction of war as it exists in our pleasantly falsifying verbiage. Our stupidity in using inappropriate language turns out, on analysis, to be the most refined cunning.

The most shocking fact about war is that its victims and its instruments are individual human beings, and that these individual human beings are condemned by the monstrous conventions of politics to murder or be murdered in quarrels not their own, to inflict upon the innocent and, innocent themselves of any crime against their enemies, to suffer cruelties of every kind.

The language of strategy and politics is designed, so far as it is possible, to conceal this fact, to make it appear as though wars were not fought by individuals drilled to murder one another in cold blood and without provocation, but either by impersonal and therefore wholly non-moral and impassible forces, or else by personified abstractions.

Ignoring the facts, so far as we possibly can, we imply that battles are not fought by soldiers, but by things, principles, allegories, personified collectivities, or (at the most human) by opposing commanders, pitched against one another in single combat. For the same reason, when we have to describe the processes and the results of war, we employ a rich variety of euphemisms. Even the most violently patriotic and militaristic are reluctant to call a spade by its own name. To conceal their intentions even from themselves, they make use of picturesque metaphors. We find them, for example, clamouring for war planes numerous and powerful enough to go and "destroy the hornets in their nests"—in other words, to go and throw thermite, high explosives and vesicants upon the inhabitants of neighbouring countries before they have time to come and do the same to us. And how reassuring is the language of historians and strategists! They write admiringly of those military geniuses who know "when to strike at the enemy's line" (a single combatant deranges the geometrical constructions of a personification); when to "turn his flank"; when to "execute an enveloping movement." As though they were engineers discussing the strength of materials and the distribution of stresses, they talk of abstract entities called "man power" and "fire power." They sum up the long-drawn sufferings and atrocities of trench warfare in the phrase, "a war of attrition"; the massacre and mangling of human beings is assimilated to the grinding of a lens.

A dangerously abstract word, which figures in all discussions about war, is "force." Those who believe in organizing collective security by means of military pacts against a possible aggressor are particularly fond of this word. "You cannot," they say, "have international justice unless you are prepared to impose it by force." "Peace-loving countries must unite to use force against aggressive dictatorships." "Democratic institutions must be protected, if need be, by force." And so on.

Let us take the sentences quoted above and translate the abstract word "force" into language that will render (however inadequately) the concrete and particular realities of contemporary warfare.

"You cannot have international justice, unless you are prepared to impose it by force." Translated, this becomes: "You cannot have international justice unless you are prepared, with a view to imposing a just settlement, to drop thermite, high explosives and vesicants upon the inhabitants of foreign cities and to have thermite, high explosives and vesicants dropped in return upon the inhabitants of your cities." At the end of this proceeding, justice is to be imposed by the victorious party—that is, if there is a victorious party.

The next two sentences may be taken together. "Peace-loving countries must unite to use force against aggressive dictatorships. Democratic institutions must be protected, if need be, by force." Let us translate. "Peace-loving countries must unite to throw thermite, high explosives and vesicants on the inhabitants of countries ruled by aggressive dictators. They must do this, and of course abide the consequences, in order to preserve peace and democratic institutions."

The alternatives confronting us seem to be plain enough. Either we invent and conscientiously employ a new technique for making revolutions and settling international disputes; or else we cling to the old technique and, using "force" (that is to say, thermite, high explosives and vesicants), destroy ourselves. Those who, for whatever motive, disguise the nature of the second alternative under inappropriate language, render the world a grave disservice. They lead us into one of the temptations we find it hardest to resist—the temptation to run away from reality, to pretend that facts are not what they are. Like Shelley (but without Shelley's acute awareness of what he was doing) we are perpetually weaving

A shroud of talk to hide us from the sun
Of this familiar life.

We protect our minds by an elaborate system of abstractions, ambiguities, metaphors and similes from the reality we do not wish to know too clearly; we lie to ourselves, in order that we may still have the excuse of ignorance, the alibi of stupidity and incomprehension, possessing which we can continue with a good conscience to commit and tolerate the most monstrous crimes.

Aldous Huxley, *Words and Behaviour*

Political language—and with variations this is true of all political parties, from Conservatives to Anarchists—is designed to make lies sound truthful and murder respectable, and to give an appearance of solidarity to pure wind.

George Orwell, *Politics and the English Language*

The Breakfast Special

a toasted english muffin
with whipped creamy butter
and a steaming mug
of mountain grown coffee
it all sounds so good on the menu
fresh ranch eggs
conjuring up pictures of
mother, father and i on an outing
flying through a summer countryside
in an open tin lizzy
mother holding her floppy hat in the wind
laughing. . . . banjo music playing
and chickens everywhere! scattering
scurrying back to a barn
full of sunshine cracks and aromatic shadows
where clucking hens nest in secret places
laying eggs for children to find
put into baskets and bring us for breakfast
yes i'll have some of that this morning.

pretending i've not
been to the concentration camp
and seen the eyes staring through the wire
and seen the miles and miles
of shopping basket cells
with barely room enough to move or sleep
forgetting how they helplessly stand for days
eating off tin trays
drinking from galvanized tanks
watching their lifes work roll away like teeth

taken out of the circle of things
crispy bacon strips
and country cured ham
have nothing to do with the slaughter.

we eat words   and no one says grace
                      and no one gives thanks

Ric Masten

Euphemisms and You

This exercise is going to take some honesty on your part and may hurt just a bit.

1 Form groups of five people, and share the times you use euphemisms to avoid facing up to unpleasant facts about yourself.

2 Remember, euphemisms are a device for fooling ourselves and others—they're defense mechanisms. If you're honest and dig a bit, you'll do doubt find a few that you use.

3 Here are a few examples to get you started:
   a. Do you call cheating on your tax "finding loopholes"?
   b. Do you "borrow" things you've no intention of returning?
   c. Do you say you're "tipsy" or "relaxed" when you're drunk?
   d. Do you pretend that an argument is a "discussion"?
   e. Do you make "suggestions" that are really commands?

4 Have your group make a list of all the euphemisms you've shared.

5 Bring all the groups together, and compile a master list of all the euphemisms you've found.

Language Shapes Our World

At the beginning of this chapter we said that meanings rest more in people than words. Although this statement is true, it shouldn't lead you to think that labels aren't important; just the opposite is true. In many cases the name we give something determines the way we'll look at it—whether we'll regard it as attractive or unpleasant, respectable or contemptible, desirable or repellent. For the next few pages we'll explore the way in which language shapes ideas.

We already hinted at how this process works when we talked about euphemisms and how they can make an unattractive idea or thing more pleasant. By changing the labels we use, the euphemism changes our perception of the world and thus our behavior. But language shapes our attitudes in other ways too.

Advertisements are probably the best example of how attitudes can be created through the use of words. Semanticists like to tell a story that illustrates this point: In a department store experimenters set up two stacks of handkerchiefs side by side on a table. The merchandise in each was identical, the only difference being the signs above each pile. One read "Fine Linen Handkerchiefs—$1.50 each," while the other said "Nose Rags—35¢." As you might expect, the "handkerchiefs" sold out quickly, and the "nose rags" were hardly touched. In this case names didn't reflect reality so much as create it.

FRANCHISING: WHAT'S IN A NAME?

There are Halston suitcases, his-and-hers Halston towels, Halston Ultrasuede quilts, Halston wigs and Halston gloves. The Bill Blass name and his back-to-back initials appear on fur coats, after-shave cologne and Lincoln Continentals. Anne Klein's "Mark of the Lion" decorates umbrellas, belts, espadrille shoes and clutch purses. And John Weitz's imprint graces bathing suits, ties, shirts and even cigars. American designers seem to be slapping their signatures on high-ticket products of virtually every description in hopes that the name of the game is a famous name.

European designers learned long ago that selling their names to an independent soap or perfume manufacturer was much easier—and almost as lucrative—as coming up with new clothing styles each season. But most American designers are just beginning to catch on to the license ploy.

□ □ □

There are many different licensing contracts but the format is basically the same. As a binder when the contract is signed, the designer is either paid "front money" from the distibutor, ranging from $5,000 to $50,000 depending on the status of his name, or a percentage of the projected first-year royalties. From then on, royalty contracts pay the designer from 5 to 10 percent of net wholesale sales, and there is usually a guaranteed annual minimum. "Royalties are all gravy," says Jack Maurer, business manager of Bill Blass, whose twelve licenses brought in nearly $2 million last year. "No costs are taken out."

□ □ □

John Weitz, one of the founding fathers of American franchising, has grown less particular and more practical over the years. "I'll put my name on a product if the company convinces me it will make money even if I don't find it particularly palatable—as long as it's not vulgar," says the 54-year-old Weitz, whose 48 accounts, including cigars, generate $100 million in worldwide retail sales a year. "I mean how much design goes into a navy-blue tie?" Sometimes nothing extra goes into a franchise product except the signature. "Most customers who buy designer names are being ripped off," says Vince Thurston, manager of T. Anthony, a top New York luggage shop. "I've got an all-leather knapsack for $65, and the same one is selling with Cassini's name on it for $95." What's in a name? Says Thurston: "A 35 percent markup."

Newsweek

317

Advertising isn't the only field in which words shape attitudes. Not too long ago a new kind of course was introduced into high schools and junior highs across the country. In the course students learned such things as the biology of human reproducton, the causes and dangers of venereal disease, and in some instances methods of preventing unwanted pregnancies. School administrators usually called the course Sex Education, and almost everywhere it was taught a large number of parents and other community members raised protests. Their arguments usually centered around the theme that "School was no place to teach kids about sex." Often these protests developed into mass meetings, newspaper editorials, and letter-writing campaigns that opposed the teaching of such a "delicate" and "personal" subject.

The protests threatened what educators thought of as a tremendously important program, one that would ensure the future health and happiness of many students. Being well acquainted with the course, they knew that nothing in them would threaten the moral values that the protesters felt were under attack. But somehow the public had to be shown the true aims of the program. As time passed, many teachers and administrators began to realize that much of their problem was caused by the name of the course they were offering. Once they recognized that it was the word "sex" that seemed to threaten so many people, the solution was simple. Rather than

"It's called bananas flambeau, not a bunch of burned bananas."

Semantics: Where Words Go Astray

SIRS: I read with interest the article by John Shlien, "Mother-in-Law: A Problem in Kinship Terminology" (*ETC.*, July 1962). My step-daughter married a fine young man during her last year of college. The three of us were on the same campus, and I ran into Paul, the husband, often. After the wedding his attitude toward me completely changed. He acted ill at ease in my presence and would avoid me if possible.

My attendance at a seminar on general semantics gave me enough insight into the situation to lead me to suspect what was the trouble. The next time he came, rather reluctantly, to our home, I fixed a bite to eat, and over the coffee said, "Paul, I am so glad that I'm not really your mother-in-law so that we can be friends." It worked like magic; he began to relax, started coming to our house at every opportunity. And today, I don't believe I have a better friend than Paul. I certainly had not changed that quickly, but I had stumbled on a way of removing my obnoxious label.

ETC.

teach Sex Education any more, the schools announced that they would offer classes in Social Hygiene or Family Health. There was no basic change in the subjects taught, just the name. And amazingly, most of the protests died away. Now that the public no longer felt that the schools were dabbling in sex, they were satisfied.

We don't give names only to things. The words we use to describe a person's role or function in society can shape the way he feels about himself. Much of our self-esteem comes from the importance we feel our work has, and this perception of importance often comes from the title our role has. For example, we've heard of a theater owner who had trouble keeping ushers working for him for more than a week or two. They seemed to tire quickly of their work, which consisted mostly of taking tickets, selling popcorn, and showing people to their seats. Then, with only one change, the manager ended his personnel problems: He simply "promoted" all his ushers to the "new" position of "assistant manager." And believe it or not, the new title was sufficient to make the employees happy. It seemed that the new name made them think more highly of themselves and take new pride in their work.

But the significance of words in shaping our self-concept goes beyond job titles. As the following article shows, the name by which we think of ourselves can be tremendously important.

Identity Crisis

Black? Afro-American? Negro? Or colored?

The NEWSWEEK Poll shows that name calling is a matter of considerable concern to the sampling of 22 million U.S. citizens. And news media mirror this concern, shifting from black to Negro and back frequently in the same story (colored seems passé).

This identity crisis seems superficial, but beneath the surface are far more complex questions of how white men view non-white men—and how non-whites view themselves. Involved too is a largely unconscious set of perceptions sometimes used by white newsmen to describe what they think they see.

Throughout American history words of racial identification have gone through cycles of popularity and disrepute. The first freed slaves preferred to be called "Africans" and periodically there have been attempts to establish the term "Afro-American." But even though Afro-American parallels such expressions as Irish-American and Italian-American, such attempts have never been very successful. The Amsterdam News in Harlem momentarily tried Afro-American, but dropped it in favor of black. "Colored" was a respectable word in the last century but is now avoided almost everywhere. (An exception: The National Association for the Advancement of Colored People founded in 1909).

Until the twentieth century, the lower-case "negro" was considered derogatory. But in the early 1900s civil-rights activists campaigned for and successfully popularized "Negro." And the word achieved a certain legitimacy in the white community when in a March 7, 1930 editorial The New York Times noted: "In our stylebook "Negro" is now added to the list of words to be capitalized . . . it is an act of recognition of racial self-respect for those who have been for generations in 'the lower case'."

More and more these days newsmen and broadcasters are using "black," a word that only a few years ago was considered contemptuous. Beginning with Stokely Carmichael's speeches in Mississippi in 1966, "black" has become increasingly acceptable and now many newsmen (NEWSWEEK's among them) use Negro and black interchangeably. The momentum has been shifting to black and, significantly, it is black newsmen who are leading the way. "Black is more prominent, it's easier to say and the young people prefer it," observes Tom Picour, editor of The Chicago Defender, a black daily.

Pride: "Black" is now associated with youth, with unity, with militancy (black power), and with pride ("Black is beautiful"). At the same time, "Negro" has come more and more to connote middle age, the status quo, complacency. "At one time it didn't matter to me whether I was called Negro or black," says Hans Massaquoi, managing editor of Ebony. "But now it does matter and I prefer to be called black. As I read copy, I am aware that when certain writers say Negro they are describing someone they *see* as a Negro—an Uncle Tom."

"'Black' is a much more honest word for us," says Henry Hampton, 28, a political commentator for WGBH in Boston. "It conjures a state of mind to cope with the long tradition of what the word used to mean. When I was 12 my mother used to play 'Old Black Joe' on the piano. Black used to be a word that was used against us. Now we've turned it around and made it into a positive weapon."

On most "white" publications, editors are taking their cue from black reporters. "One of our black reporters turned in a story and in the rewrite where he had used black it was changed to Negro," recalls Ed Cony, managing editor of The Wall Street

Journal. "When he saw the rewrite he said he'd like all those 'Negroes' changed back to 'blacks' and we did it."

William Raspberry, a black columnist for The Washington Post, believes that in general people who are over 30 prefer 'Negro,' while most who are under 30 would rather be called 'black.' "Only the older generation would accept the term 'colored'," says Raspberry, "and Afro-American is just too unwieldy." Leo Addie, director of WTOP-TV News in Washington, says that the station generally uses the word "Negro," but adds, "We leave it up to the reporter's judgment in cases where the subject insists on being called 'black'."

Heritage: Chris Borgen, a 38-year-old CBS-TV newsman, says that his rule-of-thumb is that no militant will be offended by the word "black" and that anyone displaying signs of African heritage, such as wearing a Dashiki, can properly be called an Afro-American. "To the militant," he explains, "any person of color in the U.S. who is, by his own choice, a member of the Establishment and does not agree with the militant, is a Negro." Borgen adds that he considers himself a Negro. "Black and Afro-American imply to me that I need an identity which transcends the one that I already have."

Often the galling thing to blacks—and Negroes—is the over-all context and tone of a story or broadcast.

White writers and editors, it seems, tend to put out papers that have a distinctly "white" viewpoint. The current issue of the Columbia Journalism Review cites several not so subtle examples. An editorial in The New Haven Register stated that the community had tried to give "its Negro citizens the things they have asked." The implication, the Review points out, is that "those" people are not really part of "our" community. Well-intentioned white reporters take great pains to point out that a certain Negro is "well-dressed" or "articulate" but in so doing they imply that most other Negroes are not. A New York Times article wrote of the white female lead in "The Great White Hope": "Playing a part in which she has to kiss a Negro doesn't faze her." The Journalism Review advised that "white readers should substitute 'white' for 'Negro' to understand the insult." Fortunately, there are indications that whites are beginning to understand. The man who culled the samples of "white thinking" is Robert E. Smith. He is an editor for the Newsday feature syndicate, 28 years old—and white.

KELLY by Jack Moore

THE HUSBANDS IN MY LIFE

A Greek named Heraclitus claimed that you never see the same river twice because the water that was there one minute is not there the next. In this respect, it seems to me, husbands are like rivers. For example, my husband Tom.

Tom_1 is of course the lover; Tom_2, the man of business. Both these Toms are substantially the same today as when we were married in 1948.

Tom_3, the father, is different. He wasn't born until 1950. I watched his birth with some pity, a little resentment, and a strong upsurge of motherly feeling toward him. He was almost as bewildered as was Tom, Jr. But, whereas the baby took strong hold in his new world, Tom_3 stood at the edge of fatherhood for a while, until I felt like taking him by the ear with an old-fashioned motherly grip and leading him to his son. Today, though, Tom_3 bears little resemblance to $Tom_{3\ (1950)}$. Actually, I feel a little shut out now when Tom_3 and Tom, Jr. are especially close, as when they're planning a fishing trip.

Tom_4, the fisherman, is a loathsome person—an adolescent, self-centered, unpredictable, thoughtless, utterly selfish braggart. Yesterday, he bought Junior a fishing rod.

"Pampering him," I said. "He needs other things so much more—his teeth straightened, summer camp."

"He needs a fishing rod." Tom_4 said.

"You're teaching him to become a thoughtless husband," I charged.

"Oh, I don't know," Tom_4 said. "Maybe he'll marry a girl who likes to fish."

That stopped me for a minute. I'd never thought of there being such girls. Perhaps Tom_4 was disappointed in me. I was just wondering what I could wear on a fishing trip when Tom_4 shattered my good intentions by saying, "A fishing trip for Junior is a good deal more important than a permanent for Nancy."

This came as a surprise. Tom_{3b} as father of Nancy was not the Tom_{3a} father of Junior. Usually Nancy could get away with anything. At five, she had known better than to cut up the evening paper before her father had seen it, but Tom_{3b} had just laughed. He was certainly no relation to the husband-at-breakfast Tom who would scream if his wife got the pages of the morning paper out of place. He'd always been a little too indulgent with Nancy and too severe with Junior, but now he was begrudging Nancy a permanent.

"Do you want to have an unattractive daughter?" I asked, but Tom_{3b} wasn't there. Tom_5, the amateur plumber and ardent do-it-yourselfer, had taken over. He was at the sink fussing with the garbage disposer, promising to fix it Saturday.

"Why don't you buy Nancy a fishing rod?" I suggested.

And who looked back at me? Tom_6 the bewildered husband. "Are you joking?" he asked.

"Certainly not," I said indignantly. "You should train her to make a good wife."

Tom_6 laughed. Then Tom_7 took over. Tom_7 is the appreciative husband. He's a very determined fellow. He laughs loud and long.

"Very funny," he said. "I always appreciate your sense of humor. I always tell my—"

"Don't overdo it," I snarled. "I'm not being funny. Maybe she should have a fishing rod."

"She has her permanent," Tom_8 said with a laugh. "When she gets a little older she can fish with that." Tom_6 is a clown, the life of the party. Some day I may murder him.

I poured the coffee and resisted the temptation to drip a little on Tom_8's balding head. "Polygamy's wonderful," I murmured with a sigh, as I set the coffee pot down.

Tom_7 looked at me with concern. "Have you seen your doctor lately?" he asked.

"No, there are enough men in my life," I answered. But Tom_2 was looking at his watch. I realized that my remark had been wasted. Not one of my husbands was listening.

Mary Graham Lund

"... I proceed. 'Edwin and Morcar, the Earls of Mercia and Northumbria, declared for him: and even Stigand, the patriotic Archbishop of Cantebury, found it advisable ...'"

"Found *what?*" said the duck.

"Found *'It'*," the mouse replied rather crossly: "Of course you know what 'It' means."

"I know what 'It' means well enough, when I find a thing," said the Duck; "It's generally a frog or a worm. The question is, what did the Archbishop find?"

"The mouse did not notice this question, but hurriedly went on, ..."

Lewis Carroll,
Alice's Adventures in Wonderland

Different Languages, Different Worlds

In addition to individual words, the grammar and vocabulary of a language can influence the way we think about the world. The late anthropologist Benjamin Lee Whorf is probably the leading authority on the relationship between language and perception. After spending several years with various North American Indian cultures, he found that their entire way of thinking was shaped by the language they spoke. For example, Nootka, a language spoken on Vancouver Island, contains no distincton between nouns and verbs. Because of this the Indians who speak it view the entire world as being constantly in process. Where we see a thing as fixed or constant (noun), they view it as constantly changing. Thus, instead of calling something a "fire," the Nootka speaker might call it a "burning"; where we see a house, he would see a "house-ing."* In this sense our language operates much like a snapshot camera, while Nootka works more like a moving-picture camera.

But what does this have to do with communication? How does our language influence the way we relate with each other? Because of the static, unchanging nature of our grammar, we often regard people and things as never changing. Suppose, for example, that you've just returned from a visit to New York, and someone asks you what kind of place it is. "Oh, it's a terrible place," you say. Now look at this response. By saying that New York *is* terrible (or great, or any other adjective), your language implies two things: First, that your judgment is a total one—that it covers everything about the city, and second, that New York is an unchanging place. The word *is* implies eternal sameness, when in fact the "things" we give names to are really changing, dynamic processes. New York today isn't the same place it

---

*It's extremely difficult for those of us who've never experienced any languages besides our Anglo-European ones to understand how another system works. We take our system so much for granted that to us it's much the way water is to a fish—we can't conceive of existing without it.

Semantics: Where Words Go Astray

was last year or will be tomorrow, and your experiences there aren't the same ones that other people might have had. You'd have been more correct if you'd answered by saying, "My experiences while visiting New York in January 1975 were that the streets were crowded, the people I encountered behaved rudely, and that the prices for food, lodging, and entertainment were too high." Now of course this way of talking isn't always practical, but it's certainly more accurate than judging New York in absolute terms.

Alfred Korzybski, who originated the discipline of General Semantics, suggested a linguistic device to remind us of the way all things change. He proposed that we qualify important words by attaching subscripts to them. For example, instead of saying "I didn't like Joe," you might say "I didn't like Joe last Tuesday." This would make it harder to think in abstract, overly general terms.

The real culprit we're talking about is the word *is*. It leads us to think of people or things as if they were absolute and unchanging. Saying that "John *is* handsome, boring, immature, et cetera isn't as correct as saying "The John I encountered yesterday seemed to be . . ." There's a big difference between saying "Beth is a phony" and "Beth seemed phony the other night." The second statement describes the way someone behaved at one point in time, and the first categorizes her as if she had always been a phony. It's this kind of verbal generalizing that causes teachers to think of students as "slow learners" or "troublemakers" because of past test scores or reports.

Some cultures allow their members to change names whenever they wish. Perhaps this practice makes it easier to see how none of us are the same person, how we all change.

Is Is What Was Was?

An is is just a was that was
    and that is very small. . .
And is is was so soon it almost
    wasn't is at all.
For is is only is until
    it is a was—you see. . .
And as an is advances—to
    remain an is can't be. . .
'cause if is is to stay an is
it isn't is because
another is is where it was
    and is is then a was.

                Tom Hicks, *Etc.*

The Un-Isness of Is

For several years now, D. David Bourland Jr. has conscientiously scrubbed from his discourse and his writing all forms of the verb "to be." The first time he tried to do this, it gave him a headache. Now the practice comes so naturally that Bourland's listeners and readers are not likely to notice the omission. On the contrary, they are likely to be struck by the lucidity of his expression, which is commendably unambiguous if not always very lyrical. Where most people might render harsh judgment on themselves with "I'm no good at math," Bourland would express the thought with far less immutability: "I did not receive good grades in math," or "I did less well at math than at other subjects."

Unlike the California musician who once wrote a novel without the letter "e" just to see if it could be done, Bourland, 40, is not an eccentric visionary. He is the highly skilled president of Information Research Associates, a McLean, Va., think tank that does classified systems development for the U.S. Navy. Bourland, who has a master's degree in business administration from Harvard, was also a student at the Institute of General Semantics in Lakeville, Conn., where he became an ardent disciple of the linguistic theories of the leading prophet of general semantics, Alfred Korzybski. In Korzybski's view, the verb "to be" was a dangerous and frequently misused word that was responsible for much of mankind's semantic difficulties. Going the master one better, Bourland has led a one-man crusade for the adoption of "E-prime"—which is his name for the English language minus "to be."

All Is Change The semanticist's objection to the verb "to be" is based on certain philosophical convictions. One is a stern rejection of an axiom of classical logic, the principle of identity—that A is A, or a rose is a rose. In fact, argued Korzybski, the basic principle of life is not identity but, as the elliptical pre-Socratic philosopher Heraclitus put it, that all is change. Time and movement are inexorable, and in the fraction of a second that a rose is described it has already begun to alter.

The second philosophical conviction is that language influences behavior. Mankind is much less aware of the implacable reality of change simply because his language is dominated by the verb "to be," which implies a static quality of illusory permanence. "Our language," says Bourland, "remains the language of absolutes. The chief offender remains the verb 'to be.' The spurious identity it so readily connotes perverts our perception of reality."

One semantic harm done by "to be" is that it tempts man into erroneous value judgments. Korzybski noted dryly that a rose is not at all "red" to those afflicted by color blindness, and that redness itself is not a reality but a quality of reflected light to which the description "red" is arbitrarily assigned. Better to say, Korzybski suggested, "I classify the rose as red," or "I see the rose as red."

Undemonstrated Conclusions E-prime, Bourland firmly insists, has certain advantages over conventional English. Certain questions that semanticists as well as many analytical philosophers regard as poorly structured—"What is man?", "What is art?", or Hamlet's famous "To be or not to be"—simply disappear as unaskable. Another is the elimination of essentially empty phrases—"Boys will be boys," for example, or "We know this is the right thing to do." A third advantage is that the E-prime user cannot blandly take refuge in waffling statements based on factually undemonstrated conclusions—sentences that begin with, say, "It is known that," or "It is certain."

Despite the stirring rhetorical flair of the Declaration of Independence, Bourland is even willing to rewrite it, in the interest of semantic clarity. In the standard text, the first sentence reads: "We hold these truths to be self-evident, that all men are created equal, that they are endowed by their Creator with certain inalienable rights, that among these are Life, Liberty and the pursuit of Happiness." A somewhat more prosaic E-Prime version: "We make the following assumptions: All citizens have equal political rights. All citizens simply by virtue of their existence have certain inalienable rights, including life, liberty and the pursuit of happiness."

Bourland notes with some satisfaction that a number of scientific papers, not all done by Korzybski disciples, are now being written in E-prime; he is currently writing a book on how to speak and write without recourse to Isness. From personal experience, he claims that the use of E-prime can force a self-conscious but salutary revision in the speaker's outlook on life. "Once you realize that every time you say 'is' you tell a lie," he says, "you begin to think less of a thing's identity and more of its function. I find it much harder to be dishonest now."

Time Magazine

IS IS OUT

It really does make a difference to stop using *is* in your language, but using it can be a hard habit to break.

To see what effect eliminating this word might have on you, try this experiment:

1 Take a page or so from any book, newspaper, letter, et cetera and try to change all forms of the verb *to be* into more acceptable word concepts.

2 Next, try to write a paragraph about two of the following subjects without using any form of *to be*.
   a. A description of someone you dislike
   b. What you think about this class
   c. Your pet peeve
   d. Your position on abortion

3 Was this as easy a task as you supposed it would be?

4 Could you notice a difference in the writing after you eliminated *is?* Was it less dogmatic, less definite sounding? Can you see better now how the structure of a language can shape our thinking?

Throughout this book we've switched back and forth between masculine personal pronouns—he, him, his—and feminine ones—she, her, and hers—when talking about people in general. As we pointed out earlier, we're aware of what we've been doing. We're not happy with this style of writing, but we've used it because we couldn't think of anything better.

The following article shows one solution to this problem and illustrates how the grammar of a language can shape our thinking. See what you think about the solution Ms. Miller and Ms. Swift propose.

Rock-n-Roll

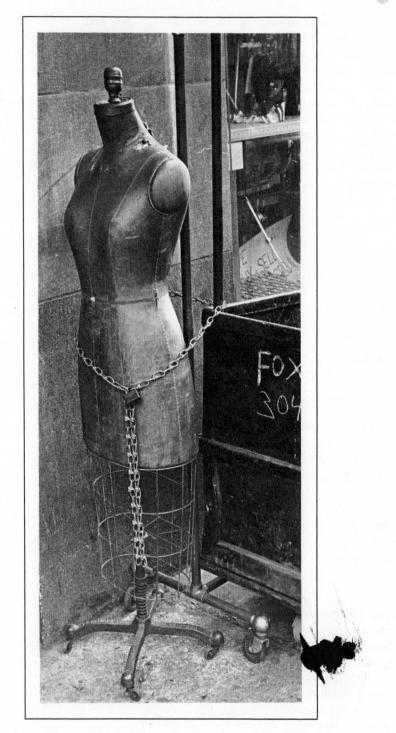

De-Sexing the English Language

On the television screen, a teacher of first-graders who has just won a national award is describing her way of teaching. "You take each child where you find him," she says. "You watch to see what he's interested in, and then you build on his interests."

A five-year-old looking at the program asks her mother, "Do only boys go to that school?"

"No," her mother begins, "she's talking about girls too, but—"

But what? The teacher being interviewed on television is speaking correct English. What can the mother tell her daughter about why a child, in any generalization, is always *he* rather than *she*? How does a five-year-old comprehend the generic personal pronoun?

The effect on personality development of this one part of speech was recognized by thoughtful people long before the present assault on the English language by the forces of Women's Liberation. Fifteen years ago, Lynn T. White, then president of Mills College wrote:

"The grammar of English dictates that when a referent is either of indeterminate sex or both sexes, it shall be considered masculine. The penetration of this habit of language into the minds of little girls as they grow up to be women is more profound than most people, including most women, have recognized: for it implies that personality is really a male attribute, and that women are a human subspecies. . . . It would be a miracle if a girl-baby, learning to use the symbols of our tongue, could escape some wound to her self-respect: whereas a boy-baby's ego is bolstered by the pattern of our language."

Now that our language has begun to respond to the justice of Women's Liberation, a lot of people apparently are trying to kick the habit of using *he* when they mean anyone, male or female. In fact, there is mounting evidence that a major renovation of the language is in progress with respect to this pronoun. It is especially noticeable in the speeches of politicians up for election: "And as for every citizen who pays taxes, I say that he or she deserves an accounting!" A variation of the tandem form is also cropping up in print, like the copy on a coupon that offers the bearer a 20 percent saving on "the cost of his/her meal." A writer in the New York newspaper, *The Village Voice,* adopts the same form to comment "that every artist of major stature is actually a school in him/herself."

Adding the feminine pronoun to the masculine whenever the generic form is called for may be politically smart and morally right, but the result is often awkward.

Some of the devices used to get around the problem are even less acceptable, at least to grammarians. It is one thing for a student to announce in assembly that "Anybody can join the Glee Club as long as they can carry a tune," but when this patchwork solution begins to appear in print, the language is in trouble. In blatant defiance of every teacher of freshman English, a full-page advertisement in *The New York Times* for its college and school subscription service begins with this headline: "If someone you know is attending one of these colleges, here's something they should know that can save them money." Although the grammatical inconsistency of the *Times*'s claim offends the ear—especially since "they" in the headline can refer only to "colleges"—the alternatives would present insurmountable problems for the writer. For example, the sentence might read, "If someone you know . . . etc., here's something he or she should know that can save him/her money." Or, in order to keep the plural subject in the second clause, the writer might have begun, "If several people you know are attending one or more of these colleges. . . ." But by that time will the reader still care?

In the long run, the problem of the generic personal pronoun is a problem of the status of women. But it is more immediately a matter of common sense and clear communication. Absurd examples of the burdens now placed upon masculine pronouns pop up everywhere. "The next time you meet a handicapped person, don't make up your mind

SINGULAR			PLURAL
	Distinct Gender	Common Gender	Common Gender
Nominative	*he* and *she*	*tey*	*they*
Possessive	*his* and *her* (or *hers*)	*ter* (or *ters*)	*their* (or *theirs*)
Objective	*him* and *her*	*tem*	*them*

about him in advance," admonishes a radio public service announcement. A medical school bulletin, apparently caught by surprise, reports that a certain scholarship given annually "to a student of unquestioned ability and character who has completed his first year" was awarded to one Barbara Kinder.

Since there is no way in English to solve problems like these with felicity and grace, it is becoming obvious that what we need is a new singular personal pronoun that is truly generic: a common-gender pronoun. Several have been proposed, but so far none appears to have the transparently logical relationship to existing pronouns that is necessary if a new word is to gain wide acceptance. Perhaps a clue to the solution is to be found in people's persistent use of *they* as a singular pronoun.

In the plural forms, both genders are included in one word: *they* can refer to males or females or a mixed group. So why not derive the needed singular common-gender pronouns from the plural? *They, their,* and *them* suggest *tey, ter,* and *tem.* With its inflected forms pronounced to rhyme with the existing plural forms, the new word would join the family of third person pronouns as shown in the box below.

Someone will probably object to the idea of a common-gender pronoun in the mistaken belief that it is a neuter form and therefore underrates sexual differences. The opposite is true. Once *tey* or a similar word is adopted, *he* can become exclusively masculine, just as *she* is now exclusively feminine. The new pronoun will thus accentuate the significant and valuable differences between females and males—those of reproductive function and form—while affirming the essential unity and equality of the two sexes within the species.

Language constantly evolves in response to need. It is groping today for ways to accommodate the new recognition of women as full-fledged members of the human race. If the new pronoun helps anyone toward that end, tey should be free to adopt it.

If anyone objects, it is certainly ter right—but in that case let tem come up with a better solution.

Casey Miller and Kate Swift

'Bachelor Living' Makes a Big Hit

FAIRFAX, Va. (AP)—At the George C. Marshall High School here, a course called "home economics for boys" got very little attention. Retitled "bachelor living," it has attracted 120 students.

They are instructed in cooking, sewing, care of clothes, laundry, pressing and "as much money management as they can take."

In Conclusion

Now we've come to the end of our short look at the subject of semantics. We hope that after reading this chapter you aren't as inclined as before to take words for granted.

We've pointed out the simple but tremendously important fact that meanings rest more in people than in words themselves. Because of this fact it's especially important to find out whether someone is using a word the same way we are before we jump to conclusions.

We've listed a few of the most common ways that language can trip us up if we're unaware—equivocation, overly broad terms, relative words, fiction words, and emotive terms.

We've shown how using overly abstract terms can lead you to think of people as being similar when they're really quite unique.

You've seen how we can go around in verbal circles by looking for meanings in a dictionary, and how much more precise communication can be when we use operational definitions.

You've learned how euphemisms are devices that can serve as defense mechanisms, helping us avoid facing facts we'd rather ignore.

And finally, you should see now that although words don't mean anything in themselves, the labels we attach to our experiences can shape the attitudes we hold.

Trying to cover so much ground in so short a space is a very frustrating thing. You probably still have many unanswered questions about semantics, and there maybe things we've covered that you simply don't understand or see as important. If you're willing to dig deeper and learn more, both your instructor and the following list of readings are good places to go from here.

Roads Not Taken

1 Develop case studies to show that communication can break down due to one or more of the following problems:

    a. equivocation
    b. use of relative words
    c. use of emotive words
    d. use of fiction words

2 Observe the use of euphemisms in your everyday life. Describe the impact such language has on your thoughts and those of others.

3 Research the charge that some school textbooks use sexist language. What evidence exists to demonstrate that such language exists and that it affects the perceptions of the people reading it?

4 Investigate other languages to see how they deal with the issue of pronouns for nonsexual objects. Based on your study, what do you think is the best method for dealing with this problem?

The labels we attach to people, the names and all the other things that identify the individual by distinguishing him from the masses, are just what prevent genuine knowing. For labels and classifications make it appear that we know the other, when actually we have caught the outline and not the substance. Since we are convinced we know ourselves and others, since we take this knowledge for granted, we fail to recognize that our perceptions are often only habits growing out of routines and familiar forms of expression. We no longer actually see what is happening before us and in us, and, not knowing that we do not know, we make no effort to be in contact with the real. We continue to use labels to stereotype ourselves and others, and these labels have replaced human meanings, unique feelings, and growing life within and between persons.

Clark Moustakas

5 Explore research in anthropology and linguistics that describes ways in which various languages shape the world view of their users.

6 Write a story or essay in E prime language, and comment on how its use changes the narration.

More Readings in Semantics

Bois, J. Samuel. *The Art of Awareness.* Dubuque, Iowa: Wm. C. Brown Company, 1973.

> General semantics (as opposed to just plain semantics) is a discipline that goes beyond studying language. It attempts to explore the ways in which we look at the world and to suggest some better alternatives. This college-level text about the subject provides a thorough introduction.

Carroll, John B., ed. *Language, Thought, and Reality: Selected Writings of Benjamin Lee Whorf.* Cambridge, Mass.: M.I.T., 1966.

> Writings of the most widely recognized authority about how language shapes our world view.

Chase, Stuart. *The Tyranny of Words.* New York: Harvest Books, 1938.

> A very readable account of the many ways in which semantic problems cause fuzzy thinking and get us into trouble.

Condon, John C. *Semantics and Communication,* 2nd ed. New York: Macmillan, 1975.

> The clearest introduction to the field of semantics we've found. It's neither too long nor too sort and gives good overview.

Fabun, Don. *Communications: The Transfer of Meaning.* Beverly Hills, Calif.: Glencoe Press, 1968.

> This pamphlet is an attractive, very short introduction to the study of language. If you're trying to explain some of the things in this chapter to a friend who doesn't have time to read it, this booklet might be just the thing.

Hayakawa, S. I. *Language in Thought and Action.* New York: Harcourt Brace Jovanovich, 1964.

> A clear, detailed treatment of many topics introduced in this chapter.

_____. *The Use and Misuse of Language.* Greenwich, Conn.: Fawcett Books, 1962.

> A collection of essays from *ETC.: A Review of General Semantics,* which illustrate how topics introduced in this chapter apply to everyday situations.

Lakoff, Robin. *Language and Woman's Place.* New York: Harper Colophon Books, 1975.

> Lakoff investigates those roots of our language that give us parallel words for male and the female. The structure may be parallel, but she argues that the range of use and connotation are not.

Marcus, Mary G. "The Power of a Name." *Psychology Today* (October, 1976), pp. 75–77, 108.

This interesting article illustrates how the principle of language-shaping perception applies to the names parents give their children. Do you want your son or daughter to be regarded as intelligent, clumsy, well adjusted, or neurotic? The name you choose may make a difference.

Miller, Casey, and Kate Swift. *Words and Women.* Garden City, N.Y.: Anchor Press, 1976.

Miller and Swift provide the evidence that point out how our everyday language communicates much about male and female role biases.

Newman, Edwin. *A Civil Tongue.* Indianapolis: Bobbs-Merrill, 1976.

Newman cites hundreds of examples of the semantic atrocities listed in this chapter. His stories come from politics, academia, business, and many other settings. After reading them, one doesn't know whether to laugh or cry.

Sagarian, Edward. "The High Cost of Wearing a Label." *Psychology Today,* (March, 1976), pp. 25–27.

This article shows some of the dangers of the word *is,* as described in Chapter 7. As Sagarian suggests, believing one's self *to be* a deviant can lend to an unnecessary self-fulfilling prophecy.

Films on Semantics

Berfunkle. Color. 7 min. 1967. Iowa University.

Cartoon portrayal of how one word carries numerous meanings through humorous adventures of character seeking definition of the word *Berfunkle.*

On the Difference Between Words and Things. B/W. 30 min. 1955. Iowa University.

Focuses on language, general semantics, and the fact that meanings are in people. Talking Sense Series.

Why Do People Misunderstand Each Other? B/W. 30 min. 1955. Iowa University.

Analyzes how the misconception that words have a single, fixed, universal meaning can lead to misunderstanding, tension, conflict, and interpersonal breakdowns.

8

Resolving
Interpersonal
Conflict

Not everything that is faced can be changed,
But nothing can be changed until it is faced.

JAMES BALDWIN

Now you've almost finished this book about interpersonal communication. You've seen the major barriers that keep us from understanding each other, and you've practiced some ways to overcome them. If you've learned to use the skills presented in this book, you should now find that your relationships with others are everything you've ever wanted, free from any problems, right?

Wrong!

We'd only be kidding ourselves if we pretended that it's possible to live a life without any conflicts, because just the opposite is true. Problems are bound to come up any time two people get together for more than a short while, and sooner or later some will arise that are serious enough to wreck the relationship unless you know how to handle them.

Unfortunately we can't offer you any magic tricks to resolve all the conflicts in your life. At this stage the social sciences just aren't advanced enough to be this systematic. On the other hand, we can show you some ways that constructively expressed conflict can be a sign of caring and how it can strengthen your relatonships.

The ideas we present here will have to take the form of suggestions because it's impossible to give the cookbook approach of "ten easy steps" to a happier, conflict-free life. Still, we think that if you can make use of these suggestions, you may find more constructive ways of handling the conflicts you're sure to experience in your life. The only way you'll find out is by trying, so let's begin.

□ □ □

Conflict Not Bad

We'll start by saying that without exception *every* relationship of any depth at all has conflict. No matter how close, how understanding, how compatible you are, there will be times when your ideas or actions or needs or goals won't match those of others around you. You like rock music, but your folks like Beethoven; you want to date other people, but your partner wants to go steady; you think a paper you've done is fine, but your instructor wants it changed; you like to sleep in on Sunday mornings, but your roommate likes to play his stereo—loudly! There's no end to the number or kinds of disagreements that are possible.

And just as conflict is a fact of life, so are the feelings that go along with it: hurt, anger, frustration, resentment, disappointment. Because these feelings are usually unpleasant, we sometimes try to avoid them or pretend they don't exist. But as sure as conflicts are bound to come up, so are the emotions that go along with them.

At first this might seem pretty depressing. If problems are inevitable in even the best relationships, does this mean that you're doomed to relive the same arguments, the same hurt feelings over and over? Fortunately the answer to this question is a definite no. Even though conflict is part of a meaningful relationship, *you can change the way you deal with it.*

Are you aware that anger is closely linked to love and that you can and usually do get angry at people you love? Love and anger are not mutually exclusive. You can get deeply angry at people and love them enough so that you want the very best of all things for them.

Theodore Isaac Rubin

The reason most of us fear conflict is that we've been conditioned to believe that it's bad to disagree, argue, or fight. We've seen conflict force people apart and damage their relationships. It's our belief that this happens most of the time because conflict is not handled constructively.

How can facing up to problems and disagreements bring people together? How can feelings like anger and hurt make a relationship stronger? Answering these questons will take some time, so let's get started. The first step is to take a look at some of the present ways you handle conflict.

Your Conflict Style

1   Think back over your recent history and recall five conflicts you've had. The more current they are the better, and they should be ones that occurred with people who are important to you, people with whom your relationship matters.

Turn an 8½-by-11-inch sheet of paper horizontally, and copy the following chart. To give yourself plenty of room you might extend your chart onto a second page.

I **The Conflict**	II **How I Managed It**	III **The Results**
(Describe who it was with; what it was about.)	(What happened during the conflict; how did it end?)	(How you felt. How the others involved felt. Are you happy with the results?)

3   For each of the conflicts, fill in the appropriate spaces on your chart. *Save the chart;* you'll be looking back on it later in the chapter.

4   Based on what you've written here, answer the following questions:

   a. Are you happy with the way you've handled your conflicts? Do you come away from them feeling better or worse than before?

   b. Have your conflicts left your relationships stronger or weaker?

   c. Do you recognize any patterns in your conflict style? For example, do you hold your angry feelings inside, are you sarcastic, do you lose your temper easily, et cetera?

   d. If you could, would you like to change the way you deal with your conflicts?

TRAINING LOVERS TO BE FIGHTERS

To confirm our suspicion that intimacy problems are common and not confined to "problem couples" who come to our Institute, we conducted an experiment. We asked people whom we knew through our business consulting, research, graduate teaching, and through social contacts, to help us recruit "normally happy" couples for detailed study. Our contacts were instructed: "Think of all the married couples you know. Then select the happiest of them for nomination to a 'Marriage Elite,' the imaginary Phi Beta Kappa of true intimacy."

We selected 50 "elite" couples and asked them, among other things, how they handled conflict situations. One question was: "On the few occasions when your husband is angry with you, what does he do?" Then we asked: "What do you think he would like to do?"

When such questions were put to these "happy" husbands and wives separately, the result was distressing: almost none had any notion of what was going on in the inner world of the other. Typically, the wife said: "When he does get miffed about something, he is very forgiving and thinks nothing of it"; yet the husband told us that he fought an appalling fight within himself in order to control his annoyance; and he maintained control mostly because he feared his wife might reject him for breaking their unspoken taboo against conflict.

Three groups emerged from our experiment: card-house marriages, game-playing marriages, and true intimates. The card-house partners were the largest group. They put on a fake front. They were almost totally lacking in intimacy and were held together largely by the partners' neurotic concern for appearances, social success, status, and "respectability."

The partners in the second (and smaller) group were somewhat more intimate. But essentially they had resigned themselves to game-playing and other ritualized routines. Many of these unions were held together by such outside pressures as economic advantage and fear of change. They were mutual protective associations who looked on their marriage as pretty much of a lost cause but felt that it would be disloyal and ill-mannered to complain about it, especially since the loneliness of being unmarried would probably be worse.

The third group consisted of only two couples. They checked out as natural geniuses at maintaining realistic intimacy. But when we asked them for the secret of their marital success, they said they had no idea what it was. All we discovered was that these marriage champions—unlike the other couples in our experiment but like successfully married pairs whom everybody occasionally encounters—argued constantly. They thought conflict was as natural as eating.

"Of course," they said, "we argue about practically everything!" Their special characteristic was that they had learned to live with aggression comfortably.

As we continued to study our clients' fights, evidence began to accumulate that couples who can't display their hostilities are not polite but phony. Gradually we started to distinguish between constructive and destructive aggression and learned that anger is manageable—not a dark, uncontrollable "mean streak."

George R. Bach and Peter Wyden,
The Intimate Enemy

Conflict is Natural

Whatever their style of handling conflicts, most people answer the last question on page 338 with a loud yes. It seems that whatever our strengths, one of our biggest communication problems is dealing with the conflicts that occur between ourselves and others.

At the bottom of this difficulty is the feeling most of us have that aggression is a bad thing. This attitude is most certainly something we've learned as we've grown up. If you've ever watched a baby or young child, you know that anger, frustration, and hostility are basic emotions, as are happiness, contentment, and affection. Children who get what they want are happy; if their needs aren't met, they become angry or frustrated.

But for many of us part of being socialized is the stressing of the "happy" emotions, or as the old saying puts it, "It's nice to be nice." This is true—it *is* nice to feel good, be polite and agreeable—but this cliché doesn't tell the whole story because it implies that the other half of the emotional spectrum is bad. We're often taught that nobody will like us unless we're cheerful, that ideal families and friends don't fight, that love and anger don't go together.

The main thing in life is not to be afraid to be human.

Pablo Casals

We get this message from many directions. Think back to the line that ends most fairy tales ". . . and they lived happily ever after," as if the ideal life is one of gallant princes and beautiful maidens living conflict-free lives. Many parents have an agreement never to argue in front of the children, which gives the impression that people who love each other don't fight. Situation comedies on television and many movies picture happy families in which any problems that do come up are always resolved quite neatly before the final commercial. Etiquette books, clergymen, teachers, and parents have often taught us that "Nice people don't fight."

Because they accept what they're told, children who have been raised hearing these anti-aggression messages grows up believing that conflict is the sign of a weak relationship. "If I really loved them, I wouldn't get angry," a child thinks. But all this moralizing doesn't change their feelings. When a playmate steals a toy, when brothers or sisters tease them, when parents say no or put them to be early, children still get angry. And with this anger comes the thought "They tell me anger is bad, and I'm angry. Therefore, I must be bad."

This attitude sets the pattern many of us still follow. Every day we experience the perfectly normal emotions of frustration, resentment, and anger, and yet we hate ourselves for doing so. Needless to say this isn't a very happy situation.

> When people ask you, "Am I right to be angry?", have you thought of asking them, "Am I right to be thirsty?"
>
> Theodore Isaac Rubin

Conflict Basic as Hunger?

Psychologists often find themselves in the position of proving scientifically what people have always known implicitly.

So it is with new data on the value of conflict.

Conflict, a Canadian psychologist reported in Scientific American, 215:82, 1966, may be the same sort of driving force as hunger, thirst, sexual appetite and pain. If so, it can be placed among the ranks of those conditions which are most efficient in producing learning, with important implications for education.

All of the basic drives have in common the fact that they arouse the individual physically, sharpen his faculties, motivate him to act and enhance his learning capacity. . . .

Science News

The Fairy Tale [or "Hollywood"] Ending

Here are the final paragraphs of four fairy tales. Not very realistic, but how many of us have been influenced to believe life should be like this?

Then he gave him the ship which would sail on land as well as at sea, and when the King saw it he could no longer withhold his daughter. The marriage was celebrated, and at the King's death Simpleton inherited the kingdom, and lived long and happily with his wife.

At last the Prince consented to do as he was asked. And no sooner was it done than the fox was changed into a man. He was no other than the brother of the beautiful Princess, at last set free from the evil spell which so long had lain upon him.

There was nothing now wanting to their happiness for the rest of their lives.

Then they hopped and danced about, and leapt over chairs and tables and out the door. Henceforward they came back no more, but the shoemaker fared well as long as he lived, and had good luck in all his undertakings.

The youth, delighted, started on his homeward journey and took the golden apple to the beautiful Princess, who had now no further excuse to offer.

They divided the apple of life and ate it together, and then her heart was filled with love for him, and they lived happily to a great age.

It is when we all play safe that we create a world of utmost insecurity.

Dag Hammarskjöld

How We Usually Deal with Aggression

What happens when we're faced with this dilemma of feeling guilty about feeling angry? There isn't any single answer to this question, but most of us react to some degree in one of two ways.

Some people, we can call them erupters, have short tempers. When an erupter's needs aren't met, she may react by "blowing her top" and lashing out at whoever is around, even when the bystanders aren't the real target of her anger. Because the erupter has the guilty feelings about conflict that we discussed, and because her anger is often out of proportion to the occasion and even unfairly directed, she often feels bad about her outbursts even as she's delivering them. But because she can't see any alternatives, the erupter keeps on with her explosions, disliking herself and making enemies of others.

A second group of people who react to anger are the withholders. Often because of exposure to erupters or because of upbringing, the withholder has a great fear of conflict. Even small disagreements are more than he's willing to handle, and it's unthinkable for him ever to get really mad at someone. But even though the withholder avoids expressing conflict-oriented feelings, he still experiences the same frustrations, resentments, disagreements, and hates that we all do. And so, because he doesn't express these feelings, they build up inside him, creating more and more pressure. In holding back his feelings the withholder is denying a real part of himself, and it makes him unhappy.

So both the erupter and the withholder have the same problem of dealing with their aggressions. A good way to think of their dilemma is to picture what might happen if we build a dam without proper spillways. The stream would eventually build up behind its wall until it leaked out by flowing over and around the dam's edges, eroding and eventually destroying it, or the pressure forced the dam to burst. Both these possibilities are destructive, and in the same way both the withholder's and erupter's methods of handling conflicts rarely lead to a satisfactory solution.

Crazymakers

What's your conflict style? To give you a better idea of some unproductive ways you may be handling your conflicts, we'll describe some typical conflict behaviors that can weaken relationships. In our survey we'll follow the fascinating work of Dr. George Bach, a leading authority on conflict and communication.

Bach explains that there are two types of aggression—clean fighting and dirty fighting. Either because they can't or won't express their feelings openly and constructively, dirty fighters sometimes resort to "crazymaking" techniques to vent their resentments. Instead of openly and caringly expressing their emotions, crazymakers (often unconsciously) use a variety of indirect tricks to get at their opponent. Because these "sneak attacks" don't usually get to the root of the problem, and because of their power to create a great deal of hurt, crazymakers can destroy communication. Let's take a look at some of them.

The avoider The avoider refuses to fight. When a conflict arises, he'll leave, fall asleep, pretend to be busy at work, or keep from facing the problem in some other way. This behavior makes it very difficult for the partner to express his feelings of anger, hurt, et cetera because the avoider won't fight back. Arguing with an avoider is like trying to box with a person who won't even put up his gloves.

The history of man is replete with mechanisms and attempts to control aggression. People have tried to pray it away, wish it away, or play it away. More recently they have tried to psychoanalyze it away. But it does not seem to go away.

George Bach and Herb Goldberg,
Creative Aggression

The pseudoaccommodator The pseudoaccommodator refuses to face up to a conflict either by giving in or by pretending that there's nothing at all wrong. This really drives the partner, who definitely feels there's a problem, crazy and causes him to feel both guilt and resentment toward the accommodator.

The guilt maker Instead of saying straight out that she doesn't want or approve of something, the guilt maker tries to change her partner's behavior by making him feel responsible for causing pain. The guilt maker's favorite line is "It's o.k., don't worry about me. . . ." accompanied by a big sigh.

The subject changer Really a type of avoider, the subject changer escapes facing up to aggression by shifting the conversation whenever it approaches an area of conflict. Because of his tactics, the subject changer and his partner never have the chance to explore their problem and do something about it.

The distracter Rather than come out and express his feelings about the object of his dissatisfaction, the distracter attacks other parts of his partner's life. Thus he never has to share what's really on his mind and can avoid dealing with painful parts of his relationships.

The mind reader Instead of allowing her partner to express her feelings honestly, the mind reader goes into character analysis, explaining what the other person really means or what's wrong with the other person. By behaving this way the mind reader refuses to handle her own feelings and leaves no room for her partner to express himself.

The trapper The trapper plays an especially dirty trick by setting up a desired behavior for his partner, and then when it's met, attacking the very thing he requested. An example of this technique is for the trapper to say "Let's be totally honest with each other," and then when the partner shares his feelings, he finds himself attacked for having feelings that the trapper doesn't want to accept.

The crisis tickler This person almost brings what's bothering him to the surface, but he never quite comes out and expresses himself. Instead of admitting his concern about the finances he innocently asks "Gee, how much did that cost?", dropping a rather obvious hint but never really dealing with the crisis.

The gunnysacker This person doesn't respond immediately when he's angry. Instead, he puts his resentment into his gunnysack, which after a while begins to bulge with large and small gripes. Then, when the sack is about to burst, the gunnysacker pours out all his pent-up aggressions on the overwhelmed and unsuspecting victim.

The trivial tyrannizer Instead of honestly sharing his resentments, the trivial tyrannizer does things he knows will get his partner's goat—leaving dirty dishes in the sink, clipping his fingernails in bed, belching out loud, turning up the television too loud, and so on.

The joker Because she's afraid to face conflicts squarely, the joker kids around when her partner wants to be serious, thus blocking the expression of important feelings.

The poker— DICK in the crock

The beltliner Everyone has a psychological "beltline," and below it are subjects too sensitive to be approached without damaging the relationship. Beltlines may have to do with physical characteristics, intelligence, past behavior, or deeply ingrained personality traits a person is trying to overcome. In an attempt to "get even" or hurt his partner the beltliner will use his intimate knowledge to hit below the belt, where he knows it will hurt.

The blamer The blamer is more interested in finding fault than in solving a conflict. Needless to say, he usually doesn't blame himself. Blaming behavior almost never solves a conflict and is an almost surefire way to make the receiver defensive.

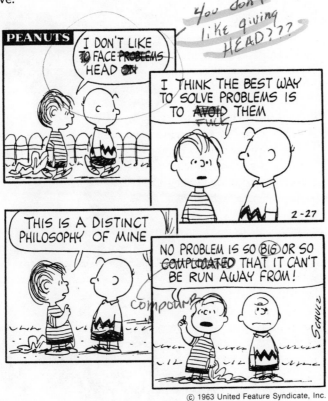

© 1963 United Feature Syndicate, Inc.

The contract tyrannizer This person will not allow his relationship to change from the way it once was. Whatever the agreements the partners had as to roles and responsibilities at one time, they'll remain unchanged. "It's your job to . . . feed the baby, wash the dishes, discipline the kids. . . ."

The kitchen sink fighter This person is so named because in an argument he brings up things that are totally off the subject ("everything but the kitchen sink"); the way his partner behaved last New Year's eve, the unbalanced checkbook, bad breath—anything.

The withholder Instead of expressing her anger honestly and directly, the withholder punishes her partner by keeping back something—courtesy, affection, good cooking, humor, sex. As you can imagine, this is likely to build up even greater resentments in the relationship.

The Benedict Arnold This character gets back at his partner by sabotage, by failing to defend him from attackers, and even by encouraging ridicule or disregard from outside the relationship.

Are there genuinely nice, sweet people in this world? Yes, absolutely yes, and they get angry as often as you and I. They must—otherwise they would be full of vindictive feelings and slush, which would prevent *genuine sweetness.*

Theodore Isaac Rubin

Who's Afraid of Virginia Woolf?

This scene from *Who's Afraid of Virginia Woolf?* provides us with excellent examples of "crazymaking" fight style. Which crazymakers can you spot here?

Martha: Hey, put some more ice in my drink, will you? You never put any ice in my drink. Why is that, hunh?

George: (*Takes her drink*) I always put ice in your drink. You eat it, that's all. It's that habit you have . . . chewing your ice cubes . . . like a cocker spaniel. You'll crack your big teeth.

Martha: THEY'RE MY BIG TEETH!

George: Some of them . . . some of them.

Martha: I've got more teeth than you've got.

George: Two more.

Martha: Well, two more's a lot more.

George: I suppose it is. I suppose it's pretty remarkable . . . considering how old you are.

Martha: YOU CUT THAT OUT! (*Pause*) You're not so young yourself.

George: (*With boyish pleasure . . . a chant*) I'm six years younger than you are. . . . I always have been and I always will be.

Martha: (*Glumly*) Well . . . you're going bald.

George: So are you. (*Pause . . . they both laugh*) Hello, honey.

Martha: Hello. C'mon over here and give your Mommy a big sloppy kiss.

George: . . . oh, now. . . .

Martha: I WANT A BIG SLOPPY KISS!

George: (*Preoccupied*) I don't *want* to kiss you, Martha. Where *are* these people? Where are these *people* you invited over?

Martha: They stayed on to talk to Daddy. . . . They'll be here. . . . *Why* don't you want to kiss me?

George: (*Too matter-of-fact*) Well, dear, if I kissed you I'd get all excited . . . I'd get beside myself, and I'd take you, by force, right here on the living room rug, and then our little guests would walk in, and . . . well, just think what your father would say about *that*.

Martha: You pig!

George: (*Haughtily*) Oink! Oink!

Martha: Ha, ha, ha, HA! Make me another drink . . . lover.

George: (*Taking her glass*) My God, you can swill it down, can't you?

Martha: (*Imitating a tiny child*) I'm firsty.

George: Jesus!

Martha: (*Swinging around*) Look, sweetheart, I can drink you under any goddamn table you want . . . so don't worry about me!

George: Martha, I gave you the prize years ago. . . . There isn't an abomination award going that you. . . .

Martha: I swear . . . if you existed I'd divorce you. . . .

George: Well, just stay on your feet, that's all. . . . These people are your guests, you know, and. . . .

Martha: I can't even see you. . . . I haven't been able to see you for years. . . .

George: . . . if you pass out, or throw up, or something. . . .

Martha: . . . I mean, you're a blank, a cipher. . . .

George: . . . and try to keep your clothes on, too. There aren't many more sickening sights than you with a couple of drinks in you and your skirt up over your head, you know. . . .

Martha: . . . a zero. . . .

George: . . . your *heads,* I should say. . . .

(*The front doorbell chimes*)

Martha: Party! Party!

George: (*Murderously*) I'm really looking forward to this, Martha. . . .

Martha: (*Same*) Go answer the door.

George: (*Not moving*) You answer it.

Martha: Get to that door, you.

(*He does not move*)

I'll fix you, you. . . .

George: (*Fake-spits*) . . . to you. . . .

Edward Albee

I was angry with my friend.
I told my wrath, my wrath did end.
I was angry with my foe:
I told it not, my wrath did grow.

And I watered it in fears,
Night and morning with my tears;
And I sunned it with smiles,
And with soft deceitful wiles.

And it grew both day and night,
Till it bore an apple bright;
And my foe beheld it shine,
And he knew that it was mine,

And into my garden stole
When the night had veiled the pole:
In the morning glad I see
My foe outstretched beneath the tree.

William Blake

Your Crazymakers

1 Pick the three crazymakers you use most often and give three recent examples of each.

2 For each example, describe
   a. the situation in which you used the crazymaker
   b. the consequences of using it, including the other person's behavior and your feelings
   c. your level of satisfaction with having used the crazymaker
   d. any alternate style of expressing your problem which might have been more satisfying

Crazymaking Diary

1 Look over the previous pages and think about the crazymakers you use. (You may want to look back at the chart you made earlier describing your conflict styles to recall some.)

2 For a week keep a record of the way you handle conflicts, focusing especially on any crazymakers you use.

3 What are the consequences of your behaviors? That is, do your crazy-making actions do anything to strengthen your relationships? to weaken them?

4 If you can, take time to talk with the person or people most important to you about the crazymakers you both use. Can you agree to try expressing your conflicts in more honest and direct ways from now on?

Clean, Fair Fights: The Fight for Growth

After reading this far, you might be confused. At the beginning of this chapter we told you that conflict between people who care for each other can be a constructive thing, that it can make your relationships stronger; yet all we've done since then is look at "dirty" fight styles. This approach is necessary because you need to understand what you're doing before you can make changes. But now that you've had a chance to see some of the unconstructive ways in which people handle aggression, it's time to look at some better alternatives.

In the following pages we'll introduce you to a new approach to fighting, one that should give you a chance to express the frustrations that come between you and others and yet not threaten your relationships. We'll call this approach the fight for growth. It's patterned after a technique developed by George Bach and has proved successful with many people, both young and old, who've participated in his "aggression labs" for the past several years.

Before we introduce you to the fight for growth, there are a few ideas you should keep in mind. This technique of fighting is a highly structured activity. While you're learning how to fight for growth, it's important that you follow all the stages carefully. Each step is essential to the success of your encounter, and skipping one or more can lead to misunderstandings that might threaten your meeting and even cause a dirty fight. After you've practiced the fight for growth a number of times and are familiar with it, this style of conflict will become almost second nature to you. You'll then be able to approach your conflicts without the need to follow the step-by-step approach, but for the time being try to be patient and trust the value of the following pattern.

As you read the following steps, try to imagine yourself applying them to a problem that's bothering you now.

Step 1—Thinking about the problem Before you approach your partner, try to get in touch with what's really bothering you. Often it's easy to protect an unrealistic self-concept by blaming your own shortcomings on someone else; so keep in mind the defense mechanisms of Chapter 3—especially projection and verbal aggression—and see if you're using them. Also, focus on your feelings and see what's really going on. For example, what first strikes you as anger or resentment may really be jealousy or hurt. See if you can explore your feelings and find out what's really bothering you.

Try to be as specific as you can about the exact behaviors of your partner that are causing the trouble between you. For example, you might clarify a gripe such as "inconsiderate around the house" into a specific complaint like "leaves unwashed breakfast dishes in the sink." Try to find out exactly what's bothering you.

Ideally it's very helpful to talk over your gripe with a third person who can help you clarify your feelings. *However,* the person should be a good active listener who will work at helping you understand your own thoughts rather than trying to impose her theories and solutions on you. Beware of the overly helpful friend who will try to tell you how to run your life.

Step 2—Making a date Often unconstructive fights start because the initiator confronts a partner who isn't ready. There are many times when a person isn't in the right frame of mind to face a conflict: He may be tired, in too much of a hurry to take the necessary time, upset over another problem, not feeling well, et cetera. At times like these it's unfair to "jump" a person without notice and expect him to give full attention to your problem. If you persist, you'll probably have a "dirty" fight on your hands.

After you've a clear idea of the problem, approach your partner with a request to try and solve a problem. For example: "Something's been bothering me. Can we talk about it?" If the answer is yes, then you're ready to go further. If it isn't the right time to confront your partner, find a time that's agreeable to both of you.

Step 3—Stating your problem This is a critical step. Your partner can't possibly meet your needs if he doesn't know exactly what he's doing that upsets you. Therefore try to describe your gripe as specifically as possible. For the sake of clarity, keep your growth fight focused on one specific behavior. Your statement should contain three parts: first a description of the behavior that bothers, second, the effect that this behavior has on you, and third, a description of your feelings. Thus it should follow this form: "The thing you do that bothers me is———, and when you do it———happens, and I feel———."

By expressing yourself this way, you're opening up yourself to your partner, telling him just what's going on inside you and how important it is to you. It's surprising how often people argue without ever sharing with each other the extent of their feelings.

You'll notice that this form of expressing your problem calls for the descriptive "I" language rather than more accusing "you" language. As we pointed out in Chapter 3, this is especially important if you're going to create a climate free of defensiveness. What you're saying here is that you're feeling upset, that you've a problem you want to share. You're not blaming your partner or demanding any kind of change at this point.

If possible in this stage, it's very helpful to have a friend present when you rehearse what you're going to say. Your partner can also be present for the rehearsal, but he shouldn't respond; this step gives you the chance to make sure you're stating your problem in the shortest, clearest way, and it gives him a good chance to understand clearly just what's bugging you.

Step 4—Checking back After you've shared what's bothering you and how you feel, your partner should check his understanding by replaying what he's heard you say. This process should be in two steps: First, he should repeat what you said word for word. If he misquotes you, help him recall your exact words, and thank him in some way. Next, your partner should paraphrase your complaint, restating in his own words what your complaint means. This paraphrasing might begin with "You feel. . . ."; "You think. . . ."; "You're saying that. . . ."; and so on.

Active listening for understanding is always important, but its especially critical in dealing with conflict where a person's own hurts, resentments, and expectations can so easily distort your message. Therefore it's essential that you're certain your partner understands exactly what you've said by playing it back.

Our marriage used to suffer from arguments that were too
short. Now we argue long enough to find out what the argument is about.

Hugh Prather
Notes to Myself

It may take several attempts before you're sure you've been understood, but the time spent will be worth it. Many fights get off the track because one person distorts the feelings of the other.

Bach suggests a very good idea at this point. Because being really understood is so rare and gratifying, why not express your appreciation by rewarding your partner with a "thank you," perhaps expressed by a handshake or hug? Besides reinforcing the importance of active listening, such gestures can show caring at what is most likely a tense time.

Step 5—Thinking about and practicing your request Now that you've shared what's bothering you with your partner, it's time to consider how you want him to change. You've probably thought about this before, but it's possible that your ideas have changed after confronting your partner in the earlier steps. At any rate, think about exactly what new behavior you want from your partner. Practice your request carefully, being sure that it's worded simply and accurately and that it deals only with the single issue you're discussing. If a good listener is present, you may rehearse your request with him before delivering it to your partner.

Step 6—Checking back on the request Repeat the procedure in step 4 until you're sure your partner understands your request. Remember, all your partner is doing is making sure he knows what you want. His understanding doesn't mean that he's accepting your request.

Again, don't forget to show your appreciation when you're sure you've been completely understood.

Step 7—Popping the question Now that your partner understands what's bothering you and what changes you want, it's time to simply ask him: "Will you do as I ask?" or something similar.

Step 8—Deciding the answer Now it's your partner's chance to respond. Until now he's been merely checking out his understandings, but here's when he can decide how to respond to your request. He should take some time to consider an honest answer, one he can live with. The potential responses range from completely accepting to partially accepting to totally rejecting the request.

Again, practicing the response with a third person can be helpful.

Step 9—Answering the question The answer will depend upon how your partner feels. He may want to take some time to think over his response, or he may be able to accept a modified version of the request: "I can't do all you've asked, but I'm willing to try this for now."

At this point the two partners need to find an answer that both can accept. You should notice that this process isn't the same as a compromise or a "deal." It's important that you both can truly accept the solution if it's going to work. (Refer to the sections on "no-lose" fighting later in this chapter.)

In each step of this negotiating process the partners should check their understanding of each other before adding any new requests, ideas, or responses. If you're unable to reach agreement, it may help to take an intermission and try again later.

Step 10—Planning a checkup meeting   It's always a good idea to make an appointment to meet a few days after your growth fight and check the progress of your solution. It may be that your agreement isn't working even though you made it in good faith. At any rate, your checkup meeting is a way to find out whether both of you are satisfied with how things are going.

Step 11—Closure   Now that you've successfully worked through a conflict, congratulate each other! Where before there was merely a problem, you've now worked together toward a solution.

Growth Fights at Home

1   After testing out one or two growth fights in class, try one at home with someone you care for. There are two things to keep in mind:

a. A growth fight is a serious thing. It takes a great deal of time and work by both partners. Make sure you're prepared before you start one.

b. Be sure you've a genuine gripe before starting a growth fight. This exercise isn't possible to fake.

2   In spite of a natural inclination to short-cut, be sure you follow every step exactly as it's outlined. If your partner hasn't taken this class, you'll probably need to explain many techniques as you go along. Although some of the steps may seem unnecessary, accept them as being part of the exercise and try to follow them. After you've become skilled at growth fighting you'll know what steps you can short-cut.

3   After you've finished the fight, analyze it by deciding:

a. Do you feel better or worse than before?

b. Is there less hurt in your relationship than earlier?

c. Do you understand your partner any better?

d. Is there greater trust in your relationship?

e. Do you feel less hostility toward your partner?

f. Do you find it's now easier to express your feelings in the relationship?

If your answers to some or most of these questions are positive, you can be quite sure that you're beginning to use conflict constructively.

Letting Go

One typical comment people have after trying a few growth fights is "This is a helpful thing sometimes, but it's so rational! Sometimes I'm so uptight I don't care about defensiveness or listening or anything. . . . I just want to yell and get it off my chest!"

When you feel like this it's almost impossible to be rational. At times like these probably the most therapeutic thing to do is to get your feelings off your chest in what Bach calls a "Vesuvius"—an uncontrolled, spontaneous explosion. A Vesuvius can be a terrific way of blowing off steam, and after doing so it's often much easier to figure out a rational solution to your problem.

So we encourage you to have a Vesuvius, with the following qualifications: Be sure your partner understands what you're doing and realizes that whatever you say doesn't call for a response. He should let you rant and rave for as long as you want without getting defensive or "tying in." Then, when your eruption subsides, you can take steps to work through whatever still troubles you.

We struggled together, knowing. We prattled, pretended, fought bitterly, laughed, wept over sad books or old movies, nagged, supported, gave, took, demanded, forgave, resented—hating the ugliness in each other, yet cherishing that which we were. . . . Will I ever find someone to battle with as we battled, love as we loved, share with as we shared, challenge as we challenged, forgive as we forgave. You used to say that I saved up all of my feelings so that I could spew forth when I got home. The anger I experienced in school I could not vent there. How many times have I heard you chuckle as you remembered the day I would come home from school and share with you all of the feelings I had kept in. "If anyone had been listening they would have thought you were punishing me, striking out at me. I always survived and you always knew that I would still be with you when you were through." There was an honesty about our relationship that may never exist again.

Vian Catrell

One final thought on growth fights. It might not be realistic to expect that you'll begin to use all the steps immediately. After all, this is probably a new skill for you, and as such it may not come easily. A good way to begin handling your conflicts more constructively is first to pick one step in the method and try to become proficient at using it. For example, you might try to rehearse your gripes clearly before sharing them with the other person involved or to make appointments for discussing your problems instead of dumping them on your unsuspecting partner. After you've become comfortable with the initial step, go on and add a second one. Continue this process until you've incorporated all steps of the growth fight into your life.

Winning and Losing

Let's take a look at one way you may be accustomed to managing conflict. You will, no doubt, find it somewhat different from the approach we've just been explaining. The following simulation should provide your group with a good firsthand experience to help in future discussions.

Play to Win!

1 Copy the following chart onto the blackboard:

How to Make Points

When Vote Is	Groups Score
X X X X	Each group gets +50 pts.
X X X Y {	Groups voting X get −100 pts. Group voting Y gets +300 pts.
X X Y Y {	Groups voting X get −200 pts. Groups voting Y get +200 pts.
X Y Y Y {	Group voting X gets −300 pts. Groups voting Y get +100 pts.
Y Y Y Y	Each group gets −50 pts.

Here's how to score: Each of the four groups will cast either an X or Y vote in each round. When the vote is tabulated, one of the five combinations above will result, and each group will score accordingly. (At this point there's apt to be some confusion and questions such as "What are we voting on?" may come up. Don't get bogged down here. Everyone will understand the process as you move along.)

2 Divide your class into four equal groups.

3 Each group should now move to a corner of the room so the members can talk together without interruption. There should be no communication—verbal or nonverbal—between groups except when instructions permit.

4 Your group's first task is to decide on how you'll make decisions: unanimous agreement, majority vote, decision of the leader, consensus, et cetera.

5 Place this scoreboard where it can be easily seen.

Round	Vote	Group I	Group II	Group III	Group IV
1					
2					
(N) 3					
4					
(N) 5 (2X)					
6					
(N) 7					
(N) 8					
9 (10X)					

The object of the game is for each group to score the greatest number of positive points possible.

6 Notice that there will be nine rounds of voting; in round 5 the scores will be doubled, and in round 9 they'll be multiplied by 10. The (N) that appears before rounds 3, 5, 7, and 8 means that the groups will be allowed to negotiate before voting in those rounds.

7 Take three minutes in your group to discuss how you'll vote in round 1.

8 After the three minutes, the instructor will collect a ballot from each group. Tally the votes and scores for round 1 on the scoreboard.

9 Repeat the same procedure for the remaining rounds. Before each N round one negotiator from each team should come to the center of the room, and if they desire, negotiate the next vote or votes.

10 During negotiations only negotiators can speak—group members must remain quiet so that they may hear negotiations. There will be time to discuss the vote in your groups after negotiations are completed.

11 After all rounds are completed, discuss the following questions:

    a. Who won the game?

    b. If two groups with the same goal finished with a tie score, did they both win? Both lose?

    c. In this game can there be more than one winner? Why?

    d. Did the groups coöperate during the game, helping each other reach their goals—or did they compete by trying to "beat" everyone?

    e. Did the simulation provide opportunities for you to behave either cooperatively or competitively, or did you add these as you went along?

    f. What did your behavior in this exercise tell you about how you handle conflict in your life?

This game usually illustrates some common ways people act when going after something they want. Most groups assume that to reach the goal they've chosen they must keep the others from reaching theirs, when in fact the surest way to succeed is to work together so all groups can score well. As one girl said when showed how all the groups could have reached their goal by cooperating, "But there can't be winners unless there are losers!"

It seems as if most of us grow up approaching our problems with this win-lose attitude. That is, if you and I have a problem or disagreement, the only way it can be settled is for one of us to get what he wants (the "winner") while the other doesn't have his needs satisfied (the "loser"). This is the method usually used by young children when the stronger one steals a toy from his smaller playmate; on a larger scale it's also the way many international conflicts are settled when a more powerful nation uses either military force or threat of it to get its way. Between these extremes problems come up every day that seem to call for a win-lose solution:

There's a chore around the house that has to be done, but nobody wants to do it.

A child likes to play in the mud, but the parent doesn't want to constantly wash dirty clothes.

You want to spend your vacation in the mountains and your partner wants to visit the beach.

You need extra time to finish a school assignment because of a personal problem, and your instructor has announced that any late papers will be penalized.

In a win-lose approach to such problems someone is bound to wind up unhappy. Either both people push for their solution with the strongest, smartest, most-persistent, or trickiest person coming out on top, or somebody simply gives in rather than go through the trouble of having a conflict. In either case the solution leaves at least one person an unhappy loser. And in a sense even the winners have lost in such situations because they've probably lost the goodwill, affection, and trust of the people they've just defeated.

When you look at the win-lose approach to problem-solving in this way, it isn't very appealing. In fact, much of the time you probably would try a different approach if you knew one. Fortunately there is such an approach. It's called the no-lose (or win-win) style of problem-solving, and as its name suggests, it offers a way to resolve conflicts in which everybody can come out ahead.

The no-lose approach works this way: When a conflict arises, instead of each person pushing for a solution that meets only their own needs, the participants work together creatively to find an answer that can satisfy both. This is done by trying to develop as many potential solutions as possible and then evaluating them to decide which one best meets everyone's needs.

Not long ago Ron and his wife Sherri used the no-lose approach to solve a problem that had been causing friction between them. To understand the problem you have to know that Ron is basically a tightwad, while Sherri isn't nearly as concerned with finances and doesn't worry as much as Ron does about budgets, savings accounts, or balanced checkbooks. This difference led to their problem: Every month Sherri would come home from shopping expeditions with antiques, new clothes, and other goodies. It wasn't that these things were very expensive, but it bothered Ron that Sherri seemed to feel there was something wrong with coming home empty-handed.

It got so that Ron dreaded the times Sherri would walk into the house carrying a shopping bag; and of course Ron's constant worrying about money bothered Sherri too. After what seemed like an endless number of "discussions" about the problem, they didn't seem to be getting anywhere. This was one area in which their needs came into conflict.

Eventually both Ron and Sherri realized that they had to find a solution that both could live with. So one evening they sat down and wrote all the alternatives they could think of:

1 Ron learns not to worry about money.

2 Sherri stops being a compulsive shopper.

3 Sherri and Ron discuss each purchase before it's made.

4 Sherri waits a day after first seeing something before buying it.

None of these ideas seemed workable. Since neither Ron nor Sherri could change their personalities overnight, solutions 1 and 2 were out. They had tried number 3 once or twice before and found it caused just as many disagreements as the original problem. The fourth alternative made sense, but it didn't sound like much fun, nor would it always be practical. Fortunately after some more brainstorming they came up with another alternative:

5 Each month they would set aside a certain amount of money for Sherri to spend any way she wanted.

This sounded good to both Ron and Sherri, and after figuring the best amount for an "allowance," things worked well. Now Sherri can buy most of the things she wants, and Ron can enjoy Sherri's shopping sprees without worrying about the budget.

The advantages of taking a no-lose approach to problems seem almost too obvious to mention, but we've found from experience that they're all too easily forgotten, and we automatically assume that there has to be a loser in every conflict. How many times have you found yourself in arguments that could have been avoided if you'd taken the time to look for a creative solution that satisfied everyone?

In a short while you'll have the chance to see if you're taking advantage of no-lose thinking in your life, but first let's look at how some other people have used this approach.

Gordon was a stamp collector; his wife Elaine loved to raise and show championship beagles. Their income didn't leave enough money for both to practice their hobbies, and splitting the cash they did have wouldn't have left enough for either. Solution: Put all the first year's money into the puppies, and then after they were grown use the income from their litters and show prizes to pay for Gordon's stamps.

Mac loved to spend his evenings talking to people all over the world on his ham radio set, but his wife Marilyn felt cheated out of the few hours of each day they could spend together. Mac didn't want to give up his hobby, and Marilyn wasn't willing to sacrifice the time she needed alone with her husband. Solution: Three or four nights each week Mac stayed up late and talked on his radio after spending the evening with Marilyn. On the following mornings she drove him to work instead of his taking the bus, which allowed him to sleep later.

Wendy and Kathy were roommates who had different studying habits. Wendy liked to do her work in the evenings, which left her days free for other things, but Kathy felt that night time was party time. Solution: Monday through Wednesday evenings Wendy studied at her boyfriend's place, while Kathy did anything she wanted. Thursday and Sunday Kathy agreed to keep things quiet around the house, and Friday and Saturday they both partied together.

The point here isn't that these solutions are the correct ones for everybody with similar problems: the no-lose approach doesn't work that way. Different people might have found other solutions that suited them better. What the no-lose method does is give you an approach—a way of creatively finding just the right answer for your unique problem. By using it you can

Resolving Interpersonal Conflict

tailor-make a way of resolving your conflicts that everyone can live with comfortably.

You should understand that the no-lose approach doesn't call for compromises in which the participants give up something they really want or need. Sometimes a compromise is the only alternative, but in the method we're talking about you find a solution that satisfies everyone—one in which nobody had to lose.

Steps to No-Lose Solutions

Probably the best description of the no-lose approach has been written by Thomas Gordon in his book *Parent Effectiveness Training*. Gordon suggests six steps that you can follow in reaching a no-lose solution to your problems:

1 Identify and define the conflict What's the problem as you see it? How does it make you feel? It's important here to use descriptive "I" language and not evaluative "you" words if you want to avoid a defensive argument. Also, be sure and make it clear that you want to find a solution that's acceptable to everyone, that you don't want just to argue. It's important here for each party to define the *ends* they want, and not to focus on *means* to achieve them.

2 Generate a number of possible solutions It's important to have everyone involved contribute as many solutions as they can think of. Don't stop to judge which ones are best in this step; this stifles creativity and can generate bad feelings. You'll pick the best ideas later.

3 Evaluate the alternative solutions This is the time to talk about which solutions will work and which ones won't. It's important for everyone to be honest about their willingness to accept an idea. If a solution is going to work, everyone involved has to support it.

4 Decide on the best solution Now that you've looked at all the alternatives, pick the one that looks best to everyone. It's important to be sure everybody understands the solution and is willing to try it out. Remember, your decision doesn't have to be final, but it should look potentially successful.

5 Implement the solution Here's where you work out the details of how the solution will operate. If you've decided to set up some sort of schedule, now's the time to work it out and make sure everyone understands it. If money is involved, you need to agree on the amounts involved. The point is to be sure that there are no misunderstandings about how the solution will operate.

6 Follow up the solution You can't be sure a solution will work until you try it out. After you've tested it for a while, it's a good idea to set aside some time to talk over how things are going. You may find that you need to make some changes or even rethink the whole problem. The idea is to keep on top of the problem, to keep using your creativity to solve it.

No-Lose Solutions and You

1 Make a list of the situations in your life where there's a conflict of needs that's creating tension between you and someone else.

2 Analyze what you're doing at present to resolve such conflicts, and describe whether your behavior is meeting with any success.

3 Pick at least one of the problems you listed above, and together with the other people involved try to develop a no-lose solution by following the six steps listed.

4 After working through steps 1 to 5, share the results of your conference with the class. After you've had time to test your solution, report the progress you've made, and discuss the follow-up conference described in step 6.

There you have it—probably some new and different ways of looking at conflict. We've tried to show you how disagreements are a natural part of life and how handling them well can turn what used to be frustrating experiences into encounters that can make your relationships stronger than they were before.

Of course the ideas we've presented here are only a beginning for you; you'll have to tailor them to suit your own personality. But we do believe that the general approach we've showed here works; it has for us and many people we know, and we hope it will for you.

Roads Not Taken

1 Keep a journal of the conflicts that arise in your life and the lives of those around you. Using the information you've learned in this book (defensive behaviors, listening styles, perceptual factors, crazymakers, growth fight, and no-lose) explore the ways in which these conflicts are handled and the results of such handling. How might the conflicts you observed be resolved more successfully?

2 Make it your goal to use no-lose problem-solving whenever possible over a two-week period. Keep a journal recording your successes, failures, and what you've learned.

3 Explore the concepts of zero-sum and nonzero-sum games as they relate to conflict resolution.

4 Research the subject of assertiveness training, focusing on the differences between assertiveness, direct aggression, indirect aggression, and unassertiveness.

5 Collect examples from films, poetry, and literature illustrating various conflict styles.

6 Agree with an important person in your life to apply the growth-fight method to your conflicts for a period of time. Report on the results.

More Readings on Conflict

Albee, Edward. *Who's Afraid of Virginia Woolf?* New York: Pocket Books, 1963.

In this famous play about George and Martha, a very unhappy couple, you can find nearly every type of "dirty fighting" we've talked about in the chapter.

Bach, George R., and Peter Wyden. *The Intimate Enemy.* New York: Avon, 1968.

In this very readable bestseller Bach and Wyden detail the destructive styles of dealing with conflict most marriage partners use. They then present the "fair fight" as an alternative. They present many examples of how couples have learned to deal constructively and successfully with conflicts they face in their lives.

Bach, George R., and Ronald M. Deutsch. *Pairing.* New York: Avon, 1970.

This book does for the singles, or nomarried persons, what *The Intimate Enemy* does for the married. Bach and Deutsch apply their methods of facing conflict to the problem that a single person has in finding and building intimate relationships. They attack the problems that our marriage-prone society puts on the shoulders of the single.

Filley, Alan C. *Interpersonal Conflict Resolution.* Glenview, Ill.: Scott, Foresman, 1975.

This book was written for use in the field of organizational management and is aimed at helping the reader learn to solve problems of interpersonal conflict in business. The book's strength lies in that the material presented is immediately applicable.

Gordon, Thomas. *Parent Effectiveness Training.* New York: Peter H. Wyden, 1970.
> The best-written book we've seen dealing with communication between parents and kids. An excellent introduction to no-lose styles of handling conflict.

Jandt, Fred E. *Conflict Resolution through Communication.* New York: Harper & Row, 1973.
> This is a collection of readings that are more theoretical than the other titles listed here. The first article by Jandt, "Simulation and Conflict," contains a good simulation for groups.

Leas, Speed, and Paul Kittlaus. *Church Fights.* Philadelphia: Westminster, 1973.
> This book recognizes that even churches have conflicts, and these conflicts should be faced rather than avoided. Although this book is about churches, it can be used for any organization because the ingredients of conflict are always basically the same.

Rubin, Theodore Isaac. *The Angry Book.* New York: Macmillan, 1969.
> Although anger is probably the least understood of human emotions, Rubin shows how you can use anger to build stronger, happier personalities and achieve better interpersonal relationships.

Films on Conflict

Conflict Resolution Research. Color. 30 min. 1966. PCR Pennsylvania State University.
> Psychological conflict problems are examined by Drs. Shamos, Deutsch, and Solomon. Laboratory research in interpersonal conflict is illustrated by film excerpts and demonstrations.

David and Hazel—A Story in Communication. B/W. 28 min. 1965. Central Arizona Film Cooperative.
> Presents a study of what may happen when a husband isolates his job from his family by showing how a husband's secretiveness when his job is threatened affects his whole family.

Trouble in the Family. B W. 90 min. 1963. Indiana University.

This film shows a family in therapy. The problem causing conflict is the fifteen-year-old son's performance at school, where he is not doing well. As the meetings with the therapist progress, the family becomes aware that they must improve their interpersonal communications, and this in turn provides them with the tools to deal with their conflicts.

Who am I? I am not sure.

Once I was a rabbit's grave and a basketball hoop on the garage, a cucumber patch, lilac trees and peonies crawling with ants. I was stepping stones and a mysterious cistern, grass fires, water fights and ping pong in the basement. I was a picket fence, a bed and maple chest of drawers I shared with brothers, a dog named Sandy who danced. Friends were easy to find. We climbed trees, built grass huts, chased snakes—and we dreamed a lot.

WILL YOU BE MY FRIEND? Beyond childhood.

Who am I? I am not sure.

Once I was predictable. I was educated, trained, loved-not as I was, but as I seemed to be. My role was my safe way of hiding. There was no reason to change. I was approved. I pleased. Then, almost suddenly, I changed. Now I am less sure, more myself. My role has almost disappeared. My roots are not in my church, my job, my city; even my world. They are in me. Friends are not so easy to find—and I dream a lot.

WILL YOU BE MY FRIEND? Beyond roles.

Who am I? I am not sure.

I am more alone than before, part animal, but not protected by his instincts or restricted by his vision. I am part spirit as well, yet scarcely free, limited by taste and touch and time-yearning for all of life. There is no security. Security is sameness and fear, the postponing of life. Security is expectations and commitments and premature death. I live with uncertainty. There are mountains yet to climb, clouds to ride, stars to explore, and friends to find. I am all alone. There is only me—and I dream a lot.

WILL YOU BE MY FRIEND? Beyond security.

Who am I? I am not sure.

I do not search in emptiness and need, but in increasing fullness and desire. Emptiness seeks any voice to fill a void, and face to dispel darkness. Emptiness brings crowds and shadows easy to replace. Fullness brings a friend, unique, irreplaceable. I am not as empty as I was. There are the wind and the ocean, books and music, strength and joys within, and the night. Friendship is less a request than a celebration, less a ritual than a reality, less a need than a want. Friendship is you and me—and I dream a lot.

WILL YOU BE MY FRIEND? Beyond need.

Who am I? I am not sure.
Who are you? I want to know.

We didn't sell Kool-aid together or hitchhike to school. We're not from the same town, the same God, hardly the same world. There is no role to play, no security to provide, no commitment to make. I expect no answer save your presence, your eyes, your self. Friendship is freedom, is flowing, is rare. It does not need stimulation, it stimulates itself. It trusts, understands, grows, explores, it smiles and weeps. It does not exhaust or cling, expect or demand. It is—and that is enough—and it dreams a lot.

WILL YOU BE MY FRIEND?

James Kavanaugh

Index